# HOW DEHUMANIZATION LEADS TO MURDER AND GENOCIDE

## Lessons from the Nazi Era

# HOW DEHUMANIZATION LEADS TO MURDER AND GENOCIDE

## Lessons from the Nazi Era

Stewart Gabel

BOSTON
2023

Library of Congress Cataloging-in-Publication Data

**Names:** Gabel, Stewart, 1943- author.
**Title:** How dehumanization leads to murder and genocide: lessons from the Nazi era / Stewart Gabel, MD, PhD.
**Description:** Boston: Academic Studies Press, 2023. | Includes bibliographical references and index.
**Identifiers:** LCCN 2023026258 (print) | LCCN 2023026259 (ebook) | ISBN 9798887193038 (hardback) | ISBN 9798887193045 (adobe pdf) | ISBN 9798887193052 (epub)
**Subjects:** LCSH: Genocide--Psychological aspects. | Murder--Psychological aspects. | Nazis--Psychology.
**Classification:** LCC HV6322.7 .G33 2023 (print) | LCC HV6322.7 (ebook) | DDC 304.6/63--dc23/eng/20230609
LC record available at https://lccn.loc.gov/2023026258
LC ebook record available at https://lccn.loc.gov/2023026259

Copyright © 2023 Stewart Gabel
All rights reserved.

Book design by PHi Business Solutions
Cover design by Ivan Grave
On the cover: *Menschengruppe vor der Deportation Holzschnitt um 1938*, by Maria Luiko. (In public domain)

Published by Academic Studies Press
1577 Beacon Street
Brookline, MA 02446, USA
press@academicstudiespress.com
www.academicstudiespress.com

# Contents

| | |
|---|---|
| Introduction | 1 |
| 1. A Brief History of the Jews from Antiquity through the Middle Ages | 17 |
| 2. Antisemitism and Dehumanization of the Jews in the Modern Period. Enlightenment and Emancipation. Political Antisemitism | 25 |
| 3. Dehumanization. Research. Definitions. Examples in the Nazi Era | 52 |
| 4. The Human Propensity toward Violence, Destruction, and Murder. Prohibitions against Killing Other Humans. Examples of the Tendency toward Violence and Murder in the Nazi Era | 70 |
| 5. The Progression from Dehumanization to Murder and Genocide in the Nazi Era | 108 |
| 6. Dehumanization of School-Aged Children in Nazi Germany | 132 |
| 7. Medical Implementation of Aryan Ideology: Sterilization, Euthanasia, Experimentation | 145 |
| 8. Summary and Conclusions. Alternative Approaches. Addressing Dehumanization | 166 |
| References | 183 |
| Index | 189 |

# Introduction

This book is about the relationship between dehumanization, murder, and genocide, emphasizing the characteristics and intricacies of this relationship. I use, as an example of these processes, the treatment of Jews during the Nazi era in Germany (1933–1945) and consider, to a lesser extent, the treatment of Jews in countries conquered by or allied with Germany, as well as the treatment of residents of institutions for the mentally or physically impaired in Germany.

I argue that dehumanization, applied in an increasingly severe manner to demean, subjugate, and control Jews in Nazi-dominated territories during the Nazi era ultimately led to the murder of Jews in these areas. I will consider the mechanisms and precipitants of this movement from dehumanization to murder that was associated with the Holocaust, perhaps the most horrific genocide in history.

## Background and Overview

The dehumanizing tactics used by Germany's Nazi leaders, abetted by many followers, targetted the Jewish people who had been considered a centuries-long threat. Adolf Hitler (1925/1999) and his Nazi followers argued that Jews were representative of the Semitic race and were the oldest and most formidable enemy of the German people that had ever existed. The German people, themselves, according to Hitler's view, had descended from an ill-defined Aryan race many centuries ago. For Hitler and his followers, Jews had to be eliminated from German (and European) soil if the Germanic people were to achieve world domination and the full potential of the Aryan race, although exactly what the latter meant was an ill-defined construct that, nonetheless, resulted in not only the genocide of Jews, but the murder of other nationalities, minority groups, and disabled individuals who were within the German sphere of influence.

Hitler's (1945) views on race, and on what he felt to be the Jewish menace, were fanatical. His misplaced and dangerous views spanned his political career and were included in his final political testament shortly before his death. On ascending to power in 1933, he and the Nazi party made it clear that there was no place in Germany for any Jew and that all Jews were to be eliminated from the country. It was unclear what "elimination" meant in the early stages of systematic dehumanization. At the beginning of the Nazi years, elimination was taken to mean coerced emigration. Toward the end of the Nazi era, elimination came to mean extermination through various forms of murder, such as starvation regimens in ghettos, German death squads, and gassing in concentration camps (Landau, 2016; Vasey, 2006).

The overall Nazi strategy regarding the Jews, therefore, was a policy of elimination that became total extermination, with the ultimate goal that Germany would become a country (and Europe a continent) free of Jews. The Nazi program was one of genocide, a term coined by Raphael Lemkin (1946) from the ancient Greek word (*genos*) for race and the Latin suffix (*cide*) for killing. Lemkin used this newly coined term to describe the numerous attempts to destroy national, racial or religious groups that he recognized as being common in human history. In the case of the Nazi-inspired Holocaust, the tactics to arrive at these goals of elimination or extermination involved a process of increasingly severe dehumanization that isolated Jews from non-Jews, restricted the livelihoods, activities, education, and freedoms of Jews and increasingly convinced the German public (the bystanders) that Jews were a separate, subhuman or inferior people that was a menace to them.

The Nazi leadership and those supporting its views used these dehumanizing tactics to persecute and ultimately enslave and murder the Jewish people. The Nazi leaders justified the dehumanization and killing of other human beings to themselves and to German citizens by arguing that these enslaved or murdered people were in essence inferior, subhuman, or not actually people at all. The people being killed, to the victimizers, were less than human or subhuman in either their personal, ethical, or moral development, and/or they were animals, creatures that did not have the essential characteristics (including moral or personal qualities) that human beings have.

Killing such people, who are considered to not really be people, often is justified by aggressors if the victimized person or group can be understood as hostile and dangerous to the victimizers (Smith, 2011). Not surprisingly, the group considered subhuman usually has less power than the larger, stronger individual or group that argues it has been "forced" to defend itself against what it considers to be a subhuman "monster." These deceptive tactics result in dehumanization of the victim but are often complicated and associated with other psychological processes through which victimizers deceive themselves (and others). Victimizers may engage in distortions, diversions, rationalizations, denial, and blame. Mental health professionals describe the psychological processes employed by perpetrators that allow horrendous acts to be committed against victims as "psychological defenses." These "defenses" are intended to ward off anxiety, guilt, shame, or other unpleasant feelings in the victimizers by blaming victims, making the victimizers able to believe, act, and react in ways that are satisfying or self-justifying to them, regardless of what the unpleasant truths, realities, and consequences of their actions or beliefs might be.

In the Nazi era, many Germans believed Hitler (1925/1999) when he falsely accused Jews of instigating or saboutaging WWI or of conspiring with fellow Jews in other countries to form a financial cabal to rule the world (Landau, 2016). These claims had no merit but allowed those Germans who believed them to blame Jews for their own financial insecurity and for their lack of political or military power. German citizens became increasingly able to project the blame for their failures onto Jews, a ready scapegoat, while diverting attention from a realistic appraisal of their own failures and fears. Based on these groundless assumptions of Jewish treachery, the Germans holding these beliefs, who might otherwise have felt powerless or inferior, were able to divert attention from themselves onto the Jews, thus fostering desires for revenge against Jews as a group. Dominating the Jews and "punishing" or expelling them from Germany was, from this more psychological perspective, intended to relieve the guilt and blame that would otherwise have been attributed to the victimizers or to their leaders. The Jews were an obvious target because centuries of antisemitism could be used to incite conspiracy theories about this group.

Dehumanization thereby became a potential catalyst, justification, and tactic to incite violence and murder. It was an activator for futher, increasingly severe dehumanizing actions and an instigator of what Freud called the death instinct (that was later called the death drive), a phenomenon related to mass murder and genocide. In this book, I do not employ Freud's (1920; 1930) formulation but offer an approach that views murder along a continuum with dehumanization. I argue that humans demonstrate a natural proclivity toward violence, destruction, and murder that may be stimulated by dehumanizing tactics perpetrated against those who are considered less than human or as "animals," given that animals are convenient targets for deadly aggression. These dehumanizing judgments render animals and dehumanized individuals less worthy of usual human protections against violence and aggression than it is true for one's fellow human beings. Essentially, the severely dehumanized individual or group becomes an opportune target to express the inherent potential that human beings have for violence.

The individuals and groups who harbor these types of psychological defense mechanisms may be entirely unaware or unconscious of their own reactions (or the reasons for them), making them likely to take actions they believe are justified, but that in reality they do not fully comprehend. Calling Jews or any other dehumanized group vermin or dogs, for examples, avoids an understanding of the chain of personal and social attitudes that have contributed to the aggressor's malign designations.

Hitler and the Nazis burned books written by psychoanalysts and were notorious for their antipathy to this form of psychological analysis. Had they pursued this form of understanding further, they might have concluded that dehumanization of others was in part an externalizing tactic for "resolving" their own internal conflicts and fears of inadequacy and failure that resulted in a series of behaviors and actions perpetrated against Jews. Dehumanization of Jews was also reflected as the internal state of these victimizers whose judgments rested on assumptions about the perpetrators, themselves, and the attitudes and behaviors of Jews, their would-be-and assumed enemies.

Dehumanization in victimizers is, therefore, both (1) an internal state that denigrates the victims and their attitudes and behaviors and (2) one or more external behaviors perpetrated against the victims that the perpetrators consider justified because of their own faulty assumptions about the victims and the victims' motivations. This internal denigrating appraisal results from a series of psychological defenses within the dehumanizer that are intended to shift responsibility, to whatever degree possible, onto the victims who are usually individuals or groups with less power.

Dehumanizing tactics, as indicated here, deny victims "personhood"—a sense of the value of their own humanity, their justification for being, and their own identity in its various forms (Bastian & Haslam, 2011). This denial of personhood is justified by the aggressor through blaming the victim for sins and errors, as defined by the victimizer. Often, these sins and errors, as suggested earlier, have little or nothing to do with what the victim actually has done; rather, they reflect prejudices linked to assumed innate or enduring qualities of the victim (such as skin color), religious identity/affiliation, or social status (such as living in poverty) that are used to justify the persecution of the victim, even when the malign social situation is due to the actions of the aggressors themselves. Regardless of the apparent unfairness of the immutable conditions of birth or the prejudicial actions of the oppressor, a series of moral and ethical failures are attributed by the victimizers to the victimized individual or group who are now considered to be less than human. The victim group essentially becomes dehumanized, a state that in severe form, as described throughout this book, carries considerable mortal danger.

The human proclivity to commit violence or to murder others (who may or may not be known to the assailant) is often attributed by mental health professionals to maladaptive, rageful, and unconscious reactions that are based on indivdiual circumstances of the perpetrators' lives. This tendency to focus on the characteristics or psychopathology of perpetrators, often clinical patients, inevitably results in a greater "understanding" of the individual but is often inappropriate when dealing with what appears to be a more general human proclivity toward violence, destruction, and murder that occurs in the context of broad social phenomena such as genocide. In the context of this discussion, therefore, it is well to recognize that explanations for the murder of individuals or groups in terms of motivations such as financial gain, professional or personal competition, romantic rivalries or remorse, and revenge for presumed personal slights or disrespect may have limited value. Violence and murder, in many instances in which there is a group of perpetrators who murder a group of unknown victims, such as occurred in the genocide of the Holocaust, do not fit easily into these accepted clinical paradigms.

In the formulations offered in chapters four and five, I emphasize that the human proclivity toward violence and murder refers to processes of aggression and destruction leading to death and negation of others that are intended symbolically to demonstrate dominance, control, subjugation, or retaliation against the victim. Genocidal murder, as occurred in the Holocaust, seems to be associated with (or follow) the dehumanization of the victims. There are numerous instances cited in this book and more extensively in the Holocaust witness literature (in the bibliography), which demonstrate instances of killing and murder that seem to be senseless by usual standards of human conduct, excessive to the situation, and even sadistically "joyful" for the victimizer. It is as if, under certain conditions (described in these chapters), inhibitions against murder are discarded and apparently innate tendencies toward murder are allowed, or even welcomed. Some Nazi personnel, for example, seemed to have had an almost zestful approach to the brutality they expressed or the torment they inflicted. Hilberg (1992), for example, cites instances in which Jewish children were "hurled live into pyres of burning corpses" (p. 53–54).

Jews were sometimes referred to as "playthings." Freud's (1923/1960; 1930) emphasis on the sadism that was associated with what he termed a death drive came to mind frequently as I read these accounts. The victimizer's dominance of the victim and the latter's helplessness in the face of the victimizer's actions also were striking and seemed to provide further stimulation for murder.

Freud's discussion of the death drive included a recognition of its polar opposite, Eros, or the life force. Freud argued that the death drive and Eros were counterbalancing life forces. Eros is the force of creativity, growth, and positive movement or change. Ideally, these two drives compensate for or balance each other. One can look at the Nazi era as a case study of how extreme dehumanizing tactics, such as unprovoked aggression against the Jews, forced relocation to ghettos, continued torment, and revocation of citizenship and its protections suppressed and even prohibited Eros, disabling its function of balancing the ever-present death drive. Shallcross (2020), a modern researcher, describes what she terms "necrotopographic" zones, ghetto scenes in which death and dying people during the Holocaust dominated the environment and was omnipresent.

## Background of the Author

Using Nazi Germany and the Holocaust to illustrate how extreme dehumanizing tactics activated an impulse to murder that resulted in genocide is personally significant to me. I am a Jewish person whose personal narrative and a sense of deep, personal involvement with the Jews (and others) lost in the Holocaust has been strongly affected by the events of the Nazi era. My story, and that of my immediate family, has had a happier ending than was true for distant relatives who remained in Eastern Europe after my immediate family had immigrated to America over several years but especially in the 1920s.

I did not know very much about the Holocaust growing up in America, and I now realize my parents and grandparents probably did not wish to speak of this period, a time of enormous sadness and loss, guilt and shame, a time of dehumanization and death that, as Holocaust scholars realize, is in some ways beyond comprehension. I hope that, in the pages to follow, as I convey aspects of the dehumanizing tactics that led to genocide during the Nazi era in some depth, I will be able to describe the phenomena involved and the relationship that exists on a continuum between dehumanization, violence, and murder. It is a relationship that proceeds from milder forms of dehumanization that can generally be described in attitudinal and behavioral terms to murder, the extreme form of dehumanization that involves an insistent drive to kill the progressively weakened and helpless victims.

Most of the chapters of this book deal, at least in part, with psychological tactics that accompanied the dehumanizing efforts used by Nazi aggressors. These included the lies, the distortions, the false beliefs, the projections, the blaming of others, and the self-serving assurances that were intended to accomplish nefarious goals of dehumanization and sometimes of death in the persecuted and the helpless. This book therefore describes the dehumanizing psychological and behavioral strategies Nazi aggressors used to mislead themselves and others as they intensified processes of dehumanization, resulting in genocide.

The contents and understandings conveyed here result from my decades of experiences as a psychiatrist, and also from my more recent doctoral work as a graduate student in religious studies. A earlier version of this book formed the focus of my dissertation.

The remainder of this chapter summarizes major points in each chapter in order to highlight the relationship between dehumanization, murder, and genocide and to provide illustrations how this relationship was exemplified by the Nazi era.

## Chapter One (A Brief History of the Jews from Antiquity through the Middle Ages)

This chapter is the first of the two that describe antisemitism up to, and including, the Nazi era. They provide a brief sketch of antisemitism across the millennia. Antisemitism in antiquity and antisemitism in modern times bear considerable resemblance. Blaming the Jews for problems in the "host" country, fearing that Jews will form coalitions with Jews in other countries against the host country, tolerating (and blaming) the Jews for the financial rewards Jews bring to the host country are all part of the psychological tactics that protect the power or income for the ruling group, while periodically encouraging (or allowing) angry mobs to attack Jews whose persecution can be used to divert attention from problems or anxieties present in the host society. Readers will readily see the similarities between dehumanization, a concern of this book, and antisemitic beliefs and practices through the ages. Indeed, anisemitism (and other forms of prejudice) can be understood as forms of dehumanization in which, through attitudes or behaviors, one individual or group denigrates the Other, those who are different, and proceeds to consider these "others" lesser (and dangerous) forms of humanity.

Exodus 1:8–11, for example, describes the Hebrews' sojourn in Egypt and reflects themes that reverberate across the centuries. The exodus narrative is a good example of the dehumanization of a weaker group that has become problematic for the ruling group and the subjugation of those who are considered potentially disloyal and who might in times of turmoil side with enemies of the host country. These Bible passages describe thoughts attributed to the Pharaoh and the fears he had of the foreign people who had seemingly grown too strong and whose numbers he therefore tried to limit.

Chapter one traces a similar pattern in the modern era and notes a change in host country tactics, if not strategy. Through what has come to be called political antisemitism, Jews were not universally condemned as members of a despised religion but rather were condemned as members of a despised race. As in biblical times, Jews, members of a minority that had been allowed or invited to live in the host country, became a threat to the insecure citizens and rulers of Germany, which was the host country. The status and privileges of the subjugated Jewish people had risen after the Enlightenment and Jewish Emancipation, but antisemitism, sometimes in new forms, continued.

## Chapter Two (Antisemitism and Dehumanization of the Jews in the Modern Period. Enlightenment and Emancipation. Political Antisemitism)

Chapter two discusses more fully the failed optimism of the Enlightenment that had emphasized the equality of nations and peoples. Along with this optimism came the emancipation of the Jews in Germany in the late nineteenth century and their being given rights as citizens of a now unified country. Religion seemed less important to civil society than in previous times. Counterbalancing these developments, however, was an upsurge in prejudice and dehumanization that was ascribed to racial differences between Jews and Aryans (Germans) rather than religious differences. Jews were blamed for the misfortunes of the German state, harshly criticized, and threatened with expulsion (or worse) on platforms and in writings of rightist political parties.

The Nazi era provided a harsh cessation to emancipation and emphasized the dangers of the Jews in the eyes of the regime. A severe program of dehumanization was instituted in an attempt to force Jews to emigrate from Germany, a country whose Nazi government wished it to become a pure Aryan nation. It did not matter that the Nazi conception of what "Aryan" meant was flawed or that imposed pseudo-Darwinian notions of Aryan supremacy also were flawed.

Hitler considered Jews vermin: smelly, criminal, and loathsome. These dehumanizing ascriptions were supported by the ideology of Hitler and his followers who claimed that Germans comprised a superior race and that others, such as Jews, were inferior—subhuman—and ultimately of no importance. Those Jews who did not or could not emigrate by the late 1930s or early 1940s were deported to concentration camps and ultimately killed. Dehumanization over several years involved severe social, economic, educational, religious, and professional restrictions, coupled with social isolation from other Germans. I describe the dynamics of this process of dehumanization more fully in chapter three, and its final outcome—violence, murder, and genocide—in chapter four. An important contextual factor making the ultimate murder of Jews possible was the diversion of the average German's attention toward the war effort, leaving the Nazis to do as they wished with the Jews who were helpless victims.

## Chapter Three (Dehumanization. Research. Definitions. Examples in the Nazi Era)

Chapter three focuses on the behavioral and psychological processes of dehumanization. In this chapter, dehumanization is defined and described, and its central features are highlighted. Research studies related to dehumanization are summarized. I provide my own definition of dehumanization that emphasizes the interactive power dynamics of dehumanization between victim and victimizer. I highlight historical factors noted earlier that contributed to dehumanization in the Nazi era, such as longstanding antisemitism and reactionary responses to the emancipation of the Jews in the nineteenth century. The National Socialist Workers' Party and Adolf Hitler represent the culmination of the dehumanizing power struggles of German politics of this period. Excerpts from Hitler's writings in *Mein Kampf* emphasize an ideology that led to the increasingly severe dehumanization of the Jews and, as I describe, the activation of murder and genocide during the Nazi era.

In chapter three, I also provide illustrations of the tactics used by Hitler, the Nazi party, and their sympathizers to justify the dehumanizing treatment of the Jews. Self-deluding beliefs and justifications involved the utilization of psychological defenses that avoided personal or national responsibilities for the humiliation Germany experienced in World War I and the interwar years. Blame ascribed to Jews was used by Nazis and their sympathizers to justify their anger and rage at the loss of standing and position that Germany was forced to accept following its defeat in World War I. Other dehumanizing tactics marshalled against Jews included propaganda conveying unfounded assumptions of a worldwide Jewish plot to take over the world through extensive and nefarious financial dealings; beliefs that Jews, despite being only one percent of the German population (although closer to fifteen percent in certain professions), were a threat to the civic and professional status of those identified as Aryans; and beliefs that Jewish males would "seduce" and intermarry with women identified as Aryans, thus diluting pure Aryan blood (Hitler, 1925/1999). Of course, the greatest calumny, and one among those seemingly closest to Hitler's (1925/1999) heart, was that Germans represented the racially superior Aryan race, which was eternally in conflict with Jews as members of the powerful but inferior Semitic race.

Dehumanization was a way the Nazi party attempted to demonstrate to the German people and to Jews themselves that Jews were inferior to Germans. Dehumanizing tactics were intended to elevate the social and personal status of the dehumanizer and to blame the dehumanizer's actions on the alleged misdeeds of culpable Jewish victims—a tactic that would presumably enhance the sense of superiority of ordinary Germans and reduce the sense of worth of the average Jew. Dehumanizing actions were intended also to justify to both groups why Germany was no place in which a Jew should or could live successfully.

The specific illustrations in chapter three are taken from accounts of concentration camp victims. In discussing these illustrations, I provide more extensive comments about the tactics and effects of dehumanization.

## Chapter Four (The Human Propensity toward Violence, Destruction, and Murder. Prohibitions against Killing Other Humans. Examples of the Tendency toward Violence and Murder in the Nazi Era)

This chapter briefly reviews the human propensity to act in violent and murderous ways against other humans throughout history. Sometimes gratuitous slaughter of others seems to have occurred with little or no provocation. Freud's notion of the "death instinct" is discussed as a modern approach to the understanding of human beings' tendency to kill one another. I provide my own understanding of the human proclivity toward violence, destruction, and murder that falls on the extreme end of a continuum of milder to more severe forms of dehumanization, with the most severe form of dehumanization being murder.

In the discussion of Nazi-perpetrated violence and genocide during this era, I illustrate how aggression and violence were frequently accompanied by torture, sadism, narcissistic enjoyment of the suffering of the victim, and a sense of omnipotence, as Freud (1923/1960; 1930) described. In the extreme dehumanizing tactics used in Nazi Germany, the perpetrator (or killer) clearly was the master and the victim was the slave, a condition the perpetrator wished to emphasize, at times gleefully. The actions on the part of some German guards in concentration camps, for example, served no apparent rational or functional purpose. These concentration camp guards' jocularity, sadistic amusement, and torture of Jewish (and other) prisoners may be understood as dehumanizing tactics that reinforced the guards' sense of omnipotence and superiority prior to the murder of their victims. Using dehumanizing tactics to reinforce Nazi Germany's sense of omnipotence was part of Hitler's (1925/1999) apparent strategy. He emphasized that the Aryan people might live forever, but in order to do so they must fight and win the eternal struggle against the Jews.

The chapter highlights the psychology of the Nazi persecutors who used psychological defensive operations, such as denial and projection, to act as if Jews were the aggressors rather than the Germans themselves. These psychological tactics seem to have made some German people fear for their own welfare and become enraged by the largely imagined social or financial assaults on their lives attributed to the Jews.

The dehumanizing tactics used by Nazi persecutors motivated Germans to "fight back"—to annihilate the Jew before the Jew's alleged actions, such as the instigation of war, could annihilate the Germans. In this scenario, the German people would emerge victorious from this eternal and extreme power struggle—this deeply imaginary, magical, and unconscious battle for survival and dominance—as the Aryan masters of the world, and Jews would be dealt the retribution the German persecutor believed they had long deserved.

Another important question addressed in this chapter is the role of prohibitions to murder, which make people strongly resistant to killing other people, and the tactics used by military personnel and others in the Nazi era to overcome these prohibitions. Contributions that discuss both the prohibitions to killing and the willingness to kill are discussed in an attempt to better understand the genocide at this time.

Resistance to killing Jews (and others) was overcome for those perpetrating murder and genocide in the Nazi era through combinations of ideology, propaganda, and psychology that emphasized the evils of the adversary, acceptance of the dictates of authority, social pressure, and personal concerns about various kinds of alleged threats to one's welfare and livelihood. The role of psychological defenses is important here as well. Killers were often encouraged by Nazi authorities to believe that the Jews caused their own deaths by their own acts, and it was not the heavily armed, highly resourced German forces and their allies that were "responsible" for the actual executions of unarmed civilians.

In this chapter, I provide a number of illustrations of the extreme frenzy and dehumanizing tactics that were sometimes associated with murder and genocide in the Nazi era. In one instance, Goldhagen (1997) describes a scene of mass slaughter in Kovno, Lithuania, where the butchery of Jews was open for all to see. It is clear that the drive toward uninhibited murder is enhanced in crowds or mobs when social support and encouragement for killing are present and when there is a reduction of individual consciousness or ego controls that might provide ethical or moral constraints on these actions. Goldhagen (1997) reports that:

> The immediate assault upon the unsuspecting, unarmed, and obviously nonthreatening Jewish community occurred immediately after the German army marched into Kovno on the heels of the Soviet retreat. With German encouragement and support, Lithuanians, in a frenzied orgy of bludgeoning, slashing, and shooting, slaughtered 3,800 Jews in the city's streets. . . . [T]he killings, whether wild or systematic, had a circus-like quality, with bystanders observing at their pleasure the slaying, the cudgeling to death of Jews, watching with approval as crowds once watched the gladiators slaying their beasts. (Goldhagen, 1997, pp. 191–192)

Goldhagen (1997) makes the point that many of the Germans and their allies delighted in, volunteered for, and enjoyed the killing. The Germans' "devotion to annihilating the Jews was such that they would even postpone operations against real partisans, against the people who posed a real military threat to them, in order to undertake search-and-destroy missions against the Jews" (Goldhagen, 1997, p. 228). The Germans used valuable resources, materiel, and personnel, to further and complete the annihilation of the Jews even when threatened by the Allies' military on the eastern and the western fronts. This zealous determination to pursue the murder of non-threatening victims suggests the insistent internal pressure that becomes apparent as dehumanization progresses to murder and genocide.

## Chapter Five (The Progression from Dehumanization to Murder and Genocide in the Nazi Era)

Chapter five describes the persecution of the Jews in the Nazi era and the role of extreme dehumanization in activating the murderous impulses that resulted in mass deaths and genocide. The timeline of the increasingly severe dehumanization of the Jews that led to the murder of one half of the Jewish population in Europe is presented in some detail, focusing on several domains: economic, political, social, religious, family, and personal. The events of the Nazi era are divided into three periods: 1933–1938, 1938–1941, and 1941–1945. These periods reflect the increasingly severe dehumanization that led to activation of the insistent pressure to murder and eradicate all Jews.

The first of the three periods emphasized legislative actions and other restrictions and persecutions of Jews such as harassment, violence, and propaganda efforts to force emigration, a milder form of elimination of the population. The second period is a transition to increasingly more severe dehumanization and state-sponsored murder. Kristallnacht, or the Night of Broken Glass, occurred during this time (November 1938) when it became clear that Jewish life in Germany was increasingly precarious. The first ghettos also were developed in this period. Coursing through the discussion in this section is an emphasis on the increasing social isolation of the Jewish population in Germany. The third period is a time of deportation, concentration camps, and death for Jews who did not (or were not able to) emigrate from Germany and the lands Germany had annexed or conquered.

The intense misery, anguish, and trauma expressed by the relatively few Jewish survivors of the concentration camps are reflected in well-known lines from Elie Wiesel's (1958/2006) book, *Night*, and discussed in this chapter. In what follows, Wiesel is describing his first night in Auschwitz, a concentration camp, as his mother and sisters are being taken toward the crematorium.

> Never shall I forget that smoke. Never shall I forget the small faces of the children whose bodies I saw transformed into smoke under a silent sky. Never shall I forget those flames that consumed my faith forever. Never shall I forget the nocturnal silence that deprived me for all eternity of the desire to live. Never shall I forget those moments that murdered my God and my soul and turned my dreams to ashes . . . (Wiesel, 1958/2006, p. 34).

These words express, in the context of this discussion, the result of an experience of extreme cruelty and brutal murder characteristic of the Nazi genocide. Although Wiesel was to have a highly productive life after his Holocaust experience, it is hard to imagine a full recovery from this type of trauma and the sense that his life had been deprived of the potential for joy because of the death, pain, incomprehensibility, and loss that this experience would have instilled in him.

## Chapter Six (Dehumanization of School-Aged Children in Nazi Germany)

Chapters six and seven deal with specific populations that were exposed to the dehumanizing (and in some cases, murderous) effects of Nazi ideology. Chapter six discusses the racially charged environment of school-aged children in Nazi Germany. This discussion emphasizes that Nazi Germany, in its vitriolic hatred of Jews, strove to achieve total commitment of the non-Jewish population to its view of Aryan supremacy. This resulted ultimately in the dehumanization of Jews from before their births (when pregnant Jewish women and their fetuses were killed) to after their deaths (when Jews were killed, cremated, and subject to desacration of their body parts).

Hitler (1925/1999) and the Nazi leadership were totally committed to the "education" of German youth in what they saw as the supremacy of the Aryan race and the perpetuation of Aryan blood. Public schools were a crucial vehicle in the attempt to achieve this end. The Law against the Overcrowding of German Schools that was passed months after Hitler ascended to power made clear the Nazis' intention to eliminate Jews from public schools and to orient school curricula toward an immersion in race-based doctrine. Physical health and physical fitness also were stressed, while purely academic subjects such as science were deemphasized. Teachers who were members of the Nazi party were preferred and Jewish or non-Nazi teachers were ultimately eliminated.

In an environment emphasizing the ideology of Aryan supremacy, Jewish children were dehumanized, ostracized, and humiliated. They were harassed, beaten, and denigrated. In some instances, Jewish children were forced to sit on special benches. They were banned from German lessons, given poor marks on school work that was done well, heard teachers describing Jews as criminals or traitors, and not allowed to participate in ceremonies, festivals, concerts, or plays (Evans, 2005).

These practices of dehumanization and humiliation of children resulted in the transfer of Jewish youth to Jewish schools and the large-scale emigration of Jews from Germany whenever possible. Those young people and their families who did not or could not emigrate were ultimately deported "to the East" to suffer the deadly fate of nearly all concentration camp victims.

## Chapter Seven (Medical Implementation of Aryan Ideology: Sterilization, Euthanasia, Experimentation)

Chapter seven describes medical programs of forced sterilization and "euthanasia" that involved state-sponsored medical efforts to limit the capacity of individuals whom medical authorities felt to be "unfit" to reproduce or to live in an Aryan society. These judgments were usually made because of severe medical or mental health conditions. Those affected included Poles, criminals, Jews, and others. This was not a program of voluntary euthanasia intended to relieve suffering but medically supervised programs of negative eugenics intended to limit what the Nazi party and affiliated physicians and authorities felt were individuals whose lives were not worth living, according to the subjective standards of these authorities. In this chapter I also describe the Nazis' medical experimentation involving extraordinary dehumanization and its gruesome and barbaric procedures that were conducted mainly on Jewish prisoners in concentration camps.

Physicians played a major role in many of these medical programs, and as a group they were the most highly represented of the professions in Nazi party membership (Lifton, 2000; Pross, 1991). Physicians were among the groups in Nazi Germany that displayed the greatest drive toward murder and killing of others. This was done under the rationale that the role of physicians had changed from its former emphasis on curing the individual to a new goal of curing a diseased society. In addition, this chapter discusses possible reasons for the attraction the Nazi party and its agenda had for many physicians.

## Chapter Eight (Summary and Conclusions. Alternative Approaches. Addressing Dehumanization)

The conclusion summarizes, and provides an interpretation of, the information presented in the earlier chapters. In this chapter, I reiterate and emphasize the factors described earlier, such as social isolation, social pressure, and group processes that encourage the progression from dehumanization to murder and genocide. I also raise additional questions intended to further elucidate the relationship between dehumanization and genocide. These include asking whether dehumanization is a necessary condition for genocide to occur and whether dehumanization is a sufficient explanation for the occurrence of genocide.

In addition, I make an appeal to monitor for, and combat, dehumanization in order to decrease human suffering generally and to forestall the progression of dehumanization to murder and genocide. I also recommend further research on the relationship between dehumanization and subsequent murder and genocide that extends the observations of this work beyond the Nazi era.

# CHAPTER 1

# A Brief History of the Jews from Antiquity through the Middle Ages

---

## Introduction

For most of their 3000-year history, the people we now call Jews lived among other peoples who considered them (as they considered their "hosts") to be alien or different. Usually, but not always, at least in the common era (CE), this difference or "otherness" was understood to be the result of the practice of Judaism, a different religion from that of the nations within which Jews lived. With the Enlightenment and Jewish Emancipation in the nineteenth and twentieth centuries, assumptions about race, rather than about religion, helped to maintain presumptions of difference and otherness between Jews and non-Jews. These presumptions frequently led to hostile interactions and prejudices against Jews who lived among larger and more powerful groups.

This chapter and the chapter following it should be considered one unit. The two chapters briefly review the history of the negative attitudes, prejudices, and behaviors toward Jews throughout their history that have come to be termed "antisemitism." These two chapters can also be called "a brief history of the dehumanization of Jews throughout their history," since, as noted in the Introduction, prejudice against Jews (and others) involves, through the attitudes, behaviors, and at times murderous actions of the dominant group, the development of negative stereotypes and dehumanization of the weaker subordinate group.

These first two chapters are not intended to be a comprehensive review of antisemitism across the ages. Rather, they are intended to be a précis of key issues in antisemitic thinking from antiquity through World War II that lay the groundwork for an understanding of dehumanization and elimination or murder of Jews that occurred in the Nazi era and that are described in detail in subsequent chapters. Antisemitism in Germany is emphasized. A brief summary of major periods in German history are provided for context, and brief comments on the writings of influential philosophers and others that bear on the Jewish Emancipation and/or on antisemitism in Germany are offered.

There are certain common characteristics that will be emphasized in this chapter that define the nature of antisemitism (and, as noted above, dehumanization) through the ages. These characteristics include: a) the domination over Jews, as a smaller, weaker group, by a larger more powerful group that inhabited the nation or land Jews had come to call home (sometimes at the invitation of the dominant group); b) a sense of otherness and alienation of a stateless people who were ripe for exploitation and blame from a more powerful group of citizens who were able to use the Jewish people as a vehicle for the expression of internal and external problems that had little to do with the Jews themselves; c) the frequent charges that Jews, living in a widely dispersed diaspora, were rootless and "wanderers," having no particular loyalty to any country; and d) that Jews living in one region or country could and would plot with other Jews in a different country to gain, financially, at the expense of the host countries in which the Jews lived.

It is useful to note that, while particularities and specific situations are important in understanding antisemitism across time, it is also true, as Ettinger (1988) says in speaking about antisemitic writings that ". . . anyone who reads anti-semitic writings of ancient times and then examines anti-Jewish arguments of the Middle Ages and the nineteenth and twentieth centuries will be astonished by the similarity of their arguments and reasoning" (p. 4). These patterns of domination of the powerful over the weak, of projection of blame onto those least able to defend themselves, and of suspiciousness of the motives of the Other are likely to be found more broadly in a discussion of prejudice on national or international levels, although the specific focus here is on the assumptions about, and the treatment and fate of, the Jews in the years before and during the Nazi era in Germany.

Antisemitism is a term that should be clarified at the outset. It is now applied to anti-Jewish and anti-Judaic attitudes and behaviors over the course of Jewish history. In actuality the term is more recent, having been coined by Wilhelm Marr, a German journalist, in 1878, and subsequently applied to stereotypical negative thinking against Jews through the millennia. Jews, in fact, are not considered a separate race or racial group by scholars or anthropologists: "The terms

Semitic and Aryan refer, not to racial categories of people, but to groups of languages, Hebrew and Arabic being Semitic tongues" (Landau, 2016, p. 29). These are facts that unfortunately were not accepted by what the Nazi party believed to be the "scientific racism" of the late nineteenth and the early to mid-twentieth centuries. In actuality, as the book burnings in Germany at the beginning of the Nazi era in 1933 demonstrated, Nazi attitudes about race reflected not science but misunderstood and misapplied notions about evolution.

The Jewish people seem originally to have been a Mediterranean division of the Caucasian race. Jews are not a homogeneous group phenotypically or genotypically. After the destruction of the Second Temple in 70 CE and the suppression of the Bar-Kokhba rebellion in 132 CE, the Jews, who already lived in some communities outside of the Holy Land, scattered across much of the known world. This dispersion is an important ingredient in the development of antisemitism and dehumanization practices noted above, but it is also important in understanding the varied physical appearances of the Jews, where factors such as conversion, intermarriage, and rape have contributed to a biological mixing of the Jews with local populations. This mixing of the Jews with other people in the lands of the Jewish diaspora over time has made it impossible to distinguish the Jews from other local inhabitants (Landau, 2016), a fact that became apparent when Nazi doctors and scientists attempted unsuccessfully to establish definite physical characteristics that could help differentiate between the Jews and the non-Jews in Nazi Germany (Cohen, 1990).

## Antiquity through the Middle Ages

Although the Hebrew Bible speaks of God's promise that the people whom we now call Jews would be given the land for as far as the eyes could see (Genesis 13:14–17), they were never the sole inhabitants of this Middle Eastern land of the Levant we now call Israel. Hostilities between the Jews and other Semitic peoples, such as the Canaanites and the Edomites, were the rule. Famine also was present in the Promised Land, which sometimes caused emigration: the Bible records a legendary experience of being the Other when Jews lived among sometimes hostile strangers during a several-century sojourn in the land of Egypt. This residence in a foreign land ended in hostility with the persecution of the Israelites and their ultimate escape from their former benefactors into the desert that was to be their home for forty years. The following biblical narrative and its interpretation are instructive for an understanding of dehumanization and antisemitic events to come:

> Now a new king arose over Egypt, who did not know Joseph. He said to his people, "Look, the Israelite people are more numerous and more powerful that we. Come let us deal shrewdly with them, or they will increase and, in the event of war, join our enemies and fight against us and escape from the land." Therefore they set taskmasters over them to oppress them with forced labor. (Exodus 1:8–11)

These aspects of the Egyptian sojourn broadly reflect characteristics of the anti-semitic attitudes noted above. Jews were a minority that initially was welcomed into a foreign land but later came to be feared and ostracized by the majority; Jews often were used by the "host" country for labor or taxes; Jews engendered suspicion in the Egyptian sojourn although it is not clear if this was because they practiced a different religion (monotheism or henotheism), or because they did not adopt the majority's polytheism, or for another reason.

The escape from Egypt and return of the Jews to the Promised Land was not without further conflict, albeit with different groups. Various tribes or nationalities, such as the Canaanites and the Edomites, were never fully conquered, and the Israelites lived uneasily in the land that these other people claimed as their own. Finally, the legendary King David founded a kingdom that was expansionist and fought to establish and maintain its own identity.

In fairly short order, however, this kingdom divided into northern and southern parts, both of which were conquered by larger empires to their east. The Northern Kingdom was conquered by Assyria, and its people were exiled to that country in the seventh century BCE and ultimately lost to history. Later, in the sixth century BCE, the Southern Kingdom was defeated by Babylonia, and many of its inhabitants were deported to the invaders' country. This initiated a roughly half century of exile and subjugation that, for many of their descendants, extended into a centuries-long period of diaspora and life among a far larger and more powerful nation that had different gods and customs.

Later, in 540 BCE, the Babylonian Empire fell to the Persian Empire. Cyrus, the conquering ruler, permitted Jews, and other peoples who had been deported from their ancestral places, to return to their homes in distant lands. The Jewish Temple that had been destroyed by the Babylonians in 586 BCE was rebuilt in what was a relatively tolerant period of Persian rule for the next few centuries until Alexander the Great conquered the Persian Empire in 331 BCE and established the Grecian control over the Land of Israel. After Alexander's death in 323 BCE, the Jewish homeland was ruled successively by the Ptolemies and the

Seleucids until the latter were conquered by the Romans in the middle of the first century BCE (Jaffee, 2006).

While not independent under Persia, the Jews were even less so under the Greeks. Internal conflicts, verging on civil war, centered in part on the issue of assimilation to the ideals and practices of the Greek state. This fostered a counterreaction and the rise of the Maccabean revolt in 167 BCE that was followed by a period of independence for the Jews.

The independence was short-lived, however, as the Roman Empire became ascendant. The Roman rule over the Land of Israel involved a series of conflicts, maladroit leaders, and ultimately a rebellion by the Jews. Continued opposition to Roman rule, rebellion in the first century CE that ultimately led to the destruction of the Second Temple in 70 CE, and a second disastrous rebellion that ended in 132 CE caused the banishment of the Jews from Jerusalem for a year and fostered their dispersion to other lands where their fate as outsiders without a homeland was highly variable.

From the Roman perspective, Jews seem to have been separatists, people "organized in their communities, living according to their customs, and demanding privileges based upon their religious tradition and a way of life molded by that tradition" (Stern, 1988, p. 15). Further, Jewish communities within the Roman empire had "very close ties with the religio-national center in Judaea . . . this connection was institutionalized to a great extent . . ." (Stern, 1988, p. 15). This perception was reinforced by the fact that Jews were separate and wished to remain apart from the dominant community. Indeed, "the religious and social separatism of the Jews was an argument used by their opponents" (Stern, 1988, p. 15). It was an argument based on a pattern of separation from the larger non-Jewish community in the diaspora that sometimes was desired by the Jews and sometimes required of them.

From the Roman perspective, there presumably was always the danger of cultural contagion or contamination. This remained true through the ages. Jews, at the time of the Roman Empire, were thought to be proselytizers, and this would have engendered hostility from the polytheistic Roman society. "It certainly is not accidental that antisemitism in Latin literature became fiercest in the period that Jewish penetration of the various levels of Roman society reached its peak" (Stern, 1988, p. 25). The prominence of the oppressed Jewish minority in this case, as was true in post-Emancipation Germany nearly two thousand years later, was considered an existential threat to the status quo of both the host society and the Jewish minority.

The attitude of the larger Greco-Roman world toward the Jews at this time (and earlier) suggests that considerable conflict and competition existed between the polytheistic and monotheistic religions (Ettinger, 1988), but the ascendancy of Christianity as a monotheistic religion changed the character of the conflict with polytheistic Rome for religious adherents. "Christianity began to exploit the hostility to Judaism already widespread in Greco-Roman society in order to win support and popularity among the very extensive circles in which scorn or opposition to Judaism were already deeply rooted" (Ettinger, 1988, p. 10). Church Fathers often portrayed Jews in an entirely negative light.

As Christianity spread in Europe, "the clergy became the bearers of the religious, cultural and ethical values of the entire people ... the negative stereotype of the Jews, crystallized in their writings and sermons, became the cultural 'baggage' of medieval Europe" (Ettinger, 1988, p. 10). Scapegoating of Jews became a convenient means of redirecting anger and frustration from a host of life's problems, including the oppression of the people by unscrupulous landowners.

The separation between Judaism and Christianity was not accomplished rapidly, and ties persisted for many years. Separation and the potential for conflict became stronger in the fourth century CE when the emperor, Constantine, clearly favoring Christianity (and later himself converting to Christianity), promulgated an edict that gave Christians the right to practice their religion openly. Judaism suffered through Constantine's actions that were not only strongly pro-Christian but also anti-Jewish. This combination of hostility from both Christian clergy and Roman emperor was a volatile mix that held considerable threats for the Jewish population. Jews were portrayed as being unscrupulous, deicides, and a people forsaken by God, characterizations that reflected the dehumanization and antisemitism they faced. Later, in the Middle Ages, usury, the practice of black magic, and surreptitious relations with the Devil were charges added to the earlier prejudices (Ettinger, 1988).

Rokeah (1988) argues also that, as contacts between Christians and Jews decreased over the early centuries CE, hatred expressed by Christians toward Jews increased. He believed that Christians came to despair of ever converting the Jewish people to Christianity, and therefore felt free to express their resentments toward their former potential coreligionists. A negative, demonic image of the Jew thus arose from these resentments (Rokeah, 1988). From this perspective, Christianity was dependent on Judaism and on the conversion of Jews to Christianity. "Since the origins of Christianity and the path to Christianity were intertwined with the Holy Scriptures of the Jews, the Jews' very existence, even without any action on their part, constituted a problem for the Church" (Rokeah, 1988, p. 63). This "failure" of Jews "to see the light" was an important, albeit partial, explanation for much of the antisemitism through the ages, including that of the modern era and of the Middle Ages that is discussed presently.

Despite these tensions in the early Middle Ages, however, relations between Christians and Jews were often relatively harmonious for several centuries when Christianity was establishing itself as a dominant force in the Western world.

The second half of the first millennium of the Common Era saw additional conflict and war as a new religious player entered the scene. Islam became a force during this time and ultimately became the dominant religion in the Arabian Peninsula. Jews and Christians were tolerated groups under Islam, although they were not considered equal to Muslims. As *dhimmi*, or protected people able to retain their original faith, they nonetheless had to pay extra taxes and obey certain restrictions.

Relationships in Europe between Jews and Christians became more contentious around the beginning of the second millennium of the Common Era. The church hierarchy, with increasing political power, opposed Jewish ownership of land. The Church also refused to allow Christians to charge other Christians interest on loans. This shifted economic practices between Jews and Christians. Increasingly, Jews became associated with financial practices, such as money lending, that Christians demeaned and that inevitably engendered anger and mistrust in Christian communities (Landau, 2016). As would be expected, this practice of lending to Christians and thereby having financial control over them, along with the excoriation of Jews as Christ-killers because of the charge that all Jews, for all time, were responsible for the events of almost one thousand years ago, provided fertile soil for the onset of more virulent anti-Jewish actions.

The Middle Ages were a time of often harsh and bitter enmity on the part of the Church towards the Jews (Landau, 2016). Jews became increasingly identified as "Christ-killers" and as agents of the Devil. The situation was highly variable, however, depending on time and place. Medieval Spain, under Muslim rule, was far more hospitable to Jews than other areas of Europe that were under Christian control. Jews prospered under Muslim rule and engaged actively in government, civic, professional, and cultural life.

The Crusades that occurred roughly at this time were ostensibly intended to win back the Christian Holy Land from the Muslim infidels. They failed in this purpose but established with clarity the enmity of many Christians for Jews who were massacred in their villages along the route of the Crusaders. The Crusades, from the Jewish perspective, were associated with "plundered homes, broken lives and . . . a new and depressing era for the Jewish people" (Landau, 2016, p. 42). This was an era that included "forced conversion, mass expulsion, and pariah status" (Landau, 2016, p. 42). Persecutions, expulsions and massacres were not uncommon occurrences during the Middle Ages, the expulsion of Jews from Spain in 1492 being the most well-known.

Christianity reconquered much of Spain from Islam in 1300 CE, and the treatment of Jews deteriorated. The Church made great efforts to convert Jews, and when the sincerity of their conversion and beliefs in Christianity were doubted, Jews were dealt with harshly, ultimately through torture and death at the hands of the Inquisition, which aimed to root out those *conversos* (Jewish converts to Christianity in Western Europe) who were felt to be false or insincere.

Finally, as suggested earlier, at least 150,000 Jews were expelled from Spain in 1492. At this time, "there was a discernible racial ingredient in the manic rooting out of Jewish influence . . . which, to some extent anticipate the later 'biological' criteria of the Nazi genocide" (Landau, 2016, p. 42). *Conversos* were felt to have different physical characteristics, for example, in their blood lines, that distinguished them from Christians who were not *conversos*. Increasingly, Jews held a subservient and reviled status in their communities through much of Europe. In 1215, for example, Pope Innocent III decreed that Jews must wear a special badge that distinguished them from Christians, an insignia reminiscent of the badges required elsewhere in Christian lands and, notoriously, in the Nazi-held lands in World War II and before.

Other calumnies, not tempered by any attempt at fact or truth, were characteristic of the treatment of Jews in the Middle Ages. The Black Death ravaged Europe in the fourteenth century, killing almost one quarter of the population. The Church chose to blame this tragedy on Jews, considered emissaries of Satan (Landau, 2016). Another calumny occurring at about this time was the "blood libel" accusation that Jews kidnapped and murdered Christian children in order to use their blood for ritual purposes. The diabolical Jew, in this scenario, was accused of abducting a Christian child, usually a prepubescent male, and murdering him, thus enacting symbolically the crucifixion of Christ. The child's blood, drained from his body, was supposedly used in the preparation of the unleavened bread (*matzot*) for Passover (Landau, 2016). This and other false and scurrilous claims were widely debunked but nevertheless persistent. They often were used as justifications for the massacres and violence perpetrated against the Jews during this (and later) periods.

CHAPTER 2

# Antisemitism and Dehumanization of the Jews in the Modern Period. Enlightenment and Emancipation. Political Antisemitism

## Introduction

Jews had periodically been criticized as members of a different race for hundreds of years prior to the late nineteenth and the twentieth centuries (Landau, 2016), but the notion that racial differences, rather than religious differences, were paramount in importance when considering the nature of Jews or Judaism reached its peak during the post Emancipation period. This view contributed to what has been termed "political antisemitism," a phenomenon emphasizing that different political parties and segments of society held different views on the nature of Judaism and that the fate of Jews living within the borders of nations should be determined through the rule of law rather than by monarchical dictate.

Political or racial antisemitism, coupled with traditional antisemitism based on religious differences and prejudices against Jews by other peoples who usually lived in close proximity to them, set the stage for Nazism and the Holocaust that was to come in the middle of the twentieth century. The doctrine or acceptance of a belief in racial superiority led directly to the notion that the German, an Aryan, was a member of a superhuman people while the Jew, a Semite, was a member of an inferior or infrahuman people.

## Enlightenment and Emancipation; the Unification and Importance of Germany

The coming of the period of Enlightenment in the seventeenth and the eighteenth centuries was a hopeful sign for many Jews and others that a new era of tolerance for their religious beliefs would ensue. These hopes were not fulfilled, however, and much prejudice continued. In Germany, especially, the Enlightenment and the later processes of Jewish Emancipation developed slower than in other Western European countries, and the economic and professional progress that was ultimately made by Jews was both conspicuous and resented (Landau, 2016).

Given Germany's central role in the Nazi era and the period leading up to it, a brief digression and sketch of important aspects of Germany's history provide context for understanding later events of the Nazi era. The land that we now call Germany has a long history that dates to prehistoric times. The borders of this land, situated in central Europe, have shifted frequently. There are major regional differences that are based less on geography than on various political, cultural, or socioeconomic conditions (Fulbrook, 2019).

In the Roman era, this land mass was called Germania. During the medieval period, an imperial structure provided a loose framework for the many principalities and territories that constituted what became the "Holy Roman Empire of the German Nation" in 962, an entity that lasted until 1806 (Fulbrook, 2019, pp. 16–31). A high point of this period that was characterized by a decentralized Germany was the reign of the Great Emperor Frederick Barbarossa in what has been considered "a golden age of imperial greatness" and a high point of Germanic civilization. Imperial powers declined in relation to princely territories in the late fourteenth and the early fifteenth centuries, however, and Germany continued to have a less centralized form of governance than other European regional powers, such as England and France.

In the sixteenth century, Martin Luther initiated the Reformation when he wrote a series of ninety-five theses alleging abuses by the Catholic Church and posted these for public viewing on the door of the Castle Church in Wittenberg in 1517 (Fulbrook, 2019). This, and ensuing events, shattered European cultural and religious unity and led to the major and seemingly unbridgeable schism in Christianity in Europe that has continued to the present time.

The Thirty Years War that followed in the seventeenth century (1618–1648) was the result of numerous factors, of which religious differences certainly played a part (Fulbrook, 2019). This lengthy conflict was very divisive for Europe, with enormous casualties and much devastation. It finally was settled with the

Peace of Westphalia in 1648. This settlement was a compromise to address conflicts among the Protestants themselves and between the Protestants and the Catholics. It attempted to address broader European conflicts as well, but this attempt was less successful. The peace treaty signed in Westphalia remained the essential constitution of the German Empire until the empire itself was abolished in 1806.

Military and political conflicts continued over the ensuing years, and it became clear over time that, although there were numerous regions and principalities in Germany, two main power centers had arisen there: a militaristic northern German region under Prussian domination and a southern German region under Austrian domination.

Napoleon's invasion of the region in the early nineteenth century initiated major and lasting changes that spurred revolutionary, nationalistic goals in Germany and elsewhere in Europe. As Fullbrook (2019) puts it: "attacked, overrun, occupied, reorganized, exploited, provoked, shaken up, by 1815 Germany emerged in very different shape; and the Holy Roman Empire, which had served as its loose political framework for so many centuries, had gone" (p. 96). As would be the case a century later after the end of World War I, political expectations of nations changed dramatically.

After Napoleon was defeated, there was an attempt to unite the German territories into an Austrian-led alliance of German states at the Congress of Vienna in 1815 that was strongly influenced by the Austrian chancellor and foreign minister, Klemens von Metternich (Fulbrook, 2019). One result of the Congress was the establishment of a German Confederation that replaced the Holy Roman Empire. The Confederation was a loose federation of numerous states and four free cities.

The time from the Congress of Vienna to a series of revolutions that occurred among German states in 1848 is considered a period of transition (Fulbrook, 2019). During these years, the strength of Prussia increased significantly, setting up a potential confrontation with the southern state of Austria. Industrialization and conservative political orientations were two important aspects of this transitional period.

1848 was a year of revolution across German territories (Fulbrook, 2019). Social unrest, political strivings for constitutional reforms, economic freedoms, and nationalism that involved German unification were all themes that drove the unrest of this time. Conservative leadership managed to put down areas of unrest, although some reforms did persist (such as economic liberalization).

The rise of a militarized Prussian state under the chancellorship of Otto von Bismarck resulted in the formation of a new German Empire in 1871 that was ruled by a Prussian monarch. This empire, whose unification had been delayed compared to other European territories, was highly industrialized, militarized, and nationalistic in orientation.

The unification in 1871 resulted in the submission of smaller states of southern and central Germany (save for Austria) to the leadership of Prussia in foreign affairs, defense, and the economy (Landau, 2016). Germany thus became an empire or federation under Prussian leadership. This unification was accomplished through Prussian engagement in a series of brief wars in the preceding years. In 1866, Austria was defeated in a war with Prussia that upended Austria's domination of southern German states and allowed Prussia to control these states as well. France was defeated in another brief war with Prussia in 1870, thus cementing Germany's position as Europe's foremost power. As Fulbrook (2019) notes, however, German unification in 1871 was more an expression of "Prussian expansionism and colonisation of non-Prussian Germany, in rivalry with an excluded Austria" than an expression of German nationalism (p. 125). Germany, nonetheless, was now united, and a great industrial and military force in Europe.

Although Germany had finally achieved unification in 1871, it found itself in a period of continual crisis, both politically and socially. Regionalism, economic difficulties, and religious conflicts all surfaced. Urbanization, modernization, and industrialization all contributed to potential social upheaval. This crisis continued through the Kaiserreich (the second Reich or empire) and the later ill-fated, democratic, and socially liberal Weimar Republic that proved ineffectual and unable to keep the country unified and address its many problems. The republic finally collapsed and was replaced by single-party rule with Adolf Hitler as chancellor in January 1933 (Landau, 2016). Hitler, of course, began to initiate a highly conservative and antisemitic agenda that would initially unify the country, destroy opposition groups, and temporarily improve Germany's economic condition but ultimately lead the country and much of the world into a ruinous war that dehumanized, enslaved, and killed millions.

## Enlightenment and Jewish Emancipation, Nineteenth to Mid-Twentieth Centuries. Philosophical and Political Writings

The latter part of the nineteenth century witnessed enormous social and political changes in Germany. The period of the Enlightenment and the Jewish Emancipation that was associated with greater assimilation of Jews into the mainstream society proceeded along with the increase of alienation and prejudice as noted earlier. Older and newer forms of antisemitism (involving claims of racial inferiority of Jews) came to the fore in what became known as political antisemitism (R. S. Landau, 2016) that is described below.

The Enlightenment had promised a change in how human beings viewed themselves, their world, and their God. Humankind would now apply reason and scientific thought to human problems, creating a better world for all. Rationality, tolerance, and skepticism of old beliefs were considered important for the enlightened person, country, and civilization. Traditional religion was viewed more skeptically by many (including the Founding Fathers of the United States). The church's authority over people's lives was diminished.

The values and ideals associated with the Enlightenment had far-reaching consequences throughout Western societies. They went hand-in-hand with the lessening of social, economic, and political restrictions on the Jewish people that occurred roughly simultaneously with the uneven and incomplete emancipation of the Jews in Europe during this period. Depending on the countries involved, Jews increasingly had greater freedom of movement and enjoyed integration into the social, civic, and economic activities of European societies. They were more welcome in urban life and less restricted to ghettos.

The Jewish Emancipation that was a part of the larger Enlightenment movement began in the late seventeenth century. It offered promise to the Jews and to the larger German society through changing social and economic structures and interests. As Grab (1984) writes:

> The medieval compulsory regulations could not be maintained, because the dynamic new competitive and profit-oriented system based on economic efficiency and achievement demanded changes in the social relationships and tended to regard religious faith and ethnic extraction as a private matter. (p. 225)

It seemed for a time that changing social and economic conditions would improve the lot of Jews in central Europe. Emancipation did not come about because of Enlightenment values, however, and does not seem to have been demanded by the German citizenry (unlike the situation in other European countries). German leaders felt that greater liberalization was in their own best interests. Capitalistic societies functioned better with greater freedoms. Grab (1984) continues:

> In Germany, however, where no successful revolution had taken place, the democratic consciousness of the people was less developed than in those countries which had liberated themselves from their traditional values. Without greater support of the people, the goals of emancipation would continually be threatened. (pp. 228–229)

Indeed, there was continued opposition to Jewish emancipation, integration, and assimilation in the eighteenth and nineteenth centuries, although strides were made in these directions. "The battle for securing the emancipation of Jews had been long drawn-out and bitter" (Pulzer, 1964/1988, p. xix). Many Jews eagerly became involved in the larger society as emancipation progressed, joining the professions, receiving secular education, and participating more actively in civic society. The greater visibility and activity of the Jews in German society (and in the military) created problems, however. This became apparent in the latter part of the nineteenth century as Jews became scapegoats for economic misfortune. Jews became identified with Bolshevism, on the one hand, and with capitalism, on the other.

Antisemitism seems to have been especially prominent in the latter third of the nineteenth century and into the twentieth century. Its character changed, however, from longstanding prejudice based on religious intolerance. It became more political and racial in nature. As Pulzer (1964/1988) points out, speaking of that time,

> Modern political anti-Semitism is different from any earlier, sporadic outbreaks of Jew-baiting. It was brought about by conditions which had not existed before the last third of the nineteenth century; only then was it possible to organize political movements wholly or partly on the basis of anti-Semitism, and to make anti-Semitism part of a coherent set of ideas. (p. ix)

The "objective of all anti-Semites was to reverse the legal emancipation of the Jews, as enshrined in the Law of 3 July 1869 . . ." (Pulzer, 1964/1988, p. xviii). This was not successfully accomplished, however, until enactment of the Nuremberg laws in 1935.

Religious antisemitism based on allegations against Jews for purported behaviors from centuries past did not cease, but racial antisemitism and the misuse of Darwinian theory became more prominent. Jews were subject to the familiar accusations that they were attempting to rule the world through nefarious (mainly financial) activities. As would be true later in the Nazi era when Jews accounted for about one percent of the German population (Landau, 2016) but held a much higher percentage of positions in the professions and among educated elites, suspicions of Jewish influence and designs became prominent. By the beginning of World War I, these currents were clear in German society. Jews would come to be blamed for the war or thought of as disloyal to Germany and loyal only to a worldwide web of Jews and Jewish financial interests. Many Jews, perhaps attempting to prove their loyalty to Germany in World War I through military service, served in numbers greater than their proportion in the population would suggest (Landau, 2016), but these efforts were often discounted and Jewish loyalty continued to be questioned.

For Pulzer (1964/1988), antisemitism of the empire period (1871–1914) was a necessary but not sufficient condition for the Holocaust:

> The defeat of November 1918 led to an extreme intensification of the anti-Jewish propaganda ... Pan-German nationalists who had prepared the war and hoped to attain world hegemony, laid the responsibility for the defeat upon the Jews and accused them of having stabbed the brave German soldier in the back. (Grab, 1984, p. 232)

This is language similar to that used by Hitler in *Mein Kampf* (mentioned again later) as he described the Jewish role in World War I.

The success of the Jews, despite racial and political antisemitism, was nonetheless evident through their visibility and activity in German society during the Weimar Republic (1919–1933). Jews were appointed to high positions in the government, being both foreign and finance ministers. This success was accompanied by denigration of the Jews that reached an ironic point in the post-World War I period. It was at this time, as Grab (1984) indicates, "German Jewry reached the peak of its success in the Weimar Republic and was at the same time more threatened than ever before" (p. 232). This would become apparent with the rise of the National Socialist German Workers' Party (Nazi party) in the 1920s.

It seems very likely that the antisemitism specific to antagonisms in the late nineteenth and early twentieth centuries was in part due to the rising status and emancipation of the Jews, who were given full citizenship in 1871. Germans who preferred traditional "volkish" (sometimes also written "folkish," from the German word for folk, *Volk*) life and who were threatened by the Enlightenment and the Jewish emancipation that was a part of it, would have resented and felt threatened by the rise to equality and prominence of Jews in Germany.

Hitler (1925/1999) expresses this antagonism to the integration of Jews when he says in *Mein Kampf*,

> In the course of more than a thousand years he has learned the language of the host people to such an extent that he now thinks he can venture in future to emphasize his Judaism less and place his "Germanism" more in the foreground . . . With this begins one of the most infamous deceptions that anyone could conceive of. . . . Race, however, does not lie in the language, but exclusively in the blood, which no one knows better than the Jew. . . . (p. 312)

It is clear here that, in Hitler's eyes, there was no possibility of accepting Jews into German society and that Jews were believed to be a continual threat to the German people.

Dehumanization as a result of emancipation would have been intended to demonstrably and symbolically lower the Jew's social and personal status, which would simultaneously affirm a higher status for the Aryan German citizen. Among the Nazis' first actions after assuming power in 1933 was to begin the process of withdrawing citizenship from the Jews, essentially lowering their status further compared to the Aryan. The full removal of citizenship was completed through the Nuremberg laws in 1935.

The writings of Johann von Herder (1744–1803), an influential German philosopher of the Enlightenment, convey the conflict about Jews and emancipation that was present during this time. Von Herder's writings express a sense of openness to various religions and beliefs that was characteristic of the Enlightenment (Foster, 2019). Von Herder's views, for the most part, reflected the aspirations of the humanity that he thought was nature's highest achievement. He believed in equality, individualism, and freedom but rejected notions of racial superiority that would form a crucial aspect of the beliefs of political and racial antisemitism of the next century. Von Herder (1784/1800) wrote that "Every man is ultimately a world, in external appearance indeed similar to others, but internally an individual being, with whom no other coincides" (p. 139). Nations, cultures, and individuals differed, but these differences were the result of innate differences and cultural experiences that did not reflect innate superiority or inferiority. People had infinite variety and infinite individuality.

Von Herder (1784/1800) argued that there is no such thing as immutability, contradicting Hitler's (1925/1999) later arguments in *Mein Kampf* that Jews were the eternal enemy of the Aryan people. For von Herder, to consider Jews (or any other group) the eternal enemy of the German people was a misunderstanding of the nature of life. For von Herder (1784/1800), "*all mankind are only one and the same species*" (p. 140, italics in the original). Equality among all peoples was a desired principle of the Enlightenment, and von Herder espouses it strongly.

Von Herder (1784/1800) also was a humanist who did not believe in exclusion or elimination of supposed enemies. He was not a racist, and, in contrast to the racist beliefs of those rightists, Nazi sympathizers and Nazis who would become powerful in German in the latter part of the nineteenth century and beyond, he wrote, "I could wish the distinctions between the human species that have been made from a laudable zeal for discriminating science not be carried beyond due bounds" (p. 141). Von Herder clearly did not wish to be seduced by a science that would come to support racist beliefs.

For von Herder (1784/1800), humans "are at last but shades of the same great picture, extending through all ages and overall parts of the earth" (p. 142). Innate superiority of one nation or group over another nation or group does not exist. Humanity develops through the exercise of reason, not, as the Nazis of a little more than a century later thought, through the perfection of one race and the elimination of another.

These promises of Enlightenment thinking, with their emphases on the individual and on freedom of expression and equality, remained to a large degree unfulfilled. In Germany, questions of racial superiority became important. The mid-nineteenth-century writer Arthur de Gobineau, in contrast to von Herder, represents a rejection of Enlightenment values, at least in terms of human equality.

Arthur de Gobineau (1816–1882) was an influential aristocrat, diplomat, and traveler who took a deep interest in racial differences among groups. He is considered a proponent of "scientific racism," the belief that biologically determined racial differences explain why some groups, countries, and civilizations thrive and others do not. In words that sound strikingly like those of Adolf Hitler three quarters of a century later, de Gobineau (1853/1854) states that "the racial question overshadows all other problems of history, that it holds the key to them all, and that the inequality of the races from whose fusion a people is formed is enough to explain the whole course of its destiny (p. ix)."

De Gobineau (1853/1854) emphasizes that societies do not fail because of fanatical behavior, luxurious living, corruption of the morality of the people or religious differences; they do not fail because of poor governance. Societies and civilizations fail, according to de Gobineau, because of racial mixing, degeneration and dilution of the purity of their race (Gobineau, 1853/1854).

De Gobineau's (1853/1854) conclusions were seemingly based on his own observations, experiences, and personal anthropological studies. He was convinced that "degeneration" among racial groups was due to the mixing of the races that resulted ultimately in the reduction of intellectual capabilities and other positive qualities in "hybrid" peoples. De Gobineau (1853/1854) argued there were three main racial groups: white, black, and yellow. Intermingling among these groups had been widespread and deleterious for humankind.

For de Gobineau (1853/1854), the three races differed in numerous ways, physically, socially, and intellectually. He argued that the white group was the most advanced and influential in terms of world history and that it had contributed to the majority of civilizations in the world. Arguing, at least in part from a biblical perspective and using biblical terms, de Gobineau claimed that Adam, the first human, was a white man (which meant, for him, a Caucasian, a Semite, or a Japhetic). At some point, a splitting off or branching from the original white race occurred. Other racial groups, that he terms "black" (the Hamites) and "yellow" (the Mongols) were then formed (p. 143).

De Gobineau's view of human racial evolution, therefore, involved an initial biblical event (the creation of a white man) that was a monogenetic event to explain the origin of the races. This event was followed at some point by a division of humankind into the three distinct races mentioned above, thus conceptualizing a polygenetic origin of the races.

De Gobineau (1853/1854) argues that the many racial groups that have been intermixing for generations can still be distinguished, among other ways, through their speech and language development. He emphasizes that language also helps distinguish the allied feature of intelligence, which, along with language differences, provides convincing support for the racial superiority of the Caucasian group. In his view, "with regard to the special character of races, philology confirms all the facts of physiology and history" (de Gobineau, 1853/1854, p. 197). De Gobineau (1853/1854) goes on to state that:

> there is a perfect correspondence between the intellectual virtues of a race and those of its native speech; that languages are, in consequence, unequal in value and significance, unlike in their forms and basic elements, as races are also; that their modifications . . . like people's blood, disappear or become absorbed, when they are swamped by too many heterogeneous elements. . . . (p. 198)

The mixing of races, for de Gobineau as for Hitler decades later, creates lesser forms of humankind. There is, of course, no evidence for this assertion.

The white race, for de Gobineau (1853/1854), has been shown by history to be the most influential of the three races. He says,

> All civilizations derive from the white race, that none can exist without its help, and that a society is great and brilliant only so far as it preserves the blood of the noble group that created it, provided that this group itself belongs to the most illustrious branch of our species. (de Gobineau, 1853/1854, p. 209)

De Gobineau is speaking here of the "branch" of the white race known as "Aryans," although he does not define this group in any detail, save for its seeming origins on the Indian continent and its association with the Germanic races among others. He provides no proof for these assertions, but, in his emphasis on the superiority of the white race, he necessarily dehumanizes other groups, and provides support for the dehumanizing efforts of others.

De Gobineau (1853/1854) was highly influential in the nineteenth century and beyond. He was widely studied by late nineteenth-century political racists and later by Nazi party members and sympathizers. His assertions, as noted above, often read like passages from *Mein Kampf*, especially when Hitler (1925/1999) writes about Aryan superiority and the dangers of racial mixing and the "monstrosities" that are born of the mixing of races.

De Gobineau's racial theories, inappropriately presented as facts, would seem to have had the potential to incite those who wished to believe themselves members of a "master" or superior race to protect or defend their "superior" status at all costs from contamination or mixing with other races. Incitement of this type did indeed happen later in the Nazi era as racists, using the work of de Gobineau and others, fueled the anxieties of some Germans about intermarriage with Jews, who were considered racially lesser than the Aryan but still white.

## Political and Racial Antisemitism in the Late Nineteenth and the Twentieth Centuries Prior to the Nazis' Rise to Power. Antisemitic Writings

By the 1870s, however, the promise of the Enlightenment and the Jewish Emancipation with their integration into full civic life had become more controversial within German society. The great forward movement of a society without irrational prejudices and old blasphemies against the Jews, such as the blood libel described earlier, gave way to increased anti-Jewish sentiments. These new denigrations included the "old" prejudices and outlandish beliefs of centuries past but added new deceits to them.

Wilhelm Marr, a German journalist and antisemitic writer, coined the neologism "antisemitism" in 1878 to describe the activities and behaviors of individuals who propagated these calumnies against Jews. Antisemitism in European countries seemed especially strong in Germany. Marr's term spread in part through the actions of the newly founded German Antisemitic League that focused on alleged racial distinctions between Jews and Aryans (MacMaster, 2001, p. 94). In addition to the old Jewish stereotypes that framed the Jews as using Christian blood in religious practice, being Christ-killers, and the personification of devils, Jews were now assaulted with more contemporary accusations, including the assertion that they were interested in worldwide dominance, and that there was an international cabal of Jews who were plotting to control the world through economic and financial tyranny. Jews, in this line of thinking, were not interested in the volkish (folk) traditions of Germany, which were anathema to them (and with which they could not identify), but aligned themselves only with a secular state, modernity, and an urban way of life. They were felt to have no regard for German traditions.

It did not matter to individuals who were prejudiced or frightened about their own station in life if these characterizations were hyperbolic or false, or that the term "antisemitism" was inappropriate since it did not accurately describe a people or apply to other "Semites," such as Arabs. The term "antisemitic" achieved wide usage and came to be applied not only to anti-Jewish activities of the nineteenth and twentieth centuries, but, as noted earlier, to all anti-Jewish activities throughout history. Mass murders of Jews during the Crusades would, in this way of thinking, have been antisemitic acts although Christians of the time would have considered them actions against Jews, who they believed were Christ-killers.

The term "antisemitic" had another advantage for anti-Jewish groups in the late nineteenth and the twentieth centuries. Terms such as "Semitic" and "Aryan" were used by Nazis in Germany and their predecessors, followers, and sympathizers to denote erroneous assumptions about racial differences among people. For rightwing political and social groups of this time, the term "antisemitic" did not necessarily imply actions or beliefs taken against those espousing Judaism as a religion. The term antisemitism conveyed an animus against a racial group, the Semites, who, as Hitler (1925/1999) indicates in *Mein Kampf*, were considered the eternal enemy of the Aryan race, and its "mightiest counterpart."

These beliefs and their accompanying assumptions would have been inconceivable to Jews, who were themselves, as described later, an unarmed minority comprising about one percent of the German population at the beginning of the Nazi era.

For those Germans of the late nineteenth or the early to mid-twentieth centuries who considered themselves to be modern, enlightened, and perhaps not as easily swayed by religion as previous generations had been, this "new" scientific attitude about the world emphasized that people were racially different. Racial differences, according to this view, as it had been for de Gobineau decades earlier, determined identity and worth. The Aryan race (represented, first of all, by the Germans), according to this line of thinking, had the right (and the duty) to dominate, control, and ultimately to eliminate Jews, the Semites, who were the eternal enemies of the Aryan race.

This notion of the supremacy of the Aryan race gained support from numerous rightist thinkers and politicians who inappropriately used Darwinian principles to support their beliefs. The survival of the fittest was wrongly interpreted to mean that there was an eternal struggle for survival between the Aryan and Semitic races. The term "antisemitic" became largely synonymous with being anti-Jewish for these groups, and being Jewish was a matter of birth, rather than a reflection of asserted or demonstrated religious beliefs.

As with the Inquisition centuries before, asserted religious beliefs were suspect. Jews by birth were Semites and were therefore automatically considered mortal enemies of the Aryan race by those who traded in these false "scientific" theories, Darwinian or otherwise. As stated throughout this book, those who are dehumanized and considered "lesser" provide an opportune target for the malicious and violent impulses of anxious and malevolent members of the dominant group.

The inconsistency of using old religious hostilities to define the now objectionable racial group was apparently of little concern to those who chose to emphasize false notions of race to fuel their prejudices. These groups argued that Jews were Semites who should be eliminated from Germany (and Europe) one way or another. Those who espoused this view to varying degrees came to use political platforms to advocate their positions, as indicated in subsequent paragraphs.

The condition of Jews in Germany in the Early Modern period before emancipation was one of isolation, servitude, and dehumanization. Jews were often forced to live in ghettos, discrete areas in a given location to which they were restricted for the most part. Ruderman (1997) identifies Venice as the city having had the first Jewish ghetto that was instituted about 1516, but Fulbrook

(2019) identifies Speyer, in Germany, as having the first walled ghetto that dated to at least 1084.

There was certainly much to criticize about the actuality, the dehumanization in, and the symbolism of ghettos over the centuries of their existence. Ghettos clearly expressed the goals of the Christian community that feared the "contamination" and influence of the Jews on the Christian population. Ghettos were known to be cramped, dirty, disease-infested, and insular, characteristics often attributed to Jews themselves by their Christian neighbors. On the other hand, the physical safety of Jews was often a question in medieval (and later) communities in Europe, and living a sequestered and segregated existence behind a large wall that was locked at night was reassuring for some Jews who were afraid of or who did not wish to have contact with the larger Christian community (Ruderman, 1997).

Grab (1984) describes several additional dehumanizing conditions under which Jews lived in Germany prior to emancipation. Immigration and emigration were controlled by state authorities; there was a prescribed number of Jews who could marry in a given period. Jews could earn a living only through certain means. Jews were not allowed to produce material goods for sale; they could not cultivate the soil or join an artisan association or a handicraft guild. They were, however, allowed (encouraged) to become involved in the economic activities of the state. Some Jews became financiers for the state, facilitating financial and business transactions and state activities such as wars. Some functioned as bankers, pawnbrokers, or traders of cattle. They charged high rates of interest for loans, but this was in turn regulated by authorities who required high rates of taxation from the Jews.

The period following emancipation in the 1870s was a time of limited assimilation of Jews into the German federation. Assimilation and integration were met with degrees of resistance both in the larger society and in Jewish communities, although greater integration offered potential benefits (as well as drawbacks) both to the society and to Jews themselves. The backlash against this integrationist scenario saw old stereotypes and prejudices coming strongly to the fore.

Mosse (1978) comments that:

> The mystery of race transformed the Jew into an evil principle. This was nothing new for the Jew; after all, anti-Christ had been a familiar figure during the Middle Ages. But in the last decades of the nineteenth century and first half of the twentieth, the traditional legends which had swirled about the Jews in the past were revived as foils for racial mysticism and as instruments of political mobilization. (p. 113)

As we see, accusations of ritual murder, blood libel, and rootlessness had been leveled against Jews for centuries. Jews were castigated as members of a worldwide conspiracy. These calumnies, and the threats implied by them, were revitalized in the last decades of the nineteenth century and new canards added.

The notorious *Protocols of the Elders of Zion*, for example, was a tract written in Russia in the early years of the twentieth century purporting to describe a secret meeting of Jews who were plotting worldwide domination. The *Protocols* was a new and exceedingly influential addition to older conspiracy theories and antisemitic accusations that came to the fore during this period (Mosse, 1978).

Racial insults, while not new invectives hurled against Jews during this time (Landau, 2016), also arose with great force in what was seen by some to be a new pseudo-scientific and "rational" era. These calumnies were examples of the inappropriate and simplistic use of Darwinian theories applied in a sociocultural sense. Nazism in the 1920s would take these views to greater extremes and hammer the ostensible linkage between race, blood, and the Aryan people: "The legends about the Jews ... were kept alive, now as part of the race war that seemed imminent" (Mosse, 1978, p. 121).

This racialization of antisemitic discourse "was one element within a complex ideology that was essentially an expression of the anti-modernist and anti-democratic sentiments of social groups faced with crisis" (MacMaster, 2001, pp. 86–87). These groups included "conservative Christians, decaying aristocratic land owners, the *petite bourgeoisie*, small shopkeepers and artisans in decline" (MacMaster, 2001, p. 87). The concerns of these groups ranged "from xenophobia and radical nationalism to nostalgia for the passing of a traditional rural order" (MacMaster, 2001, p. 87). Antisemitism, for many individuals at this time, became a popular ideology spread by politicians, writers, academics, educated elites, and others. It helped these various groups, from conservative Christians to politicians, to shift blame onto Jews (and others) for aspects of their worlds that they were not able to control.

An important aspect of the evolution of antisemitism in Germany and elsewhere in this period was the development of political parties whose platforms contained, at times, harsh antisemitic rhetoric. Antisemitism replaced anti-Judaism as a way to express criticism, rejection, and at times violent inclinations towards Jews. As Pulzer (1964/1988) indicates, "The period of 1867–1914 becomes important because during it the movements and ideologies developed which matured after 1918" (pp. ix–x). While the Nazi party did not develop fully until after World War I, it, like other less "successful" political parties, had its roots in this period that emphasized nationalism, volkish (folk) interests, fascism, anti-Marxism, anti-liberalism, and racist and blood ties to agrarian and traditional German values.

The large number of rightist political parties that formed in this period contrasted with leftist and more central parties. Among them, the Nazi party was distinctive especially through the use of violence to achieve its objectives; this party was notable for its sadism, cruelty, and "lack of scruples" that was used actively to rouse the masses and attract those of the middle class that felt dispossessed or disillusioned. They were also effective in breaking down barriers between older right radical groups and the working class (Pulzer, 1964/1988). While other rightwing groups emphasized rhetoric rather than action, the Nazi party was clearly also interested in action. Pulzer (1964/1988) reports that there were over 100 Jewish cemetery desecrations and forty synagogue desecrations from 1923 to 1931. Most of these seemed to be connected with the Nazi party, an ominous sign of what was to come.

The main party of the left prior to the rise of Adolf Hitler and the third Reich was the Social Democratic Party whose views were progressive and more egalitarian. Not surprisingly, this was the party that attracted Jews, many of whom had become involved in banking and financial interests, commerce, and industrialization after the Jewish Emancipation. This involvement would prove to be a decidedly mixed blessing, as it allowed the continuance of the stereotyping and criticism of Jews as "bankers" and financial dealers who wished to control the world through money webs and worldwide networks dominated by international Jewry.

The assimilated, successful Jew in the capitalistic society of twentieth-century Germany was rejected by the rightist parties, although the unassimilated Jew of the eighteenth and the nineteenth centuries was also not acceptable.

> The nationalist anti-Semites of the nineteenth century attacked the Jew for retaining his separate identity: they wanted him to be assimilated. The racialists of the twentieth century frantically tried to prove that the Jew must always remain different. What offended them was his all-too-successful assimilation. (Pulzer, 1964/1988, p. 318)

It is clear that Jews would be criticized by rightist and racist segments of the population regardless of social or economic conditions in the society.

These shifts toward a new form of antisemitism and away from the traditional anti-Jewish bias on religious grounds were accompanied by, and in some cases depended upon, advances in science and industrialization, as well as a greater acceptance of secularism and a greater disaffection with traditional religious views. Pulzer (1964/1988) points out that early Christian conservative antisemitism rejected Darwinism on religious grounds; with the turn of the century, however, "survival of the fittest" "became increasingly attractive to political anthropologists and increasingly useful to doctrines of racial superiority" (Pulzer, 1964/1988, pp. 286–287) even though Darwin's theories were misinterpreted and misapplied for political and racist purposes. Misusing Darwinian theory in these cases worked to the detriment of the Jewish segment of the society and to the benefit of those who chose to channel their prejudices along racial lines.

From these racial perspectives, the Aryan race was the world's superior race; Jews and Judaism, as examples of the Semitic and inferior race, were its enemy. Many Germans, especially those on the political right, argued that Aryans had been defeated in World War I because of the treachery of others; often this explicitly meant the Jews. These rightwing conservative parties were not only openly antisemitic, they also were against the Weimar Republic that had been formed in the wake of Germany's defeat in World War I and the abdication of the Kaiser in 1918. One of the reasons the rightist groups were opposed to the Weimar Republic was because participation in governance was open to and, in their eyes, associated with Jews. These rightist parties wished to reverse the humiliation of Germany in the war, and considered Jews, now more socially noticeable and prominent than ever before, convenient to target as enemies of the German Aryan state.

Arguments and vitriol against Jews were thus an attractive antidote for the challenges of the changing times that included increased secularization, industrialization, economic catastrophe, social dislocation, loss of the monarchy, and humiliation around the defeat in World War I.

Another painful misfortune associated with the military defeat was a significant loss of German territory (Fulbrook, 2019). Germany's area had increased significantly with unification of the German Empire in 1871. As a result of the Treaty of Versailles that ended World War I, however, Alsace-Lorraine was to be returned to France (from which it had been taken during the war preceding German unification); Poland, a newly reconstructed country, was to receive West Prussia, Upper Silesia, and Posen; Danzig was to become a free city that would be supervised by the League of Nations; and a "Polish corridor" that separated East Prussia from the larger German land mass was developed. African colonies that Germany controlled were lost. In addition, any union between Germany and Austria was forbidden (Fulbrook, 2019).

The various stressors of the post-World War I period provided fertile opportunities for scapegoating, which always found a comfortable resting place in speaking of Jews, perhaps especially those who wished to become socially mobile in the post-unification environment. Considering the attitude of one of these many rightist groups, the Christian-Social Party, Pulzer (1964/1978) comments,

> Most of the party did not bother their heads about questions of detail. For them, anti-Semitism was an emotional and electoral necessity. They neither did, nor could, decide whether they hated the Jew as a capitalist or a Socialist, as the member of a false religion or of a foreign race. (p. 310)

Nazism and other rightwing parties thus benefitted from, and seemed to foster, incoherence and social disruption as means to further their political aims.

Illustrative of the split in German society between rightist antisemitic parties and leftist secular parties during the post-unification period are the following excerpts from the Antisemitic People's Party platform of Otto Bockel (1859–1923) and a resolution of the Social Democratic Party (reprinted in Pulzer 1964/1978). Bockel's People's Party says: "The Anti-Semite Party is faithful to emperor and Reich, Prince and fatherland. It aims at the repeal, by legal means, of Jewish emancipation, the placing of Jews under an Aliens' Law, and the creations of healthy social legislation" (p. 328–329). The party platform later says, "Only Christian German men (of non-Jewish extraction) are to be elected into legislative bodies and to be employed in state or municipal offices" (p. 329).

In contrast, the Social Democratic Party resolution states:

> Anti-Semitism springs from the discontent of certain bourgeois strata, who find themselves adversely affected by the development of capitalism.... Social Democracy fights anti-Semitism as a movement directed against the natural development of society ... the petty bourgeois and peasant strata stirred up against the Jewish capitalists must come to recognize that not only the Jewish capitalist but also the capitalist class generally is their enemy and that only their realization of Socialism can free them from their misery. (p. 333)

These two excerpts from political party statements show diametrically opposed views in German society at this time, and the divergent, and perhaps irreconcilable opinions about the Jewish role in society.

Another way to understand the turbulent political and social period that included the years from the 1870s through the pre-Nazi era is to review prominent writings of this time. One of the famous political theorists of this period was Georges Sorel (1847–1922). Sorel's work was notable for many reasons, including an instability of views that reflected at least in part the shifting political and social winds of his time. Sorel's writings have been described as "dispersed and unsystematic" (Vernon, 1978, p. 5) but are especially interesting here for their emphasis on the value of violence to promote revolution and social change and his later adherence to conservative, anti-republican, and antisemitic views.

Sorel's best-known work, *Reflections on Violence*, published originally in 1906 during the period of his greater interest in socialism, emphasizes the importance he attaches to violence. Sorel's sympathies seemed to lie with "those who argued for the violence of a conspiratorial band aiming to reestablish traditional authority . . ." (Shils, 1950, p. 22). In this work, Sorel (1906/1950) states, "It is to violence that Socialism owes those high ethical values by means of which it brings *salvation* to the modern world" (Sorel, 1906/1950, p. 249). Violence for Sorel, at least at this stage of his writings, is a means to a higher social and ethical good. His later adoption of rightwing authoritarian Catholicism was accompanied by antisemitism, however, and serves as a prelude to fascist totalitarianism that is part of his legacy (Antliff, 2005).

The Dreyfus affair, in which Captain Alfred Dreyfus, a Jewish officer in the French army, was accused in 1894 of passing military secrets to Germany, fueled the writings and polital agitation of antisemitic forces at this time. Dreyfus ultimately was found to be innocent, but not before he was convicted and sent to prison on Devil's Island. The Dreyfus affair and the apparent antisemitism that was associated with his prosecution split the French public. The charges against Dreyfus "reflected both a climate of paranoid nationalism, as well as a consistent theme in European anti-Semitism which viewed the Jews as a treacherous internal enemy" (MacMaster, 2001, p. 111). By the end of the century, the affair was the stimulus that split French internal opinion into disparate factions. Jews were associated with post-Enlightenment, rationalistic, egalitarian, universalistic, and sectarian views. These perceptions were of course pitted against conservative Catholic and traditional forces (MacMaster, 2005). Antisemitism surged with writers such as Sorel, who was clearly on the side of the traditional, reactionary forces that lamented the loss of religious and social mores of the past.

Another social commentator and writer at this time who had great influence through World War I and beyond was Houston Stewart Chamberlain (1855–1927). Chamberlain's writings added a strong racial, mythic, and spiritual dimension to the Germanic emphasis on the greatness and spiritual journey of the Aryans. Chamberlain was an English citizen who became disenchanted with his homeland. He travelled extensively as a young person and was strongly influenced by Richard Wagner, who himself "blended the racial mystique and the concept of Christian salvation most effectively" (Mosse, 1978, p. 104). Chamberlain met Hitler and greatly admired him. He ultimately became a German citizen, settled in Bayreuth, Germany, and married one of Richard Wagner's daughters.

Chamberlain believed that "the Germanic race entered history as the saviors of mankind and as the heirs of the Greeks and Romans" (Mosse, 1978, p. 106). For Chamberlain, the essence of German religion was to bestow "infinite vistas upon the soul and . . . to keep science within narrowly defined bounds" (Mosse, 1978, p. 105). It was the Aryan "race-soul" that the Germans shared. Christ, in Chamberlain's view, had not been a Jew but rather an Aryan prophet with an "Aryan race-soul" who lived among other Aryans in Galilee. Aryans, for Chamberlain, were destined to wage struggles against their enemies in order to fulfill their mission in life. He considered Catholics an enemy of the German Aryans although he held that the greatest enemy of the Aryans were the Jews, who embodied all that was negative in the world (including materialism and immorality) in comparison with the Aryans. Chamberlain believed the "Jews were the devil and the Germans the chosen people" (Mosse, 1978, p. 106). For the world to experience a spiritual revolution, the Jews would have to be defeated and the Aryan race-soul would then dominate the world (Mosse, 1978, p. 107).

Chamberlain's writing, in his influential *Foundations of the Nineteenth Century* (1911), does not provide a factual basis for what seem to be his many outlandish racial assertions. In the midst of his writings that are intended to be historical, there is a struggle to come to grips with what he believes was the Aryan Christ growing up among the materialistic Jews who he argues have been a successful people throughout the ages. Speaking of Christ growing up among Jews, Chamberlain (1911) says,

> It was in these surroundings that Christ grew up . . . He awoke in the direct presence of God and Divine Providence. He found here what He would have found nowhere else in the world: a complete scaffolding ready for Him, within which His entirely new concept of God and religion could be built up. After Jesus had lived, nothing remained of the genuinely Jewish idea; now that the temple was built the scaffolding could be removed. But it had served its purpose, and the building would have been unthinkable without it. (pp. 233–234)

Christianity, apparently, was the new temple.

Chamberlain (1911) goes on to assert, speaking of Judaism as a materialistic religion, "... yes, assuredly the most materialistic—religion in the world" (p. 234). This is a time-worn diatribe and/or a form of misinformation against Jews for which Chamberlain does not provide factual evidence. The lack of evidence for his claims unfortunately did not stop a receptive rightwing German audience, including Adolf Hitler, from speaking glowingly of his insights.

In other passages, Chamberlain (1911) emphasizes what he considers to be the historical superiority of the pure Teutonic people that had been compromised by Jewish blood. He also seems to rail against emancipation and intermarriage when he maintains, again without facts,

> From the moment the Teuton awakes, a new world begins to open out, ... one in which, in the nineteenth century especially, there have appeared new elements ... as, for example, the Jews and the formerly pure Teutonic Slavs, who by mixture of blood have now become "un-Teutonised" ... (Chamberlain, 1911, p. lxvi)

He later writes, "We are left with the simple and clear view that our whole civilization and culture of to-day is the work of one definite race of men, the Teutonic" (p. lxvii), which for Chamberlain (1911) is "the one great North European race..." (p. lxvii). Race is for Chamberlain, as it was for de Gobineau, and as it will be seen to be for Hitler, the defining feature of human existence.

The Teutonic people and Christianity are inevitably superior for Chamberlain, and of course, being superior and "chosen," these entities are continually challenged by the inferior Semitic race whom they have allowed at times to defeat them. Chamberlain's writings expose the reader to calumny and diatribe that has no evidence to support its claims but that does have the potential to harness anger, and in some cases, rage, against the Jew, whose religion is considered "beggarly-poor" (Chamberlain, 1911, p. lxxix).

Political parties and political activities that advocated virulent antisemitism reached their greatest influence under Adolf Hitler (1889–1945) and the Nazi party, whose efforts were influential in the 1920s even before the Nazi era (1933–1945). The best-known example of immensely influential antisemitic writing around this time is of course Hitler's *Mein Kampf* (1925/1999), a book Hitler wrote (or dictated) while serving a prison sentence for his part in a failed insurrection against the German government (the Beer Hall Putsch of 1923).

## Ideology of National Socialism and Adolf Hitler. *Mein Kampf*

*Mein Kampf* is a work of great passion, anger, and vitriol. Repetitive, forceful, and devoid of documentation or historical support, this polemic castigates more than one enemy (Jews, Socialists, those Germans who "stabbed" the volkish people "in the back" in World War I) but has a major focus on the issue of Jews and race. Hitler says, "Without the clearest knowledge of the racial problem and hence of the Jewish problem there will never be a resurrection of the German nation" (Hitler, 1925/1999, p. 339). Again, there is no evidence provided for the denigration and hatred toward Jews that is expressed here. This reader is left with the impression, amplified in other paragraphs and chapters of this book, that the fear of the Jews was an irrational and at times delusional anxiety about being undone or destroyed by them. In this sense, Hitler felt forced to eliminate the Jews because he feared they would eliminate him.

The development of the Nazi party and the beliefs that governed the expression of its power and the power of its leader, Adolf Hitler, were based less on a carefully thought-out philosophy and more on the implementation of actions based on romantic and mystical ideas that rejected the positivism and materialism present elsewhere in Europe at the end of the nineteenth and the beginning of the twentieth century (Mosse, 1978). Romanticism had deep roots in German culture, and many of German citizens were unwilling to leave this cultural tradition behind under pressures of materialism and capitalism that arose during the Enlightenment.

For many Germans who would come to value goals, ideals, prejudices, and aspirations of the Nazi party and its precursor rightwing and ultraconservative groups, a clue to understanding and experiencing a sense of meaning in life did not come through Enlightenment goals and practices but through "a belief in nature's cosmic life-force, a dark force whose mysteries could be understood, not through science, but through the occult" (Mosse, 1978, p. 81). This ideology promised a national renewal and emphasized a unified German nation and a German people (*Volk*) that placed their native country above all else.

Many late nineteenth- and early twentieth-century Germans believed individuals saw best with their souls rather than through the lens of modern rationality. The rightist views of the time, latching onto the much-maligned Jewish Emancipation of 1871, became fused with a glorification of an Aryan past. Views about the importance of mystery in understanding the world drew from both a romanticized vision of the past and from contemporary sources, such as the theosophy of Helena Blavatsky, and the writings of Guido von List and Lanz von Liebenfels, which were deeply influential in promulgating the idea that the Aryans were a master race that should rule the world, but they were constantly thwarted by a materialistic and sinister Semitic race of Jews who continually plotted worldwide rule (Mosse, 1978).

In this way of thinking, the Jew stood in opposition to the *Volk*: "The Jew, as an alien disrupter of the volk, represented capitalism and the Jewish ghetto . . ." (Vasey, 2006, p. 39).

> The volkish irrationality on which National Socialism was based found its epitome in the occult societies which flourished in nineteenth and early twentieth century . . . this activity took the form of a fusion of German volkish neo-pagan romanticism and the doctrine of Theosophy. . . . (Vasey, 2006, p. 39)

National Socialism would provide a home for these unfounded but influential mystical traditions.

Theosophy "postulated a prehistoric past ruled by an elite of mystic initiates and inhabited by a succession of superior races . . . the latest of these superior races was the Aryans" (Vasey, 2006, p. 43). From a fusion of theosophy with occultism, volkish nationalism, Aryan racism, and antisemitism there developed a theory known as Ariosophy (Vasey, 2006, pp. 67, 68).

> The Ariosophists . . . combined volkish nationalism and racism with occult notions borrowed from the theosophy of Helena Petrovna Blavatsky, in order to prophesy and vindicate a coming era of German world rule. Their writings described a prehistoric golden age, when wise gnostic priesthoods had expounded occult-racist doctrines and ruled over a superior and racially pure society. (Goodrick-Clarke, 1985/2004, p. 2)

It is clear that the notions of Aryan supremacy had centuries-old roots.

Hitler (1925/1995) presumably did not object to Jews on the basis of religion, as had so many before him. Hitler's antisemitism was based on previously discussed notions of race and the eternal conflict between the Aryan and the Semitic race. According to this view, Jews threatened the Aryan or Nordic race through assimilation, contamination, and intermarriage with unsuspecting Aryans. Jews therefore had to be eliminated. Race, for Hitler, was the key to understanding all of human history:

> The blood of every person and every race contained the soul of a person and likewise the soul of his race, the Volk. Hitler believed that the Aryan race, to which all 'true' Germans belonged, was the race whose blood (soul) was of the highest degree. (Vasey, 2006, p. 59)

It was not only a cleansing of the German people that Hitler sought, however. His aim was a fulfillment of what he saw as Aryan destiny:

> *What we must fight for is to safeguard the existence and reproduction of our race and our people, the sustenance of our children and the purity of our blood, the freedom and independence of the fatherland, so that our people may mature for the fulfillment of the mission allotted it by the creator of the universe* (Hitler, 1925/1999, p. 214, italics in the original).

For Hitler, the Jew was the greatest impediment to the aspirations of the Aryan race. He wrote, "The mightiest counterpart to the Aryan is represented by the Jew" (Hitler, 1925/1999, p. 300). Hitler felt it was crucial for the Aryans to focus on what he considered to be the malign presence of the Jews in order to combat the influence of the Semitic menace. In his view, the destruction of the Jews was necessary to achieve the true destiny of the Aryan people and to produce a heightened form of civilization that would result after a successful confrontation with the Jewish threat. "Without the clearest knowledge of the racial problem and hence of the Jewish problem there will never be a resurrection of the German nation" (Hitler, 1925/1999, p. 339). Hitler's writing here seems ominous for the future of Jews in Germany.

For Hitler and the Nazis, "Aryans were, in essence, god-men on earth, but through blood poisoning lost their ruling position" (Vasey, 2006, p. 62). The greater mission of the Aryan race (and the German people) was to regain leadership in the world and to produce a higher civilization and higher Aryan culture. As Vasey (2006) writes, "If this were done, racially and thus spiritually pure human beings could be produced, ensuring Aryan world domination" (p. 62). The one major obstacle to the fulfillment of Aryan destiny was the Jew, "the poisoner of the blood (soul) of the Aryan race, thus inhibiting its spiritual growth and endangering its divine destiny" (Vasey, 2006, p. 62). Hitler believed that: "Once the Jew was purged from Europe, Germany would be able to produce pure Aryans, who would be physically and spiritually perfect human beings ... demigod rulers ..." (Vasey, 2006,

p. 63). In *Mein Kampf*, Hitler (1925/1999) emphasizes: "I believe that I am acting in accordance with the will of the Almighty Creator: *by defending myself against the Jew, I am fighting for the work of the Lord*" (p. 65, ital. in original). For Hitler, the conflict with the Jews was, apparently, a holy crusade, a spiritual quest.

This desire or, one might say, "obsession" to raise the Aryans to their "rightful place" as the master race of the world required a lowering or reduction of the Jew's status and the elimination of Jews from Europe. Hitler believed that the Aryans' fate was to rise above mere humans to become what they really were, or could have been: the master race. This aspiration required a dehumanization and diminution of the Jew, a member of the inferior Semitic race. The Nazi leader believed that, as the Jew was dehumanized, humiliated, broken down, and eliminated through various means (such as emigration or death), the Aryan's superiority over the eternal enemy would be confirmed. A cosmic war between good and evil, the spiritual Aryan and the materialistic Jew, would be decided once and for all.

Hitler (1925/1999) wrote:

> *Thus, the highest purpose of a folkish state is concern for the preservation of those original racial elements which bestow culture and create the beauty and dignity of a higher mankind. We, as Aryans, can conceive of the state only as the living organism of a nationality which not only assures the preservation of this nationality, but by the development of its spiritual and ideal abilities leads it to the highest freedom.* (p. 394, italics in the original)

For Hitler, the integrity of the Aryan race was paramount and must be defended at all costs.

Hitler argued that Jews, the eternal enemy, were the major threat to the Aryan people and the vision he held for them. "Only the total destruction of the Jews could thus save the Germans and enable them to enter the promised land" (Goodrick-Clarke, 1985/2004, p. 203). Hitler believed that the Jews must voluntarily leave the European soil, be driven from it, or be eliminated. Dehumanization of increasing severity was the road to this end.

In *Mein Kampf*, Hitler repeatedly condemns Jews as an inferior race, a designation that he believes is based on science and rationality. The Jewish religion is not Hitler's stated concern. Hitler is concerned with race and the bloodline of the Jew. He argues that the Jewish bloodline has been kept, for the most part, pure through the centuries, but now, in his view, it attempts to infect the unsuspecting Aryan who already has been contaminated by the degenerate Jew in other parts of the world.

For Hitler (1925/1999), the Jew is the "eternal mushroom of humanity" (p. 123), ugly, despicable, unclean, and smelly. He believes that it is the Jew who threatens to bring down the German people, the volkish citizens of the pure Aryan race. Jews intend to accomplish their goals, he states, through a worldwide financial conspiracy in which Jews will conspire with one another internationally. He claims that Catholics will fight Protestants and countries will fight with one another, but in his view the inspiraton for the destruction of the Aryan race is actually the international financier of destruction, the wandering, worldwide Jew. "Catholics and Protestants wage a merry war with one another, and the mortal enemy of Aryan humanity and all Christendom laughs up his sleeve" (Hitler, 1925/1999, p. 561). Likewise, he charges that

> while the Jew sold the freedom of the nation and betrayed our fatherland to international high finance, now again he succeeds in causing the two German denominations to assail one another, while the foundations of both are corroded and undermined by the poison of the international world Jew. (Hitler, 1925/1999, p. 562)

Hitler urges potential religious foes to unite against the Jew, who he claims is really their (and his) greatest enemy.

In Hitler's (1925/1999) view, Jews comprise a nation within a nation, they are the leaders of the communist movement and the advocates for civil rights and equality for all. These are political positions that Hitler considers inimical to the German state because they place the continuance of the pure Aryan race at risk. Jews, he claims, are advocates for the demise of the volkish state; they are considered parasites who choose an international Marxist order that is, somehow, also simultaneously capitalist. Hitler emphasizes that it is the state's responsibility to preserve only the fittest of its citizens. Human rights mean preservation of the Aryan state,

> *No, there is only one holiest human right, and this right is at the same time the holiest obligation, to wit: to see to it that the blood is preserved pure and, by preserving the best humanity, to create the possibility of a nobler development of these beings.* (Hitler, 1925/1999, p. 402, italics in the original)

These last statements contain implicit threats against disabled individuals, Jews, and others who Hitler thinks do not "contribute" or are detrimental to the ideal Aryan state.

Marriage, in Hitler's view, should not lead to the defilement of the Aryan race but must reflect *"the consecration of an institution which is called upon to produce images of the Lord and not monstrosities halfway between man and ape"* (Hitler, 1925/1999, p. 402, italics in the original). Speaking of Jews, Hitler (1925/1999) says,

> This contamination of our blood... is carried on systematically by the Jew today... these black parasites of the nation defile our inexperienced young blond girls and thereby destroy something which can no longer be replaced in the world.... The significance of this for the future of the earth does not lie in whether Protestants defeat the Catholics or the Catholics the Protestants, but in whether the Aryan man is preserved for the earth or dies out. (p. 562)

Hitler was not concerned with religious denominations but rather with everyone's willingness to support his notion of the supremacy of the Aryan people.

The atrocities to come in the Nazi era, including the dehumanization of the Jews (and others) and the ultimate sentence of genocide and indiscriminate death for millions can readily be imagined from reading *Mein Kampf* (1925/1999). This work culminated a tradition of political and racial antisemitism in pre-World War II Germany that built on centuries of antisemitism, which focused originally on religious prejudice but later also included harsh racial bigotry.

The following chapters discuss steps taken by Hitler and the Nazi government to add racial invective to the longstanding antisemitism in order to dehumanize Jews and convince German citizens that Jews were an inferior, subhuman people who had always been aligned against the superior Aryan race. Hitler (1925/1999) argued that interactions between Jews and Germans would in the end produce beings who were not really human at all, beings who were, as noted above, *"monstrosities halfway between man and ape"* (p. 402, italics in the original). Jews therefore were threatening and dangerous to the Aryan race and, from Hitler's perspective, they were appropriate for, and deserving of, "elimination," a term that can be taken to suggest physical removal from Germany and Europe, or extermination and death. Both of these interpretations proved to be well-founded.

# CHAPTER 3

# Dehumanization. Research. Definitions. Examples in the Nazi Era

## Introduction

Jews were considered immoral, ugly, and corrupt by Nazis and their sympathizers during and before the Nazi era. They were denigrated as animals, vermin and as racially inferior beings, constantly scheming to take over the world. They were felt to be subhuman, and therefore could be treated as less than human by those who wished them ill. These attributions and the behaviors that resulted from them reflect a process termed dehumanization, a process Haslam and Loughnan (2014) describe as "the most striking violation of our belief in a common humanity: our Enlightenment assumption that we are all essentially one and the same" (p. 401).

This chapter will describe dehumanization in greater detail. It will offer a definition of this phenomenon and indicate centuries-old themes, as well as factors unique to the Nazi era and the decades before it that contributed to the dehumanization of the Jews. Illustrations from Jewish conditions during the Nazi era will be given. The perspective offered is that increasingly severe dehumanization of the Jews led to and facilitated the murder and genocide that was the Holocaust.

## Dehumanization—Definitions, with Specific Reference to Germany and the Nazi Era

Dehumanization is a widely used concept, but one that has been studied relatively infrequently (Smith, 2011). According to Smith (2011), who provides a comprehensive approach to dehumanization, this phenomenon refers to

> the act of conceiving of people as subhuman creatures rather than as human beings.... When we dehumanize people we don't just think of them in terms of what they lack, we also think of them as creatures that are less than human. (p. 26)

Subhumans are believed to lack something special, a particular essence, often difficult to define, that makes them and members of their "outgroup" different and far less worthy and valuable than those who are in the "ingroup" (Smith, 2011, pp. 33–39). Members of the "ingroup" think of themselves and their own group as being more human than "others" who are in the "outgroup" (Smith, 2011, pp. 49, 71). Subhumans, according to this line of thinking, "can be enslaved, tortured, or even exterminated—treated in ways in which we could not bring ourselves to treat those whom we regard as members of our own kind" (Smith, 2011, p. 2; Volpato & Andrighetto, 2015).

Dehumanization for Smith (2011) is a psychological experience that is rooted in the biology, culture, and architecture of the mind. Although it is not clear what is meant by "architecture," this presumably relates to the biological structure of the brain. To the degree that biology and culture (especially) are involved, there must be various factors, personal, social, and/or cultural, that contribute to, and influence, dehumanizing attitudes and behaviors.

Leyens (2009) and his colleagues (Leyens et al., 2007) also have emphasized that ingroup members consider themselves to have a particular essence that differentiates them from outgroup members. Their studies fall in the realm of "infrahumanization," a less severe form of denigration than dehumanization (Haslam & Loughnan, 2014; Leyens, 2009). The development of the concept of infrahumanization is related to essentialism; ingroups believe that they alone have a fully human essence. Leyens (2009) says that essentialism is "to be understood as *fundamental, essential differences* between groups leading to the belief that the ingroup is more fully human than another group" (p. 808, italics in original).

This view of essentialism potentially leads directly to the concept of "essential" racial differences among groups, as emphasized by the Germans in the period before and during the Nazi era. Using this formulation of essentialism emphasizes that the ingroup is more "human" and inherently better or superior to the outgroup, which is racially inferior and morally and ethically deficient. Jews, who were felt to be crafty, scheming, and corrupt, were considered subhuman, having characteristics that made them less worthy than other humans (even if these beliefs had no objective basis). Hitler (1925/1999) and other German leaders believed that these attributions based on race must not be allowed to contaminate the pure and "essentially superior" German race.

For Leyens (2009), human "essence is what people are beyond contingencies," that is, once an "essence" is considered (such as being a member of the Aryan race), particular social constructions or individual or group efforts or qualities, are not important (p. 808). In this context, the notion of essences is "completely opposite to the idea of groups as social constructions" (Leyens et al., 2007, p. 142). Essences are therefore considered immutable—for better or worse.

Leyens and his colleagues have conducted a number of experimental studies focused on the perception of emotions in ingroups and outgroups. These experiments have shown that subjects believed that more positive as well as more negative uniquely human emotions are found in ingroups than in outgroups (Leyens et al, 2007). Leyens (2009) says that members of the ingroup see themselves as sharing "basic, human characteristics that mark them as inherently different, more human than outgroup members" (p. 814). An important aspect of the development of a sense of essence may be that people infrahumanize others or groups they do not like or with whom they do not wish to affiliate. Essentialism, then, is at the core of infrahumanization. It is also characteristic of dehumanization, which is considered a more severe form of infrahumanization.

For Leyens et al. (2007), "The belief in human essence is a poisonous symbol..." (p. 167). It is poisonous because it separates people and creates ingroups and outgroups that act upon their own sense of uniqueness. Both groups think of the other group as different. This sets up mischaracterizations, distrust, and notions of superiority and inferiority between the groups. In the Nazi era, these "poisonous" symbols of superiority and inferiority were related to presumed racial differences that were used to justify the murder of Jews by those who called themselves Aryans.

This formulation posits a basic sense of difference that members of both the ingroup and outgroup have about themselves and the other. For the ingroup, the imprecise sense of being somehow different, more human than those in the outgroup, seems potentially to have significantly harmful consequences for the outgroup when pressed beyond the bounds of infrahumanization to the more severe dehumanization. This point will be illustrated in a subsequent section in this chapter on dehumanization and ideology in the Nazi era where a belief in Aryan superiority and uniqueness had "poisonous" consequences. It will also be important in considering the effects of "lesser" forms of dehumanization in a later chapter.

Haslam (2006) and his colleagues (Haslam & Loughnan, 2014; Haslam & Loughnan, 2016; Haslam & Stratemeyer, 2016; Haslam et al., 2013) have conducted a series of experimental studies to elucidate the nature of dehumanization and to be precise about difficult-to-define terms such as "essentialism" and "humanness." Haslam (2006) has argued that an understanding of dehumanization requires "a clear sense of what is being denied to the other, namely humanness" (p. 255). Using participant ratings of a large number of traits, Haslam and colleagues found two senses of humanness: firstly, a series of personality traits that were uniquely human (UH) and that did not apply to other species and secondly, a series of traits that the investigators felt were characteristic or representative of some aspect of human nature (HN). UH characteristics

> define the boundary that separates humans from the related category of animals, but humanness may also be understood noncomparatively as the features that are typical of or central to humans. These normative or fundamental characteristics might be referred to as human nature (HN). (Haslam, 2006, p. 256)

Each of these two broad dimensions (UH and HN) can be characterized along what might be considered positive or negative dimensions.

Positive qualities of the UH dimension include civility, refinement, and moral sensibility. Negative (or opposite) aspects of this dimension include coarseness, amorality, and irrationality. Positive qualities of the HN dimension include emotional responsiveness, interpersonal warmth and cognitive openness. Negative (or opposite) aspects of these characteristics include coldness, rigidity, and passivity (Haslam, 2006).

These two forms of humanness are related to corresponding forms of dehumanization when the corresponding qualities are not present. Haslam (2006) indicates that: "When UH characteristics are denied to others, they should in principle be seen as lacking in refinement, civility, moral sensibility and higher cognition" (p. 257). Their behavior is less cognitively mediated, and therefore more motivated by appetites and instincts. From a moral dimension, people lacking in UH characteristics are thought to be immoral or amoral. These individuals reflect animalistic dehumanization. When dehumanized, these individuals are often considered to be "unrefined animals" (Haslam, 2006, p. 258). When HN is perceived to be lacking, individuals are considered to lack warmth, cognitive flexibility, and emotionality. They are considered cold, rigid, and superficial. When dehumanized, these people are considered automatons or mechanistic; they may be seen as "soulless machines" (Haslam, 2006, p. 258) who are "distant, alien, or foreign" (Haslam, 2006, p. 259).

Haslam and colleagues have made an important contribution in distinguishing between two forms of dehumanization: animalistic and mechanistic. Both forms are apparent in narratives of the treatment and perceptions of the Jews in the Nazi era. As Haslam (2006) says, it is not clear, however, whether this model provides a valuable framework for further research. Does a preponderance of one dimension distinguish between attitudes or behaviors toward a particular outgroup compared to the other dimension? The question of what is "essential" also remains unclear, although Haslam (2006) generally links it with the HN form of dehumanization.

In more recent work, Smith (2020) emphasizes the relationship between dehumanization and violence that is of primary interest in the study of genocides. He does not confine his studies to the Holocaust but does write that the Holocaust "represents the most explicit and thoroughly documented example of the dehumanization of a whole people" (Smith, 2020, p. 23). Smith goes on to write that much of what can be learned from the Holocaust is applicable to other cases of dehumanization, given the similarities of patterns of dehumanization in various conflicts. It therefore seems that lessons of dehumanization and its importance to the Holocaust appear broadly applicable to other genocides, while recognizing that each instance of dehumanization and genocide has its own specific features to some degree.

Smith (2020) writes that it is the desire to harm victims that results in their dehumanization. He argues that dehumanization lets loose antagonisms that already exist and that subsequently result in violence toward the victim. In other words, as described in this book, when dehumanization becomes severe, and other factors such as social isolation (that is described later) become prominent, the drive toward murder and extreme violence may find its target in the victims. The course of dehumanization in the Nazi era suggests this is likely to be the case, at least in many instances. Hitler and the Nazi party certainly hated Jews and possibly desired their extermination even before the Nazi era began but were constrained from large-scale efforts toward this end until the German public was primed by the dehumanization that resulted from the Nazis' actions over several years. As social isolation and indifference to the plight of the Jews progressed, and as the German public became distracted by the onset of the war, planning and institution of mass murder and genocide became more feasible.

Consistent with the view expressed here, Smith (2020) argues that dehumanization may clear the way for "viciously destructive moral fury" (p. 93). As indicated above, it is not clear in the case of the Holocaust whether dehumanization was a conscious or unconscious preparation for genocide, or a strategy to coerce Jews to leave Germany, or both. When it became clear that not all Jews could or would leave Germany, various factors, including dehumanization and its accompanying social isolation of Jews, paved the way for genocide. Smith (2020) argues correctly, I believe, that dehumanization facilitates a disinhibition of our "worst impulses." In accord with the understanding presented here, dehumanization reduced inhibitions against murder in Nazi leaders and their many sympathizers, resulting in the murder of millions.

## Toward an Expanded Definition of Dehumanization

Haslam et al. (2013) have said that "Any theory of dehumanization needs an account of what it is that dehumanized people are denied or seen as lacking. 'De-humanization' implies that something is removed or lost in the process, presumably something to do with being human" (p. 27). Leyens et al. (2007) and Leyens (2009) have focused on what is essential to being considered human and studied more subtle forms of emotionality as offering clues to this question. Haslam and colleagues (see, for example, Haslam, 2006; Haslam & Loughnan, 2014) have posited two forms of humanness (UH and HN) that, when denied, may result in the potential for corresponding forms of dehumanization: animalistic and mechanistic. The differences between these two dimensions are not always clear, however, although both these types of dehumanization are corroborated by the narrative descriptions of Jewish sufferings during the Nazi era.

Haslam et al.'s studies focused on questions of what traits raters felt constitute humanness and, derivatively, what perceived traits are associated with those who might be dehumanized. These are important questions, although after reading numerous witness accounts of the treatment of Jews (and others) in the Nazi era, I question whether a purely experimental approach is able to capture the full impact of the experience of dehumanization that includes victims and perpetrators. Experientially, dehumanization of the victim affects several aspects of what it means to be human, including the victim's identity and self-worth. The experience of perpetrators is also important but rarely studied.

My own contribution to a definition of dehumanization does not emphasize difficult-to-define terms that are associated with much ambiguity and debate, such as "essentialism." It does offer an experiential understanding of what might be considered "essential" aspects of the human experience from both the perpetrator's and the victim's experience and their interactions.

With these points in mind, the following definition that emphasizes phenomenological and psychological aspects of dehumanization is presented:

> **Dehumanization is the process by which a powerful individual or group (the victimizers) actively deny or withdraw a second group's (the victim's) sense of human worth or personal value. The process may reflect external actions taken by the victimizer group and/or internal attitudes held toward the weaker or maligned group. The victimizers' actions are intended to reflect actual and/or symbolic dominance over the victim group and to increase the victimizers' own sense of power and personal worth at the expense of the victimized individual or group. Dehumanization results in the loss of the victims' sense of personal value, self-worth or "personhood." In extreme cases, dehumanization becomes murder as the victims' identities, lives, and "personhood" are taken from them.**

It is important to emphasize that this definition of dehumanization involves a sense of relationship between victimizer and victim. This relationship may be recognized or unrecognized by the parties involved. It may be overt or covert. It may be acknowledged or unacknowledged. In any case, it requires the existence of persons who are perceived to be more powerful than their victims and persons who are perceived to be less powerful than their victimizers.

The victimizer's actions against their victims are often associated with extreme cruelty towards, and suffering of, the victim. Violence and a sense of revenge against the victim often accompanies dehumanization. The form dehumanization takes may reflect, both directly and symbolically, particular grievances of the perpetrator. Examples in a subsequent section of this chapter will be used to illustrate this definition and the importance of unique conditions before and during the Nazi era that were reflected in the dehumanization of the Jews during this time.

## Psychological and Social Contributions to Dehumanization of Jews in the Nazi Era

Dehumanization is a likely reaction when severe psychosocial stressors, such as war, poor economic conditions, or social upheaval occur. This was especially true in the case of the Jews in Europe given the history of longstanding intolerance and antisemitism against the Jews that had dated back over 2,000 years. When these types of difficulties occur, as discussed earlier, many people tend to assign blame for intractable or frightening conditions to a potentially vulnerable target, in this case the Jews, who controlled at least some access to loans, banks, and other financial activities. The sources of dehumanization in and prior to the Nazi era therefore had familiar and longstanding roots as well as more contemporary ones.

## Illustrations and Comments about Dehumanization, Death, and Murder of Jews in Ghetto and Concentration Camp Environments

The following accounts are mainly from Nazi survivor (witness) writings. They reflect instances of dehumanization, as I have defined it earlier.

Primo Levi (1996) was an Italian chemist. Speaking of his time after arrival at a concentration camp, Levi (1996) says:

> One learns quickly enough to wipe out the past and the future when one is forced to . . . I push wagons, I work with a shovel, I turn rotten in the rain, I shiver in the wind; already my own body is no longer mine; my belly is swollen, my limbs emaciated, my face is thick in the morning, hollow in the evening; some of us have yellow skin, others grey. (pp. 36, 37)

There are several examples of dehumanization in this paragraph. Conditions were apparently so horrible and frightening, with little food or suitable clothing, that Levi learns to wipe out the past and the future. He is living in a timeless state, brought on by these physical conditions and the trauma-induced numbness he is experiencing. He is denied living conditions suitable for a human being; his treatment is "inhumane." The usual human experience consists of a past, present, and anticipated future. But Levi is no longer human and has only the wretched present of starvation, pain, and useless work on which to focus. Levi's body is "no longer mine." His body, an essential aspect of identity, is no longer his. It has been separated from his sense of himself. He is dehumanized.

The following is Levi's (1996) description of the loss of identity one may experience as a result of being tattooed with a number:

> He is Null Achtzehn. He is not called anything except that, Zero Eighteen, the last three figures of his entry number; as if everyone was aware that only a man is worthy of a name, and that Null

> Achtzehn is no longer a man. I think that even he has forgotten his name, certainly he acts as if this was so. When he speaks, when he looks around, he gives the impression of being empty inside.... (p. 42)

People's names are essential aspects of their identity. The disregard for a person's name dehumanizes that person and humiliates them. An aspect of their human identity has been stolen. Compared to others who have names (the camp guards), the prisoner is nothing, "Zero Eighteen." Levi was tattooed with this number, his body again being used by others for clerical purposes and camp procedures. The tattooed number that is used to call him begins with a zero, "nothing," as if that is who and what he is. As he says, he is no longer a man. He has described the loss of further aspects of his identity as a human. He has been dehumanized and treated like an animal, perhaps like a cow who is herded into a cattle car and branded with numbers to keep track of the herd. The man who is described seems empty inside. He has lost his human vitality, his soul. The man in Levi's self-description has been dehumanized.

In this witness account, Levi, as is often the case, says nothing about his tormenter. His energy, or what is left of it, seems focused on himself. Consistent with the bidirectional approach to dehumanization emphasized here, however, it seems appropriate to ask how the guard who tattooed Levi's arm and gave him a number he did not want might have reacted, or what a guard staring at a man who seemed "empty inside" might have experienced? We do not know the answers to these questions with certitude.

Browning (1992; 2017) does report that members of a police battalion commandeered to kill Jews generally (but not always) came to consider this a routine part of their jobs that most did not experience with either appreciation or revulsion. From a more analytic perspective, however, it must have been apparent to these men whose orders were to kill others, however dehumanized, that they, themselves, retained their names, ate suitable meals, had suitable surroundings, and had not suffered trauma sufficient to make them "empty inside." On the other hand, the guards were presumably "Aryan" men whose sense of superiority compared to the inferior Semitic Jew must have been reinforced for them. They were reminded through these measures that Aryans were supposedly meant to subjugate and dehumanize Jews who were considered subhuman and not really people in any case. In many small ways, through the replacement of their names with numbers or the meager rations of food, for example, even in this one concentration camp, the Aryan won the eternal battle with the Jews and dehumanized and humiliated them in the process. It was not the other way around.

The "Muselmann" is another example of individuals who were so dehumanized that they seemed to exist in a state somewhere between the living and the dead. The Muselmanner were concentration camp prisoners who had been starved by highly inadequate rations; they had been beaten, tortured, and humiliated. They apparently reflected the most severe results of extreme dehumanization and trauma experienced by concentration camp prisoners.

The exact origin of the term "Muselmann" is not known. Levi (1996) describes the Muselmanner as individuals who have lost the "divine spark" and as individuals who are "empty," weak, existing but no longer suffering. He goes on to write: "One hesitates to call them living: one hesitates to call their death death, in the face of which they have no fear, as they are too tired to understand" (p. 90). The Muselmanner, feeble, emaciated, and unable to do significant amounts of work, were among the first condemned to the gas chambers when regular exterminations were carried out. This is not surprising. According to the Nazis' conception of human worth, the Muselmanner would be considered "useless" since both physical strength and motivation had left them.

For nearly all concentration camp inmates, food was rationed, hard labor was expected, illnesses went untreated, and medical experimentation was torturous for those selected for the often heinous procedures that are described further in chapter seven. These dehumanizing procedures were intended to demonstrate their (the Jews') inadequacy and guilt in relation to their Aryan tormentor guards. All of these factors contributed to what would have been physical, emotional, and spiritual dehumanization. It does not seem from the accounts of Levi and others that this final Muselmanner stage, stepping from being barely alive to being totally dead, a heap of ashes in the crematoria, was at that point of much concern to the Muselmann whose fight for life had seemingly left him (or her) well before the gas was turned on. It is likely that both physical and mental changes were at play in the exhausted and saddened condition of the bent-over Muselmann who was often (but not always) shunned by fellow prisoners.

Bruno Bettleheim was a well-known psychoanalyst in America who had spent nearly a year (1938–1939) in Dachau and Buchenwald concentration camps. Bettleheim (1960) describes the Muselmanner as "walking corpses" (pp. 151–152). They felt helpless and unable to affect their environment. Bettleheim (1960) considers the Muselmanner as "people who were so deprived of affect, self esteem, and every form of stimulation, so totally exhausted, both physically and emotionally, that they had given the environment total power over them" (pp. 151–152). The Muselmanner had been cruelly and willfully dehumanized. Their dehumanized state had made clear that their deaths were imminent, although, based on these accounts, they would have at times been indifferent to their own deaths—if even their impending death was a part of their awareness.

It must be recognized, however, that these accounts are based on a few descriptions from the mid-twentieth century of individuals who witnessed the Muselmanner directly. While not plentiful, there has been some recent scholarly work on the Muselmanner from others who have reviewed archival records, photographs, other writings, or witness accounts of the period. In general, these reports do not significantly challenge earlier accounts, but they do add nuance and details.

Becker and Bock (2020) emphasize that the Muselmanner could not always be considered mute and passive prisoners. Not all Muselmanner were men, although it is likely that most were. Becker and Bock (2020) also report that some Muselmanner were pitied and allowed to rest from their duties, thus fostering rebound from their imminent demise.

While it seems from other accounts that the Muselmanner were often avoided by fellow prisoners, sometimes they were integrated into the social system of the camps. It is likely that whether the Muselmann was integrated into the social system of the camp prisoners depended on the particular situation, the particular camps involved, and the psychological and physical condition of the Muselmann. Becker and Bock's (2020) report that Muselmanner were sometimes able to regain their will to live suggests the importance of social support for humans and the very negative impact of the loss of social support on prisoners.

Ultimately, however, it was death and dying, and the horrific and dehumanizing tactics that led to the outcomes that defined the Muselmann. As Becker and Bock (2020) write, the Muselmanner embodied a "shift of death into the realm of life" (p. 173). It was also the other way around, the Muselmanner exemplified a shift of life into death in the gruesome visions of their horrific conditions and their almost inevitable passage to gas chambers that surprised no one after the dehumanizing tactics they had endured.

Shallcross (2020) also places an emphasis on the death of the Muselmanner as she writes about the "necrotopography" of the ghetto. She indicates that she coined the term "necrotopography" to indicate the presence of corpses as characteristic of the physical space of the ghetto. She considers necrotopography to define Holocaust spaces that "are saturated with either dying, or already dead, people" (p. 220). Death was omnipresent in the ghettos she describes, a conclusion that is not new or surprising but striking when the focus is placed squarely on death, one of the characteristics of the Nazi era that is the subject of this book.

Jews cramped into ghettos were in unlivable conditions. Extreme crowding, illness-infested rooms, exhausting work, unsustainable food rations, isolation from others, torture, and death were the norm. Shallcross (2020) reports on the "Muselmanization" produced by the physical and psychological trauma present in the camps. She describes the Holocaust's "hostile sphere of isolation" (p. 222) and the corpses and near-corpses that seemed to be omnipresent. All of this, of course, represents extreme dehumanization.

Shallcross (2020) studied archival photographs, prisoner diaries, and writings that provided verbal or visual images of people lying on the street, emaciated, looking diseased or nearly dead, sometimes begging for handouts and sometimes too far into their Muselmann trance-like state to seemingly be aware of passersby who tried to avoid glancing at the horror of death and near-death all around them. Shallcross (2020) emphasizes that there were attempts, consistent with Jewish tradition, to care for the most downtrodden, to provide food for the needy, but it seems that, at some point, much of the residents' energies of necessity went to caring for themselves and their families. This resulted in the isolation of the dead and the dying Muselmann, as well as in the isolation of other residents (temporarily in better conditions) from their even more unfortunate brethren.

Most important, from the perspective of this discussion, is the sense that everything about the ghetto (and the concentration camp) ultimately revolved around dehumanization leading to death. These were its ultimate purposes. As Shallcross (2020) writes in speaking about the horrific conditions set up by the Germans to sooner or later result in the deaths of all Jews in the ghetto:

> It is such conditions that produced the necrotopographic zone: dead and dying people collapsing suddenly and everywhere—in alleys, passageways, courtyards, gates, squares or on sidewalks—and becoming a common, variable, and sustainable physical presence that defies all past connotations of public space. (p. 225)

Death, fear of death, and impending death commandeered the attention of all the dehumanized residents of the ghetto until some, such as the Muselmanner (or at least some of them), no longer seemed to have the mental or physical capacity to be concerned with such things.

Terrence Des Pres was a historian who was not, himself, a Holocaust survivor. His writing about the Holocaust is nonetheless deeply reflective and psychologically insightful. Des Pres (1976) comments about the treatment of Jews in concentration camp environments that were isolated and hidden from public view, which made them tempting spaces for heinous abuses as well as unacknowledged exterminations (Pingel, 1990). Phrased somewhat differently, these were environments in which the urge to murder, not balanced by more usual civilizing and life-enhancing and life-generating forces, had free reign. They were, as Shallcross (2020) suggests, necrotopographic areas, zones in which activities devoted to death, dying, and murder commanded nearly all available space and time, as well as all physical and mental activities.

Des Pres (1976) writes,

> Within the camp world all visible signs of human beauty, of bodily pride and spiritual radiance, were thereby to be eliminated from the ranks of the inmates. The prisoner was made to feel subhuman, to see his self-image only in the dirt and stink of his neighbor. . . . In Auschwitz prisoners were forced to march in the mud, whereas the clean roadway was reserved for the SS. (p. 61)

Des Pres (1976) goes on to discuss the reasons for this extreme dehumanization and prisoner degradation:

> . . . here is a final, vastly significant reason why in the camps the prisoners were so degraded. This made it easier for the SS to do their job. It made mass murder less terrible to the murderers, because the victims appeared less than human. They *looked* inferior. (p. 61)

Dehumanized people, as Des Pres suggests, are viewed as less human, thus opening the door to their murder, death and genocide.

Des Pres writes about aspects of what it means to him to be human. There is human beauty; there is bodily pride; and there is spiritual radiance. Dehumanization robbed the concentration camp inmate of all of these human characteristics. This theft of what it means to be human was intentional. The Jews were to think that they were dirty, unclean, and unfit to share the roadway with their SS guards. They were inferior beings whose ongoing exploitation was justified by the victimizer. The SS guard was privileged compared to the Jewish prisoners because, according to this line of thinking, the SS guard was a member of the superior race and therefore entitled to walk on the clean roadway.

The intentionally dehumanized Jews were required to walk in the mud, a symbol for them and their victimizers of their perceived worthlessness as human beings.

As indicated earlier, dehumanization should be understood from a relational, interactive perspective, whether this is direct or symbolical. The SS guard who walked on the clean roadway was made to feel superior to the prisoner marching in the mud. The SS guard and his life therefore were worth more in the sense of human currency than the life of the Jews, who saw their self-image and worth in the dirt and stink of their neighbors. Individual Jews were members of a herd, whether coming to the concentration camps like animals on cattle cars, working as a part of a road gang, living and sleeping in dense, disease-infested, and crowded conditions, or dying en masse in the crematoria. Dehumanization robbed the victim(s) of their individuality and, as the witness literature attests, interactions among them were sometimes of the lowest common denominator. As dehumanized humans who were now considered akin to animals, they came to compete like animals for resources (such as food) among themselves.

Human self-image is fostered in large part through human interactions. The self-images of the dehumanized Jews were now to be recreated through their own dirt and stink as well as the dirt and stink of their captive neighbors. The Jews' interactional frame was of necessity that of the herded human animals, required to interact with other Jews as competitive animals and unable to communicate in any meaningfully engaged way with the dominant guards who walked on clean roadways.

The interactional frame by which dehumanization is understood in this chapter shows the coarse and subhuman interactions of the prisoners among themselves and the necessarily subservient posture of the prisoners towards the Nazi guards. The brief vignettes quoted here also reveal that, while dehumanization was horrific for the Jew, and potentially elevating for the Nazi guards, even the Nazi guards could not escape the fact that dehumanization was a fragile strategy for dominance. Des Pres (1976) comments that the prisoners were dehumanized in part to make them appear less human to the guards who murdered them indirectly as a result of the inhumane conditions of the concentration camp or directly in the gas chambers. The human interaction with the degraded, dirty, starving Jews made killing easier for the guards but did not eliminate entirely the difficulty of killing another human being, however inferior and threatening the guard was made to believe the Jew was. Dehumanization as a strategy to make genocide easier was only partly successful, as discussed in the following chapter. At least for Des Pres, dehumanization of the Jews affected both the victims and the victimizers, although obviously in vastly different ways and to vastly different degrees.

Emil Fackenheim was a Jewish theologian and philosopher whose emphasis on the importance of maintaining Judaism after the Holocaust has been important in post-Holocaust Jewish thought. He, himself, was imprisoned briefly in a concentration camp after Kristallnacht and ultimately made his way to Canada where he practiced as a Reform rabbi and wrote extensively. Later, he emigrated to Israel.

Fackenheim's (1982/1996) understanding of the Holocaust and the motivation and psychology of the Nazis aligns well with the emphases in this book. He condemns the moral vacuity of the Nazi enterprise and writes of the dehumanized Muselmanner being the end product of the Nazi effort to murder human souls while their bodies were still alive. He emphasizes that the concentration camp was the "inmost essence of the Third Reich" (Fackenheim, 1982/1996, p. 99), during which torture and murder were committed on a scale previously unknown.

Unbelievably to Fackenheim (1982/1996), the "worship" of both torture and murder were the regime's goals. As he describes it, for the Nazi enterprise, murder was the goal, and torture and the zest for killing were features that accompanied gratuitous murder. The ends of "degradation, torture and murder... had no higher purpose but were themselves both highest and 'unshakable'" (p. 182). As Fackenheim (1982/1996) points out, even Himmler's desire to stop the genocide of Jews at war's end in order to use them as bargaining chips to make peace with the Allies was unacceptable to Hitler. The zealous pursuit of murder, death, and genocide was blind in its tenacity and fury, possibly rivalling in importance even the fate of the Third Reich itself. Fackenheim (1982/1996) writes: "the 'extermination' of the Jewish people became an end more ultimate than the Third Reich's very survival" (p. 231).

As indicated in the next chapter, although Hitler and the Nazi leaders may not have planned for genocide with precise forethought, dehumanization served in many cases to demoralize and weaken the resolve of the Jews, deaden or enlist the response of the "ordinary" German people (the bystanders) to the ultimate fate of the Jews, and prepare both groups for the actualization of murder and genocide that was enacted through the Holocaust. Ordinary people developed new ideals, which to Fackenheim (1982/1996) resulted in dehumanization, torture, and ultimately in murder. The Muselmanner are considered the most characteristic and original product of this delusional system.

The Muselmanner are also examples of the death of our notions of what we expect of human beings and how we expect human beings to treat one another. They are examples of trauma that is inflicted intentionally on other humans. For Fackenheim (1982/1996), the notion of who man is and who God is died at

Auschwitz. He explains that the horrific events of the Third Reich and Auschwitz go beyond barbarism. They are incomprehensible using usual human forms of understanding. The blind fury and incomprehensibility of the compulsion to murder and commit genocide against millions of people, to be described more fully in the following chapter, are on full display.

Freud (1920) argued that human beings, at their deepest level, want to unite with others (Eros), but they also want to destroy and kill others. People create many delusional façades to cover the predilection to kill, although Freud, and others, have argued that the tendency to kill others is a basic aspect of human nature. Fackenheim has expressed much of this understanding in his writings about the Holocaust that, itself, stands as a prime example of uncontrollable genocidal behavior.

## Summary

Dehumanization is the psychological withdrawal or removal from a person or group of that which the victimizer (and often, the victim as well) considers to be essential to the victim's identity or human value. This brief statement provides an important but partial description of dehumanization, while it raises immediate questions such as what is "essential," what is "human," or what is "essentially human." Several investigators have tried to address these questions, most notably Haslam (2006) and his group (see, for example, Haslam et al., 2013) who have concluded that a series of traits distinguish two forms of humanness, human uniqueness (UH) and human nature (HN). Haslam and his group have argued that dehumanization occurs when either of these two forms of humanness are denied to others. Haslam et al. (2013) emphasize that: "Human uniqueness-based dehumanization represents the other as animal-like and human nature-based dehumanization represents the other as machine- or object-like" (p. 31).

My approach to a definition and greater understanding of dehumanization has been experiential and has emphasized victims' experiences as well as the experiences of perpetrators in what can be understood at least in part as an interactional paradigm. The literature on witness accounts and testimonies related to the Nazi era provide many examples of dehumanization and the reactions of victims and, to a lesser degree, of perpetrators. Comments such as those of Des Pres (1976) provide a deeply emotional and broad view of the dehumanization experience that can enhance and supplement experimental studies. As noted earlier, Des Pres (1976) says, "Within the camp world all visible signs of human beauty, of bodily pride and spiritual radiance, were thereby to be eliminated from the ranks of the inmates" (p. 61). Dehumanization here entailed loss of at least three aspects of personal identity: human beauty, bodily pride, and spirituality.

In this and the previous chapter, I have suggested that the specific focus of dehumanization in the Nazi era went beyond the traditional dehumanization of centuries before that was based, at least in part, on religious concerns and also came to reflect what was believed to be racial differences between the Jews and the "Aryans". Other precipitants for the vitriolic dehumanization of the years before and during the Nazi era were the harsh socio-economic conditions of the post-World War I years and their associated economic instability and loss of morale among the German people. Additionally, the emancipation of the Jews, itself a product of the Enlightenment, may have contributed to an environment of fear about loss of position, status, and stability that a segment of the German population was unwilling to accept. When dehumanization is understood in the relational paradigm suggested above, it seems that many Germans dehumanized the Jews, or further withdrew human status from them, to maintain the German citizenry's position of dominance. Dehumanization, in this sense, diminishes the status of the Jew in order to maintain or enhance the more exclusive position of the non-Jew.

I have also considered a more subtle but similar hierarchical and interactional approach to dehumanization and its manifestations when discussing ideological and spiritual aspirations of Germans during and prior to the Nazi era. The additional factor considered in this chapter is the development of Nazi ideology, with its strongly occult and spiritualistic influences that were prominent toward the end of the nineteenth and the beginning of the twentieth century. The development of Nazi ideology emphasized that history was now calling the Aryan people to live out their destiny and establish themselves as the world's dominant, master race. They were the chosen ones, destined to combat the Semitic Jew, their eternal enemy and competitor for this status. In this view, the Jew had to be defeated if the Aryan people were to prevail. Dehumanization was a direct and symbolic step on this path to mastery of humanity.

Jews, of course, had long encountered hostility and been criticized for purportedly considering themselves to be God's "chosen ones" (see, for example, Deuteronomy 14:2), who were somehow superior to others. Dehumanization of the Jews by the Nazis created a clear image and statement that refuted the notion of Jewish superiority and replaced it with Aryan superiority. Aryans now subjugated the Jews and gained revenge for centuries of Jewish statements of "chosenness." Aryans had come to see themselves as existing on a higher, ascendant plane of human evolution that looked down upon the Jews, who were lowered further into a dehumanized, subordinate, and subhuman position. Given the conditions (and opportunities) of war, dehumanization fostered through a false ideology supplemented other, more traditional as well as newer, prejudices that had denigrated the Jews. Dehumanization and its effects on Jews and Germans ultimately facilitated the murder of the dehumanized Other that is characteristic of genocide. These points are discussed further in the next chapter.

Before proceeding to discuss the progression from dehumanization to murder, its ultimate form, a cautionary note about the thesis that dehumanization of victims is associated with increasing likelihood of mortal harm being inflicted on these individuals is appropriate. Over (2021) terms this assertion "the dehumanization hypothesis" and presents a series of challenges to this view. These challenges emphasize that comparisons to non-human entities are not restricted to members of outgroups and are not necessarily negative (friends and enemies in the ingroup can be thought of, favorably or not favorably, as "lions or tigers"); that not all outgroups are described in non-human terms; that denying outgroup members some mental attributes does not necessarily deny them other "human" traits that may be positive; and that being seen as less than human does not automatically predict the ingroup's desire to inflict harm. These challenges appear to me to express appropriate caution about overvaluing and overestimating the ability of dehumanization to explain particularly harmful or adverse outcomes but do not invalidate the pernicious effect that increasingly severe dehumanization may have on the uncovering of the human proclivity to murder, with the subjects of dehumanization becoming the murder victims.

Goldenberg et al. (2021) respond to Over's (2021) challenges by agreeing about the importance of specificity in describing the effects of dehumanization. They continue to consider the dehumanization hypothesis valuable but recognize that it is not always true or applicable to particular situations. They recognize that dehumanization is not the only way outgroups (or ingroups) are marginalized. They point out that dehumanization alone may not be sufficient to result in harm to members of the outgroup. Characteristics of the ingroup and the outgroup, as well as the conditions and beliefs of the parties involved, are all important. Goldenberg et al. (2021) emphasize that "the challenge . . ., in our opinion, is to understand when out-group (and in-group) members are at risk of being dehumanized and when this is especially likely to lead to harm" (p. 17).

This chapter has pointed out some of the conditions, such as longstanding antisemitism, resentment toward emancipation, the emergence of "political" antisemitism, and socio-economic and political stressors, such as the German humiliation in World War I, that likely led to the dehumanization of a particular outgroup (the Jews). The following chapter will emphasize conditions that appear to have further facilitated the progression from dehumanization to genocide and mass murder of the "others."

CHAPTER 4

# The Human Propensity toward Violence, Destruction, and Murder. Prohibitions against Killing Other Humans. Examples of the Tendency toward Violence and Murder in the Nazi Era

## Introduction

It is hopefully clear from the material presented in the previous chapter that increasingly severe dehumanization may be a precursor to murder. The mechanism(s) by which this occurs may not always be clear, however. It may be that, with increasingly severe dehumanization, murderous impulses and death for the victim become almost routine, expectable and uneventful, a final step on a continuum of destructive impulses that fortunately are generally aborted. In this scenario, as Smith (2021) suggests, the desire to kill the victim may have been present from earlier in the victim/victimizer interaction, but the victimizer was not able to actually murder the victim at that time because of personal interdictions or social pressures. Ultimately, in this view, murder follows on the path of denigration and malice as a further dehumanizing action.

On the other hand, it must be noted that killing another human being is abhorrent to most people, and religious, social, and cultural taboos, as reflected in the Sixth Commandment in the Bible, prevent killing in many cases. In most situations, a great deal of pressure, psychologically and socially, must therefore be exerted on the victimizers to overcome psychological resistances and taboos and have them allow themselves to kill another human being. In this scenario, which may not involve a previous period of dehumanization, we can see the importance of social support and social pressure for the victimizer as being among the important factors supporting the murder of the victim. An example here are the ordinary men who became murderers (often reluctantly) during World War II (Browning, 1992/2017). Probably, both scenarios occur: dehumanization sets the stage for murder as a final dehumanizing act, but murder also results from other forms of incitement, such as social pressure or obedience to authority, as may occur during a war. Regardless whether earlier forms of dehumanization precede a final murderous act or not, it seems that human beings have a propensity toward violence, destruction, and murder. This chapter discusses this apparent human propensity for killing others and factors that support or inhibit this tendency. Illustrations from the Holocaust are provided.

## The Human Tendency toward Violence and Murder; Evolutionary, Anthropological, and Historical Considerations. Psychoanalysis and the Work of Sigmund Freud

### Evolutionary Considerations

Various fields of study, such as anthropology and evolutionary psychology, emphasize that human behavior seems to have precursors in non-human primates that provide models for a greater understanding of our own behavioral patterns. Jane Goodall (1990/2010) is probably the best-known chimpanzee researcher of our times. She has spent decades following and studying generations of chimpanzees at Gombe National Park in Tanzania. Goodall points out that the chimpanzee is the "closest living relative" to humans (p. 275). She emphasizes similarities in chimpanzee and human behavior, including her findings around aggressive territoriality.

There are several developmental and behavioral stages in the life of male chimpanzees that may shed light on the origins of violent and aggressive male behavior in humans. These areas include strivings for alpha male prerogatives and status among male chimpanzees; the male chimpanzees' pursuit of power, dominance, and control; aggressive, unprovoked, and threatening displays of the males against members of their own community; unprovoked chimpanzee male aggression against members of the same or outside groups; and subjugation and control of females, who are weaker and of lower rank in the chimpanzee community. Sousa & Casanova (2008, p. 86) emphasize that, in chimpanzee communities, "an adult male organizes his whole life around issues of dominance." Dominance, as pointed out in the previous chapter, is a crucial goal of those who would dehumanize (and murder) others.

Male chimpanzees feel an imperative to protect (and often patrol) the borders of their community's "territory." If they have an advantage in terms of strength and numbers, they will act violently against actual or feared territorial interlopers (who might be termed "others"). Goodall (1990/2010) points out that chimpanzees, like humans, engage in warlike activities. "Chimpanzees show hostile, aggressive territorial behavior that is not unlike certain forms of primitive human warfare" (p. 238). Chimpanzees have "an inherent fear or hatred of strangers; sometimes expressed by aggressive attacks" (p. 238–239). Young adult male chimpanzees find intergroup conflict alluring. These young adult males are likely to team up with age-mates and those of similar rank (Mitani et al., 2004). Ostracism or forced withdrawal of defeated alpha males from the community signifies a loss of status and position and is an example of a behavior that Goodall (1990/2010, pp. 96, 282) has called "dechimpization" (p. 282) to reflect isolation and loss of acceptance in the chimpanzee community that can be compared to the social isolation and dehumanization of rejected humans.

The descriptions Goodall (1990/2010) provides of aggressive chimpanzee behavior in a chapter entitled "War" are illustrative of aggressive behaviors that may become lethal when chimpanzees of different but neighboring communities encounter one another. Goodall (1990/2010, pp. 118–119) comments, "It seems, then, that the attacks are an expression of the hatred that is roused in the chimpanzees of one community by the sight of a member of another."

Goodall (1990/2010, pp. 120–126) describes another instance of "war" that bears on the type of violence perpetrated against the Other when a particular community splits apart. In 1974, the chimpanzee community that Goodall was following began a split into two communities, a northern and a southern group that over time became separate and increasingly hostile to one another. During the initial phases of this split, the males of the two communities related to one another with many insults and hostile displays when encounters occurred in the overlapping zone of the two communities. At some point, for reasons not described (or perhaps not known), some males of the original group who were on patrol suddenly and viciously attacked a single male from the second group who soon died. Over the next four years, four more assaults on chimpanzees from the breakaway group were witnessed. The killers returned to their northern home and seemed to be extremely excited. "Repeatedly they drummed on tree trunks, hurled rocks, dragged and threw branches. And all the time they called out, as though in triumph" (p. 123). Ultimately, all of the adults, males and females, of the breakaway group disappeared and were thought to have been killed. In this way, the breakaway community disappeared and its territory was annexed by the initial community.

Supporting the discussion in this book about dehumanization's relationship to murder, Goodall (1990/2010, p. 239) writes,

> Among humans, members of one group may see themselves as quite distinct from members of another, and may then treat group and non—group individuals differently. Indeed, non-group members may even be "dehumanized" and regarded almost as creatures of a different species. Once this happens people are freed from the inhibitions and social sanctions that operate within their own group, and can behave to non-group members in ways that would not be tolerated amongst their own. This leads, among other things, to the atrocities of war.

Smith (2011, 2020) expresses a similar understanding in describing human behavior that dehumanizes and potentially murders the Other. The weaker victim comes to be considered non-human and is therefore attacked or killed with impunity.

Goodall (1990/2010) emphasizes that chimpanzees' sense of group identity is strong. Non-community members may be fiercely attacked, and not simply because of the fear of strangers. For example, she mentions that a solitary member of a breakaway group was killed by a member of the chimpanzees' original group. It seems to Goodall (1990/2010) that, by separating themselves from their original group, the breakaway chimpanzees forfeited their right to be treated as members of the group. In some sense, based on the ferocity with which they were attacked, these "deserters" were treated even more viciously than members of other chimpanzee communities who had not been associated with the original group.

As mentioned earlier, Goodall (1990/2010, p. 240) uses the term "dechimpized," as a pun to substitute for "dehumanized," in describing the hatred reserved for breakaway members of the original chimpanzee community. Speaking again of humans, Goodall (1990/2010, p. 45) states that "We carry in our genes, handed down from our distant past, deep rooted aggressive tendencies." These aggressive tendencies may be activated even more strongly by "others" in close proximity to the predominant group or perhaps those in some way related to the predominant group. This dynamic of murderous aggression towards members of weaker (but closely associated) groups who come to be considered "others" brings to mind Hitler's (1925/1999) fear of the "powerful" Jewish, or Semitic, "menace" that, in his mind, had existed in proximity to the Aryan people and had always threatened Aryan supremacy.

Wrangham (2019) also stresses the aggressiveness of chimpanzees. He states that sometimes, for reasons that reflect mainly a quest for status,

> Chimpanzee males fight often with other members of their community. Sometimes they fight over valuable foods such as hunks of meat. Sometimes they fight over mating privileges. Mostly, however, they fight over nothing more than status. They regularly charge at one another in displays intended to demand clear expressions of subordinacy. (p. 88)

Dominance, power and control are primary pursuits.

Wrangham (2019) goes on to say, "Interactions between chimpanzee communities are never relaxed or friendly" (p. 89). "The only relationship that has ever been seen between males from neighboring territories is instant hostility, leading to flight, shouting or fight" (p. 91). Human behavior is, of course, far more nuanced and complex than that of prehuman primates. Still, some features of chimpanzee-like behaviors, such as the fear of the Other, bring to mind intercommunity interactions among humans.

Wrangham (2019) discusses further possible implications of male chimpanzee behavior for understanding aggression in humans. He considers "coalitionary" killing, that is, murderous attacks by several chimpanzees against a smaller number of weaker chimpanzees, to have massively destructive consequences when applied on a human level. "Coalitionary proactive aggression is responsible for execution, war, massacre, slavery, hazing, ritual sacrifice, torture, lynchings, gang wars, political purges, and similar abuses of power" (p. 246). He emphasizes, however, that "Violence responds to circumstance, not to unstoppable genetic instructions" (p. 253). "Evolution has made the killing of strangers pleasurable, because those that liked to kill tended to receive adaptive benefits" (p. 257). These benefits, in human terms, may include high position, parades, and heroic status. Wrangham (2019) also argues in a similar vein to Goodall (2010/2020) and to Smith (2011, 2020) that, in essence, human strangers are dehumanized and reduced to non-human status, thus enabling the murderer to kill with impunity or even joyfully, given that the object of the kill is not "really" human. He emphasizes, "To enjoy a successful attack makes grisly sense" (p. 257).

Wrangham points out that "We are inclined to label callously planned violence such as the Holocaust as 'inhuman'. But phylogenetically, of course, it is not inhuman at all. It is deeply human. No other mammal has such a deliberate approach to mass killing of its own species" (p. 260). As Wrangham (2019, p. 260) states, "Coalitionary proactive aggression can be responsible not only for execution of selected individuals but also for the deliberate killing of larger groups."

## Preliterate and Ancient Civilizations

Keeley (1996) has studied ancient civilizations from historical and archaeological perspectives. He finds that war and violence among prehistoric and primitive peoples were common, merciless, and deadly, seemingly more so than is true even in the present day. The myth of the "peaceful savage" is simply a myth. "Peaceful prestate societies were very rare; warfare between them was very frequent, and most adult men in such groups saw combat repeatedly in a lifetime" (p. 274). In a description that is quite like Goodall's (1990/2010) description of chimpanzee battles between neighboring groups, Keeley describes primitive warfare as "war reduced to its essentials: killing enemies with a minimum of risk, denying them the means of life via vandalism and theft (even the means of reproduction by the kidnapping of their women and chidren), terrorizing them into either yielding territory or desisting from their encroachments and aggressions" (pp. 174–175). The picture that emerges suggests that humans have always resorted to violence, sometimes catastrophic violence, to address problems related to the Other.

Ralph (2013, p. 5) emphasizes that violence in prehistoric times (as is true today) may help the creation of a group's identity, and that violence may help to define the Other, and to enable distinctions between "us" and "them." In warfare and in genocide, for examples, tensions around ethnicity and identity have been manipulated in order to justify violence. Ralph's (2013) emphasis here is consistent with the definition of dehumanization offered in the previous chapter. Violence, murder, and dehumanization are often used to clarify or establish the identity and dominant status of the stronger group in relation to the subjugated or weaker group.

Otterbein (2013) addresses another issue related to the study of violence when he reviews our understanding of genetic and cultural contributions to violent behavior. He has studied prehistoric warfare and argues that warfare is a culturally learned phenomeon, "but that *Homo sapiens* have many features based on anatomic and neuropsychological traits that facilitate warfare" (p. 278, italics in the original). These neuropsychological traits include the brain's triggering a fight or fear response, an impulse to respond aggressively to perceived challenges, and a tendency to take revenge on perceived enemies. These impressions are in accord with the view stated in this book: humans have a predisposition to violence, but this predisposition is activated when particular cultural, social, or personal conditions are met. In the context of the discussion of Nazi Germany and the Holocaust, these associated conditions would include German humiliation in the post-World War I period and its associated economic and social uncertainty.

Gat (2006), in a voluminous text, addresses numerous questions about violence and war across civilizations and over time. He summarizes some of his findings about the nature of violence and aggression by arguing that violence and severe aggression are innate in human nature, "but only as a skill, potential, propensity, or predisposition" (p. 39). Aggression is "optional" rather than fixed, but "while being optional, aggression has always been a *major* option, and thus very close to the surface and easily triggered" (p. 40, italics in the original). There is, therefore, what might be considered an ongoing pressure toward severe aggression and violence in human beings that is evolutionary in origin. This predisposition leads readily to war but can be surmounted by factors that resist these violent urges. The final chapter in this book discusses the prevention of severe violence through various efforts including a reduction in dehumanization perpetrated against susceptible individuals and groups.

## Psychoanalysis and Sigmund Freud

The discussion of violence and murder now turns to the modern period. In 1920, shortly after World War I had claimed millions of lives and a tumultuous interwar period was in process, Sigmund Freud proposed a controversial addition to his understanding of the human mind. He was now considering whether there was a "death instinct" that would stand in contrast to Eros, or the life force that was a pillar of psychoanalysis.

Freud (1920) did not rigorously define the death instinct, nor did he provide details as to when or under what conditions it became manifest. He did argue that activities and behaviors reflecting the death instinct interacted with its opposite, Eros or the life force, to produce a variety of behaviors that included milder forms of violence or destruction, as well as more severe forms of violence, such as occurred in war (Freud, 1930).

Freud's "death instinct" came to be termed the "death drive" to avoid the assumption that the term "death instinct" suggests an "instinct" that is of unproven biological origin. The existence of a death instinct/drive, nonetheless, has been controversial from its beginning (Money-Kyrle, 1955; Parens, 2011), with many psychoanalysts continuing to refrain from employing the term at all. Others, such as Kernberg (2009), consider the term valuable in a clinical sense. Laub and Lee (2003) argue that the term "death instinct" is indispensable in describing the clinical condition of individual patients who have suffered trauma, although they too demur from using the term in a more general sense.

In this section, I address controversies that exist in psychoanalytic circles around the existence and nature of this concept. I avoid using the term "Thanatos" that is often used synonymously with the death instinct/death drive since Freud, himself, apparently did not use this term in any of his writings (Lind, 1991). The following provides a description of the death instinct/drive, as conceptualized by Freud (1920; 1923/1960; 1930; 1933).

Freud's (1920) first attempt to describe the death instinct/drive in some detail was in his *Beyond the Pleasure Principle* as he grappled with a number of questions, including the recurrent dreams of traumatized soldiers. He ultimately speculated that perhaps he had come upon a universal attribute of instincts, and perhaps of organic life in general, which had not hitherto been clearly recognized or at least not explicitly stressed: "*It seems, then, that an instinct is an urge inherent in organic life to restore an earlier state of things* which the living entity has been obliged to abandon under the pressure of external disturbing forces . . ." (p. 36, italics in the original). Proceeding further, Freud postulates that the "'*aim of all life is death*' and, looking backwards, that '*inanimate things existed before living ones*'" (p. 38, italics in the original).

These highly speculative assumptions soon led to the conclusion that, while sexual instincts conform to the well recognized pleasure principle, another instinct that came to be called the death instinct does not. Freud (1923/1960) reviewed his notions of Eros and the death instinct in a subsequent work, *The Ego and the Id*. He reiterates his hypothesis that the task of the death instinct "is to lead organic life back into the inanimate state. . . . The emergence of life would thus be the cause of the continuance of life and also at the same time of the striving towards death; and life itself would be a conflict and compromise between these two trends" (Freud, 1923/1960, p. 38). Unfortunately, Freud (1923/1960) attempts to support his hypothesis by using biological analogies without sufficient support or proof of their relationship to the psychological processes he describes.

Freud (1933) goes on to describe aspects of the death instinct in its internal and external manifestations. He suggests that violent, aggressive, and destructive actions against others reflect an individual's resistance to his or her own death and to becoming inert matter once again. The death drive therefore included an aggressive component that could be channeled outward in ways that produced destruction, death, and war.

Freud clarifies and elaborates on this view in his book *Civilization and its Discontents*, in which he writes, "This aggressive instinct is the derivative and main representative of the death instinct which we have found alongside of Eros and which shares world-dominion with it..." (Freud, 1930, p. 122). Freud asserts pessimistically, "It is not easy for men to give up the satisfaction of this inclination to aggression. They do not feel comfortable without it" (p. 114). War, in this view, would be a means to expresss this inclination to aggression. Dehumanization would be a weaker alternative to killing others or a precursor to it.

In usual times and circumstances that are not too stimulating to the individual, aggression is constrained through the development of "guilt," an internal state fostered by what Freud terms the super-ego or conscience. The sense of guilt and the fear of punishment are the mental states that aid civilization to obtain "mastery over the individual's dangerous desire for aggression by weakening and disarming it and by setting up an agency within him to watch over it..." (Freud, 1930, pp. 123–124).

From this perspective, Nazi Germany worked to reduce its own sense of guilt and the collective and individual guilt its citizens might have experienced in the Holocaust by dehumanizing Jews and thereby denying them the humanity that might have activated the German conscience. The Nazi program also was successful because its various efforts (including dehumanization and systemized propaganda) invited aggression and fostered the ascendency of violence and murder while it obscured the instincts associated with Eros, at least as related to non-Aryans. The situation then became favorable for what Freud called the "the greatest hindrance to civilization—namely, the constitutional inclination of human beings to be aggressive towards one another..." (Freud, 1930, p. 142).

The lack of this balance as a result of the uncontrolled actions of what would be termed the death drive and the associated destruction in the Holocaust is clear in Shallcross's (2020) discussion of places of necrotopography noted in the previous chapter. The Nazi-developed ghettos and concentration camps, including the extermination camps, were, in the terms Freud uses here, dominated entirely by the death drive. Destruction, negation, sadism, torture, and killing were the omnipresent characteristics of these necrotopographic sites. Eros was shunned and death was embraced. In terms consistent with *Civilization and its Discontents*, civilization became regressed and nearly annulled.

*Civilization and its Discontents* was published in 1930, during the interwar years. Surprisingly, perhaps, the concept of the death drive expressed clearly in *Civilization and its Discontents* (as well as the topic of the death drive in relation to the Holocaust itself or to other genocides) does not seem to have gained the attention of psychoanalysts to the degree that might be expected. One of the reasons for this may involve Freud's notion that sociology is mainly individual psychology applied to groups (Lothane, 2012). Freud wrote about psychological topics that were intended to learn about and help the suffering of the individual and also about topics that might be termed "applied psychology" or "social psychology," in which he applied psychoanalytic insights to social issues and social problems. *Civilization and its Discontents* is an example of this latter effort (Lothane, 2012). Many psychoanalysts seemingly were not willing to join Freud in the social application of psychoanalytic principles that they felt were too speculative and ungrounded in clinical observations.

This may be the reason that there seems to be relatively few references to the death drive in psychoanalytic literature, given Freud's strong defense of it. Another question, and one that I believe is related to the first, is the question why there are relatively few references to the Holocaust in psychoanalytic literature given the importance of this topic. In this context, a recent text that is intended to provide a "more comprehensive psychology of the Holocaust" (Mastroianni, 2019) indexes only five out of over 400 pages total that deal with "psychoanalytic approaches" to the Holocaust. This otherwise valuable text provides no indexed references to either the death instinct/drive or to Freud himself.

Kuriloff (2014) and others have provided valuable perspectives on the question whether there has been a relative oversight or even avoidance of the Holocaust itself and the death instinct/drive in psychoanalytic literature. Kuriloff (2014) recognizes that the death instinct/drive had always been controversial among analysts even when Freud was alive. She indicates that other factors may have contributed to the avoidance of this topic, including the stress of relocation (usually to America or to England) for Austrian Jewish psychoanalysts, who, like Freud, fled for their lives during the Nazi era.

There is a suggestion here that, in addition to the controversies around the death drive noted earlier, and despite (or perhaps because of) the horrific evidence of impending death that had been around them, émigré analysts preferred not to deal further with the topic. Kuriloff's (2014) writing suggests that they may have been so severely traumatized by the events of the Nazi era that they were not able to contribute further to a psychoanalytically informed approach to the Holocaust or to what Freud had called the death instinct.

## Freud's Death Instinct/Drive: Critiques and Controversies. Melanie Klein

As I indicated above, Freud was well aware that the death drive was controversial from its inception, and not fully accepted, even by psychoanalysts (Freud, 1930). Many objections were raised to the notion of a death drive. Freud's metapsychological formulation was felt to be highly speculative, and to lack clarity or confirmation on clinical or empirical grounds. The critiques range from near total rejection to partial acceptance (especially of the aggressive component of the drive) or to the acceptance of the drive in certain clinical situations involving trauma (for examples, see Caropreso and Simanke, 2011; De Masi, 2015; Kernberg, 2009; Laub and Lee, 2003; Lind, 1991; Rechardt and Ikonen, 1993; Richards, 2018).

Specific mention should be made of another contribution to psychoanalytic literature in this era that has influenced my own conception of what I consider to be the human propensity toward violence that exists at the extreme end of a spectrum of dehumanization that may lead to murder. This is the work of Melanie Klein.

Melanie Klein (1946; 1955) was an Austrian psychoanalyst who emigrated to England during the years between the world wars. Klein had a view of the death drive that was different than that of Freud and seems to have used the term differently. It is based on her understanding of developmental considerations in infancy. Sanchez-Pardo (2003, p. 138) writes that while

> most analysts compromised with the death drive by accepting the theory of a primary instinct of aggression but rejected or ignored the self-directed aspect of the death drive theory... this was certainly not the case with Melanie Klein. She took the death drive as crucial in the psychosexual development of the individual, and it acquired a central and even founding role in her theory.

Klein (1955) argued that infants, in the first months of life, had very active perceptual frameworks that were based on their own innate characteristics as well as their treatment by caretakers (mainly the mother). One of the important characteristics of infants during the first three months or so of life was persecutory anxiety, later considered within a specific term, the paranoid-schizoid position. Experiences of birth, helplessness, and vulnerability impacted the infant to split their reactions and project emotions of love and hate onto the mother, and specifically the mother's "good" and "bad" breasts. The infant comes to introject and identify with the mother's good breast when innate endowment and caretaking is good, warm, loving, and supportive. The infant also introjects and identifies with the mother's bad breast when caretaking is frustrating and perceived to be cold, distant, or haphazard. Rage and later aggression result from anxiety and fears of annihilation that are worsened by poor or haphazard caretaking during these first months. These reactions, fearing death and annihilation when caretaking is insufficient or uncaring, continue and are expressed through childhood and adulthood.

Klein's understanding of the death drive, within the framework she developed, involves aggression and rage that might include threats against oneself and others when the perceived potential for annihilation and death of the self occurs. Klein (1946) argues that

> Some of the functions which we know from the later ego are there from the beginning. Prominent amongst these functions is that of dealing with anxiety . . . anxiety arises from the operations of the Death Instinct within the organism, is felt as fear of annihilation (death) and takes the form of fear of persecutions. The fear of the destructive impulse seems to attach itself at once to an object—or rather it is experienced as fear of an uncontrollable overpowering object. (p. 100)

Severe anxiety, along with the fear of death, therefore, occur ultimately due to the fear of annihilation. In this view, annihilation by the Other is perceived as an ever-present threat throughout life and may be the basis for the wariness and fear of others that come to figure prominently in human infants during their development. Hitler's (1925/1999) fear of Jews as a fear of the Other who is strong enough to annihilate the Aryan race is an example of how an irrational fear of annihilation may trigger rageful hatred and violence against the presumed enemy.

## Comments on Freud's Death Instinct/Drive

Freud's (1920) *Beyond the Pleasure Principle* was an attempt to shift the focus of psychoanalysis to a new metapsychology that includes the more familiar Eros as well as the newly defined drive toward death that Freud believed also was instinctual and found in everyone. He, himself, recognized that his intuitive understanding of this concept, which involved, first, the actual efforts on the part of the organism to return to an inorganic state from which it had come and, second, the organism's aggressive, destructive behaviors on internal and external levels that reflected the death impulse, was not entirely convincing (Freud, 1920). Freud continued to struggle with these concepts over the coming years, as did other psychoanalysts who provided limited or, at times, no support for Freud's arguments and speculations.

Many analysts, as De Masi (2015) indicates, ultimately settled on the existence of an independent aggressive drive that fell short of the larger and more encompassing death drive Freud continued to espouse. As Money-Kyrle (1955) wrote, "The fear of death, or of dying, and the death instinct are logically distinct" (p. 509). He, like many psychoanalysts, is unsure if there is a death instinct at all. The bipolarity of life that Freud envisioned, Eros or positive life forces allied against, and along with, a destructive death drive, reflected, in Freud's view (as indicated in a letter to Einstein [1933]), an example of the law of opposites that proved essential in understanding the variety of metapsychological principles in the world.

My own impressions are that Freud's attempts to support the notion of a death instinct/drive were largely unconvincing. His unproven speculations and the ambiguity in his writings that are based, in part, on biological assumptions in non-humans confuse the concept of a death drive that, when reformulated, might have served to foster greater understanding when the mass slaughter and destruction of World War II, the Holocaust (and other genocides) are considered (Kuriloff, 2014). Freud's notion that there is, at least in part, an intrinsic basis to human aggression and violence does gain support from the evolutionary considertaions and studies of ancient societies cited earlier in this chapter, although his own writings intended to support this notion are not effective in doing so. The following amplifies further my conception of the human proclivity toward violence, murder, and genocide that was presented earlier.

## The Human Proclivity toward Violence, Murder, and Genocide

My conception of violence, murder, and genocide inflicted on humans by other humans that reflects a continuity of dehumanizing actions on the part of the perpetrator is based on my study of the Holocaust, the literature noted above, and my understanding of the concept of dehumanization. The writings of Freud (1920, 1923/1960; 1930; 1931/1932), Melanie Klein (1946; 1955; 1957), and Rechardt and Ikonen (1993) are helpful at times, especially as related to Freud's descriptions of the associated features of mass murder, such as torture of victims, sadism, zest, and joy experienced by the perpetrators and the issue of developmental anxiety (and "paranoia") in infants formulated by Klein on this topic. It is further supported by literature on the effects of socially sanctioned and supported killing of others and survivor/witness accounts of Holocaust experiences presented in this and other chapters of this book.

In my approach to the concept of violence and murder at the most severe end of the spectrum of dehumanization leading to mass murder and genocide, I attempt to avoid definitive and controversial speculations about the propensity to violence and murder in humans. I do think that evolutionary and anthropologial perspectives support the notion of an innate human propensity to violence that can be influenced by social and external events. Overall, I emphasize phenomenology and the descriptions of events. I utilize psychoanalytic understandings of motivation and defenses that are conscious and unconscious while resisting the specifics of Freud's theoretical formulation. I recognize human interdictions against murder and the strategies and beliefs employed by the Germans (and their allies) to weaken these strictures psychologically. My focus is on the expression of dehumanization that is on a continuum the furthest end of which represents violence, murder, and genocide, as exemplified during the Holocaust.

I emphasize that, in humans, "death" can be understood both metaphorically and literally (Rechardt & Ikonen, 1993), and can be partial or total. The loss, defeat, or removal of one's sense of oneself, of individual destiny, personal potential, and the particular meaning of life that individuals and members of their group attach to life are all forms of death that are "dehumanizing."

The Holocaust illustrates how the dehumanization continuum, leading ultimately to murder and genocide of Jews and others, became manifest during the Nazi era. The German people and its leadership also had had humiliating defeats and losses that were likely to have been felt to be dehumanizing to them. These reactions probably contributed to a compensatory grandiosity and expectations of their own achievements and future potential based on flawed theories of Aryan racial superiority.

My perspective is that the genocide of the Jews (and others) perpetrated by the Germans reflected, at least in part, reactions to and fears of the perpetrators' own deaths in metaphoric terms. These fears and losses had been blamed on the Jews, an old enemy, who became the victims of the Germans and, first of all, the Nazis. It did not matter that the Nazi sense of an eternal battle between Aryans and Semites (Jews) that they must win was a delusion; that a worldwide Jewish financial conspiracy against them was a delusion; or that they had, in Adolf Hitler, a delusional leader (Coolidge et al., 2007) who seemed to place the elimination of Jews as a possibly more important objective than military victories in war.

Jews, in reality, were not responsible for the personal, collective, or national losses that were experienced by the German people, but they nonetheless were associated with the perception of these losses in the German psyche that, for Hitler, were tantamount to the death of the Aryan ideal. Quoting from *Mein Kampf* is instructive:

> *What we must fight for is to safeguard the existence and reproduction of our race and our people, the sustenance of our children and the purity of our blood, the freedom and independence of the fatherland, so that our people may mature for the fulfillment of the mission allotted it by the creator of the universe.* (Hitler, 1925/1999, p. 214, italics in the original)

Hitler and the German leadership responded ferociously to ward off losses that symbolized a form of death for them. They did this through attempts that were largely successful to kill and destroy every Jew the Nazi forces and their collaborators could find. There were death marches, "Jew hunts," crematoria, and starvation regimens that did nothing to further the war effort but were required to maintain the ideological purity of the Nazi program and establish its retaliation against the eternal enemy, the Jew (Goldhagen, 1997). Understanding the death and destruction of the Jews along these lines helps to explain the brutality, sadism and slaughter that occurred as concomitant features of mass murder.

The murder of Jews (and others) occurred in several ways, including shooting the victims, clubbing the victims, starving the victims, overworking the victims, and gassing the victims in concentration camp crematoria. These murders sometimes became "routine" for the SS member or civilian policeman thrust into a frequently unpleasant task (Browning, 1992/2017), but this was not always so. Some men could not engage in these tasks and were allowed to perform other duties (Browning, 1992/2017). Other men seemed to revel in their work and happily engaged in the extreme cruelty, barbarism, and at times joyful amusement and sadism perpetrated by Nazi SS members as they tortured their helpless victims prior to, or during, killing episodes.

Hilberg (1992) writes, "There were men who deliberately brutalized the victims, or tortured them, or derived excitement or amusement from their fate" (pp. 53–54). When the Germans were impatient, "small children were thrown out of windows, or tossed like sacks into trucks, or dashed against walls, or hurled live into pyres of burning corpses" (Hilberg, 1992, p. 54). Sadism

> emerged in face to face contacts of those men who wanted to exhibit their mastery over Jews. Essentially these individuals played with their victims . . . they handed toothbrushes to Jews to clean sidewalks . . . they cut the beards of pious Jews or used Jews as ponies for rides. (Hilberg, 1992, p. 54)

They used Jews for target practice or women as sexual slaves. Narcissism coexisted with sadism as the life and death of the prisoners centered on the will of their SS overseers.

There was a "master of life and death syndrome":

> The predominant type of German sadism was somewhat predictable and virtually institutionalized. It even had a name, "to make sport" and often enough it took the form of staging "gladiatorial" fights among inmates or of commanding prisoners to carry heavy stones from one place where they were not needed to another place where they were not needed. (Hilberg, 1992, p. 54)

This was another form of torment reflecting the inhumanity that accompanied murder and served to amuse the guards. It was they who were dominant, who had knowledge and control over the victims' lives. Exactly when they tired of the play and when the games would be over and the "action" taken to finally transport the prisoner to the gas chamber was knowledge kept from the prisoner but available at some point to the guards, who comprised the ruling class. The Nazi guards had complete control over the prisoners' lives and deaths and the dehumanizing behaviors that were required in order to live at all.

These actions on the part of the German guards served no apparent rational or functional purpose. The jocularity, sadistic amusement, and torture did serve various functions, however, such as the reinforcement of the German guards' sense of superiority over the Jews, the reinforcement of the Jews' sense of inferiority and personal meaninglessness, the reinforcement of the process of dehumanization that would make killing another human being (who now was no longer a "human") acceptable. These actions of the killer guards also served to deny (for themselves) and reverse the inhumanity in which they were participating by emphasizing joyful amusement (for the guards) that could be produced by the dehumanization of, and infliction of suffering on, the Jews whom they saw only as subhuman.

The subjugation of the Jews and others is consistent with Freud's (1933) recognition of the use of what he termed the death drive not only to kill others but to enslave the victims and use them for the perceived needs of the victimizers, as noted above. Essentially, the myriads of vanquished people throughout history who have been enslaved rather than killed outright reflect the dehumanization that is on a continuum the furthest end of which represents murder and violence. Actions that have been described and similar behavior confirmed for the Germans that they were the masters and the Jews were the slaves. For these Nazis and their sympathizers, there was only one master race and it had brought its main rival, the Jew, to heel through its control of the Jews' lives and the ability of the master race to humiliate the Jew at will. In the competition to retard death and to experience life, German "lords" exerted their power and extended their own lives symbolically as the master race as they thwarted death by sending Jews prematurely to die. The powerful Aryans, considering themselves superior beings, denied their own mortality by "enjoying" the death and tortured experiences of others. Symbolically thwarting death, the Aryan race, in this grandiose view, would continue to live, to flourish, and to enjoy the full expression of the instincts for life. It was winning the cosmic battle against the archenemy. As Hitler is quoted above saying, it is important for the people to fulfill "*the mission allotted it by the creator of the universe*" (Hitler, 1925/1999, p. 214, italics in the original).

Many of the perpetrators' joyful experiences of torture and murder that accompanied the sadistic treatment of Jews in Jew hunts, ghettos, and concentration camps were not shared by all of the perpetrators, however, and some felt guilt and stress as a result of their participation in mass exterminations. Browning (1992/2017) records the sometimes raucous entertainment and use of alcohol that awaited the killers after their murders were over for the day. "Forgetting" or denying their actions seemed to serve most of the executioners well.

A related way to understand the apparently senseless murder of Jews who were powerless in the face of the German killing machine is to consider the application and relevance of Melanie Klein's (1946; 1955; 1965) notion of the death instinct to the murderous rage that some Germans, especially Nazis, seemed to have had for the Jews. As noted earlier, Klein argued that the earliest experiences of the vulnerable infant include a fear of annihilation and death, although these fears are of course non-verbal. The substrate for this fear of annihilation and death—and the rage and aggression that becomes the infant's, child's, or adult's responses to it cannot simply be understood as erroneous or irrational behaviors from adult perspectives. Depending on factors such as the individual's biological endowment and environmental conditions, perceptions of impending personal destruction may become pervasive and severe. These reactions potentially are enacted throughout life in the personal and in the social sphere or, in the case of the Nazi era, in the socio-political sphere where the defeat and humiliation of the losses in World War I would be continuously present.

Although somewhat hampered by psychoanalytic language that makes her research less accessible to many readers, Klein basically argues that fear of annihilation and death are perhaps the most basic of human emotions. She initially termed this earliest phase of human development the "persecutory" phase and then called it the "paranoid-schizoid" position. Her concepts of good breast and bad breast, good mother and bad mother, are easily understood as indications of the later existence of polar opposites of life forces and death forces in adulthood that stem from the supportive and caring actions of the mother and, conversely, from the mother's rejecting or indifferent actions.

From these perspectives, and based on Hitler's (1925/1999) writings in *Mein Kampf* noted earlier, Nazis, on the one hand, strove for world mastery and domination to fulfill a presumed rightful place they believed they have or should have in the world but, on the other hand, they were terrified of a perceived eternal enemy, the Semitic Jew, who, in their minds, had always been out to destroy the Aryan people and render Aryans inconsequential. In Kleinian terms, the Nazis, leading for a time the most powerful military force in the world, were terrified of the Jews and feared that the Jews would annihilate them and destroy Germany, the greatest of the Aryan nations.

The German leadership argued that the Jews threatened the Aryan race through a worldwide web of financial dealings known only to the Jews themselves. Since there is no evidence for this, however, it must be concluded that the real fear the Germans (especially those in the Nazi party) had for the Jew arose from a deeper sense of vulnerability that selected particular events or situations to provide a rationale for the German leaders' actions. The need to dehumanize and then murder the Jews arose from, and was based on, this vulnerability.

In this context, it was necessary for the Nazis, fearing for their existence and enraged by the potential assault on their lives and their very beings, to fight back—to annihilate the Jew before the Jew could annihilate the German. Particularly zealous Germans might then have denied their own fears of helplessness and annihilation as they projected their anxieties and expressed their rage onto their perceived eternal enemy, the Jew. In this scenario, if the German people would emerge victorious from this deeply imaginary and unconscious battle for survival and dominance, they would become the Aryan masters of the world and Jews would be dealt the retribution they had long deserved. Understood in this way, the heavily armed German soldier who murdered the helpless and unarmed Jew saw the Jew only (or mainly) as a potentially murderous force that was out to destroy and annihilate Germans and the Aryan race. The unreasonableness of this perspective that reflects the irrationality of dehumanization and subsequent murder and genocide, as understood here, required the Nazis to destroy all Jews and accelerate the deaths of Jews in order to fulfill their inspired mission to become masters of the world.

Ian Kershaw (2000), a noted scholar of the Holocaust, describes these psychological events in somewhat different terms as he speaks of what he presumes to be Hitler's considerations around the time of Kristallnacht. Kershaw (2000) indicates that the upcoming war in Europe was coming into clearer focus for Hitler and that

> since the 1920s he had not deviated from the view that German salvation could only come through a titanic struggle for supremacy in Europe, and for eventual world power, against mighty enemies backed by the mightiest enemy of all, perhaps more powerful even than the Third Reich itself: international Jewry. (p. 130)

In actuality, international Jewry, this "mightiest" of enemies, was a rather helpless and dispersed group of people that had no land of its own, few independent resources, and few friends. Hitler's well recognized delusional beliefs (Coolidge et al., 2007) nonetheless helped lead millions to their deaths.

Germany, and Hitler's ambitions for the Aryan people, clearly were endangered in Hitler's mind. It is little wonder that the human propensity toward violence and murder became manifest during this titanic fight between one of the greatest military powers on earth and the Jew, who had achieved some social and political prominence during the interwar period in Germany. Hitler was overcome by his unrelenting quest to defeat the Jew, his greatest enemy, before this greatest enemy defeated and annihilated him.

It is important to recognize that, from these perspectives, the murder of millions of Jews (and others) should be considered an active and determined phenomenon. Smith (2011) has argued that genocidal behavior against dehumanized populations may be understood as the result of a loss of perceived humanity of the victim that "allows" the aggressor to murder dehumanized individuals or groups who are no longer considered "human." In more recent work, Smith (2020) has argued that dehumanization facilitates a disinhibition of our "worst impulses." In the context of this discussion, our "worst impulses" are the activated violence and mass murder that resulted in the greatest genocide in recorded history.

In the model I suggest here, the victimizer (Nazi Germany) dehumanized the victim (Jews and other weaker groups) and activated a further progression of dehumanization that led to the violence and murder directed at the victim, in this case the Jew. Murder, in this sense, is a continuation of the dehumanization that resulted from various historical and contemporary factors and delusional beliefs.

It is probable that many, if not most, German executioners had, at least initially, some reluctance to kill their victims. Killing another human being is usually defended against psychologically through the internalization of the taboo against murder (Smith, 2011). The violence and murder to which dehumanization leads must then overcome psychological barriers against the murder of other humans. This is discussed further in the following section.

## Killing Jews: Reactions and Behaviors of the Executioners

Freud (1930) recognized the enormous personal and social struggles that ensued when murderous aggression was unleashed in the society. Given his emphasis on the ensuing guilt and persecutory feelings of conscience that may result from excessive aggression and violence, one might predict that the victimizers and killers of Jews would have had enormous psychological burdens to endure. On the other hand, there was the charismatic (but delusional) leadership in the form of Adolf Hitler and many social forces that have been enumerated earlier that encouraged and supported the murder of Jews on individual and collective levels.

Several authors have addressed the relationship between violence and destruction in the Holocaust and psychological attitudes and reactions in those who perpetrated this violence. Tentative conclusions about the impact (or lack of it) of killing Jews in the Holocaust will be offered at the conclusion of this section.

Dave Grossman's (1995) *On Killing: The Psychological Cost of Learning to Kill in War and Society* addresses this question through the statements of veterans of wars and through a review of the literature. The situation is not directly comparable to the Holocaust, for the most part, since the latter did not involve Jews as combatants in a war between states or entities. Nonetheless, the impressions of Grossman, a retired military officer and a psychologist, are instructive. They do speak specifically to the Nazi killing of Jews to some degree. Grossman (1995) recognizes that there exists "a powerful, innate human resistance towards killing one's own species" and that there also are powerful "psychological mechanisms that have been developed by armies *over the centuries* to overcome that resistance" (p. xxi).

Grossman (1995) cites research conducted with soldiers in the World War II era that found only fifteen to twenty percent of American riflemen fired on the enemy during combat. Many soldiers would intentionally miss the enemy as they shot their guns (often firing over the heads of the opposing soldiers). These soldiers did not run from the enemy and they would act heroically to rescue comrades, but they would not fire to kill opposing forces if they could help it. It took later training and conditioning techniques in the Vietnam war to increase the willingness of American soldiers to fire on the enemy. For Grossman (1995), the resistance to killing another human being is a combination of factors that are instinctive, hereditary, rational, environmental, cultural, and social. These factors are not easily overcome for most people.

The situation is especially difficult for those who are expected to kill at close range compared to those whose job it is to kill at greater distances. Grossman (1995) writes:

> The resistance to the close-range killing of one's own species is so great that it is often sufficient to overcome the cumulative influences of the instinct for self-protection, the coercive force of leadership, the expectancy of peers, and the obligation to preserve the lives of comrades. (p. 87)

Many people are not able to kill those whom they can see directly.

Grossman (1995) indicates that destructive aggression and killing seem to require emotional withdrawal. Various factors that facilitate this emotional withdrawal include: cultural distance (for example, racial differences that facilitate dehumanization); moral distance (a sense of moral superiority), social distance (social stratification), and mechanical distance (for instance, killing through a sniper sight).

Grossman (1995) dissects factors that contribute to the psychological morbidity of combatants and the intense guilt felt by those who kill their enemies in war. He also speaks of the impact of hate in Nazi death camps and argues that the hatred the Jews felt from their Nazi guards was crucial in creating the psychiatric morbidity and post-traumatic stress experienced by Jewish survivors. Overseers in concentration camps also contained a "remarkable concentration of aggressive psychopaths . . . and the lives of victims of these camps were completely dominated by the personalities of these terrifyingly brutal individuals" (Grossman, 1995, pp. 78–79). The human propensity toward violence and murder can be seen here to express itself variably, depending on situation and person.

In remarks consistent with my discussion of dehumanization in chapter four, Grossman (1995) comments,

> the victims of these camps had to look their sadistic killers in the face and know that another human being denied their humanity and hated them enough to personally slaughter them, their families, and their race as though they were nothing more than animals. (p. 79)

In this case, victims recognized that they were not considered human, or perhaps they were even worse than a subhuman creature, not worthy of any compassionate consideration at all.

Christopher R. Browning (1992/2017) describes the killing of unarmed Jews in Nazi-held territory in World War II. *Ordinary Men: Reserve Police Battalion 101 and the Final Solution in Poland* is a narrative about a reserve police battalion of the German Order Police that was incorporated into the German military and tasked with mass murders/exterminations and deportation of Jews in Poland during the first years of World War II.

There is limited information about the men of the battalion, but it seems that about sixty percent of the rank and file were of working-class backgrounds, and about twenty-five percent of these men were party members. They were generally middle-aged. Most did not have any education beyond the ages of fourteen or fifteen and most came from Hamburg, a city that was not considered to be highly nazified. The majority of the men "came from a social class that had been anti-Nazi in its political culture" (Browning, 1992/2017, p. 48). Browning (1992/2017) comments further that recruitment of those who would commit mass murder on behalf of the Nazi world vision from this group of men would have seemed unlikely prior to their actual participation in the killings.

Browning (1992/2017) describes the first major action of these men, a "massacre" of Jews in the town of Józefów, Poland in detail. Some men, a minority, had intense emotional difficulties around the task of shooting helpless and unarmed Jewish civilians. Some found it repugnant. When they spoke up and asked to be excused, the command structure was supportive of them and allowed them to be relieved of this duty. Some policemen, as would be expected from Grossman's (1995) study above, did not formally request release from the firing squads, which was a common way to murder the assembled Jews. They took various forms of evasive actions, such as firing past their intended victims (Browning, 1992/2017). Those men who evaded or asked to be relieved of their killer duties seem to have suffered no consequences from their superiors, although their fellow policemen were sometimes denigrating to them. The leaders of the reserve police battalion were aware that these murders might be difficult for the men, and alcohol was readily available after completion of their duties to try and relieve their emotional burdens.

In reflecting on their experiences about twenty years later, the men reported that discussions about what they had done were not encouraged by either the men or their superiors at the time. Some reflection about the morality of their actions rose to the fore years later. Based on what they said, some of the men had participated in the mass murders out of fear of being called cowards by their comrades. They were not overtly concerned about what the Jews might think of them and,

> with few exceptions the whole question of anti-Semitism is marked by silence. What is clear is that the men's concern for their standing in the eyes of their comrades was not matched by any sense of human ties with their victims. (Browning, 1992/2017, p. 73)

The fate of the Jews was, in an odd way, not thought of as their responsibility.

Browning (1992/2017) estimates that, in addition to the small number of policemen who spoke up at the beginning of (or prior to) the operation, a larger number (estimated at ten to twenty percent) either tried to evade the shooting in a less conspicuous way or asked for release once the firing had begun. This would leave about eighty percent of the men who continued to shoot until all the Jews had been killed. When this was discussed nearly one quarter of a century later, "those who did quit shooting along the way overwhelmingly cited sheer physical revulsion against what they were doing as the prime motive but did not express any ethical or political principles behind this revulsion" (Browning, 1992/2017, p. 74). Nonetheless, recalling a specific early massacre, a sense of resentment and bitterness was felt by many of these men because of what they had been asked to do. Ultimately, the policemen were relieved to a degree of the horrors of the killing process itself. They became more involved in clearing Jews out of ghettos and in the deportation actions (that also entailed potential for considerable violence).

In time, after the Józefów massacre, battalion members divided into groups based on their eagerness/willingness or unwillingness to kill Jews. Browning (1992/2017) reports that:

> Many had become numbed, indifferent, and in some cases eager killers; others limited their participation in the killing process, refraining when they could do so without great costs or inconvenience. Only a minority of non-conformists managed to preserve a beleaguered sphere of moral autonomy that emboldened them to employ patterns of behavior and stratagems of evasion that kept them from becoming killers at all. (p. 127)

Ultimately, the killings, deportations, and hunts for Jews came to an end.

> With a conservative estimate of 6,500 Jews shot during earlier actions like those at Jozefow and Lomazy and 1,000 shot during the "Jew hunts," and a minimum estimate of 30,500 Jews shot at Majdanek and Poniatowa, the battalion had participated in the direct shooting deaths of at least 38,000 Jews. (Browning, 1992/2017, pp. 142–143)

The battalion also had been involved in the deportation of about 45,000 Jews to Treblinka. In sum, as Browning (1992/2017) points out, a battalion of under 500 men had been responsible for the ultimate deaths of at least 83,000 Jews. The policemen's obedience to authority and perceived social pressure appear to have been important aids in their willingness to kill the Jews.

Daniel Jonah Goldhagen's (1997) *Hitler's Willing Executioners: Ordinary Germans and the Holocaust* exhibits none of the grayness of motivation that Browning finds in those "ordinary men" turned executioners. Goldhagen reviews much of the material that Browning has considered, although his published work is more detailed, and less willing to give the ordinary German leeway in considering genocidal motives.

Goldhagen (1997) emphasizes the widespread involvement and complicity of ordinary Germans in the huge killing operation that was the Holocaust. He implicates Germans at all levels, be they lower-level administrative personnel, or higher-level commanders, or the actual executioners and those deporting Jews to concentration camps in the killing operation that emptied Poland of its Jewish inhabitants. Jews had accounted for about ten percent of Poland's prewar population. Goldhagen emphasizes the massive nature of the operations involved in the largely successful elimination of Jews from Europe that ultimately resulted in their deaths (Goldhagen, 1997, p. 167). There were, for example, at least 10,005 German "camps" (including ghettos), not all of which housed Jews; 941 forced labor camps in Poland that were specifically for Jews; and 230 additional camps for Hungarian Jews that were not in Poland itself. There were nearly 450 ghettos in Poland (mainly), and in Galicia and Lithuania. Main concentration camps numbered 52, with over 1200 satellite camps. Auschwitz had 700 guards at various times; over 400 guards and other personnel were at Dachau, with many other German personnel staffing various other locations. It is clear that all of these sites, with their thousands of prisoners at any one time, required an enormous expenditure of German energy and resources that was devoted heavily to killing those people whom they considered undesirables, including the Jews whom the Nazis considered subhuman.

Goldahgen (1997) also chronicles the "requirements" of the institutional killing machines that were mobile, such as the Einsatzgruppen, an "itinerant killing institution" that followed the German army on its invasion of Eastern Europe and sought Jews in newly conquered territories for murder. He also reports on the thirty-eight police battalions having at least 19,000 men that participated in the slaughter of European Jews through deportations, elimination campaigns and "Jew hunts." Ultimately, and this is Goldhagen's (1997) main point,

> Unknown thousands of other Germans contributed to the genocide in their roles as administrators of many varieties: railroad officials; army soldiers; police and other security forces who deported Jews from, among other places, Germany and western Europe; and the many who contributed to the slaughter of Jewish slave laborers working under them in production facilities. (p. 168)

Goldhagen (1997) concludes that "the number of Germans who contributed to and, more broadly, had knowledge of the regime's fundamental criminality was staggering" (p. 168). Goldhagen (1997) argues that antisemitism was broadly and deeply resident within the German psyche, and that the various murderers of the Jews willingly engaged in the completion of a task that essentially was willed and supported by the German people. Goldhagen's observations suggest also that, as the killing increased, it seems likely that the murder of Jews came to involve the activities of an increasingly large percentage of the German population that was no longer shocked (or perhaps dismayed) by the genocide in which they participated in an indirect way.

Goldhagen's (1997) report of the killing operations of the battalions of the Order Police describes the willingness, or rather the frequent eagerness, of these men to ferret out, kill and/or deport Jews to their slaughter. In one example, he reports that after a group of Jews had been transported to the execution area, each member of the police battalion involved in the executions "would choose his victim—a man, a woman, or a child" (Goldhagen, 1997, p. 217). The pair would walk to a clearing where the killing would occur and await the squad leader's orders. Goldhagen (1997) writes that:

> The killing itself was a gruesome affair. After the walk through the woods, each of the Germans had to raise his gun to the back of the head, now face down on the ground... pull the trigger and watch the person, sometimes a little girl, twitch and then move no more. The Germans had to remain hardened to the crying of the victims, to the crying of the women, to the whimpering of the children. At such close range, the Germans often became spattered with human gore. (p. 218)

Blood, bone, and brain would sometimes spatter against the German executioner. Nonetheless, the executioners returned to fetch more victims, "and to begin the journey back into the woods. They sought unstained locations in the woods for each new batch of Jews" (Goldhagen, 1997, p. 218). Except for the period after the initial executions when (or earlier) a minority of men had opted out of this task, many of the executioners seemed to enjoy their murderous duties.

In another execution, Goldhagen (1997) describes the scene of mass slaughter in Kovno (now Kaunas), Lithuania, where the butchery of the Jews was open to all to see.

> The immediate assault upon the unsuspecting, unarmed, and obviously nonthreatening Jewish community occurred immediately after the German army marched into Kovno on the heels of the Soviet retreat. With German encouragement and support, Lithuanians, in a frenzied orgy of bludgeoning, slashing, and shooting, slaughtered 3,800 Jews in the city's streets. . . . [T]he killings, whether wild or systematic, had a circus-like quality, with bystanders observing at their pleasure the slaying,

the cudgeling to death of Jews, watching with approval as crowds once watched the gladiators slaying their beasts (Goldhagen, 1997, pp. 191–192)

Goldhagen (1997) asks, in discussing an incident that involved torture, beating, and humiliation of old men before killing them, "Why degrade and torture the Jews and especially these old Jews? . . . Cold, mechanical executioners would have just killed their victims" (p. 228). He makes the point that the Germans were not just functionaries. Many of them actually delighted in, volunteered for, and enjoyed the killing.

One answer, or at least a partial answer to Goldhagen's (1997) rhetorical question is that these killers, and the higher-level officers and leaders of the German regime, were consumed by and acting in accord with what has been called here a propensity of human beings to kill other humans. Accompanying this tendency are various attitudes and reactions including sadism, enjoyment, a sense of dominance and a sense of omnipotence. The frenzy of the slaughter and the killing spree loosened the killers' ego or "civilized" controls and unleashed the barbarous violence that lay beneath it. Being in a mob or group of zealous and unrestrained individuals loosened an individual's inhibitions against murder and supported the now murderous people's heinous, violent, and genocidal actions.

Goldhagen (1997) comments that the Germans' "devotion to annihilating the Jews was such that they would even postpone operations against real partisans, against the people who posed a real military threat to them, in order to undertake search-and-destroy missions against the Jews" (p. 228). Germany's leaders believed they must engage in an "exterminatory pursuit of the remnants of a particularly pernicious species that needed to be destroyed in its entirety" (p. 238). German leaders thus used valuable resources, material, and personnel to further and complete the annihilation of the Jews. From the perspective proposed here, the Nazi leadership and the German army felt compelled to fight a crucial battle against their eternal enemy, the Jew, despite having to fight simultaneously the Russians in the East, and the Allies, ultimately including the United States, in the West.

The elimination of the Jews had been a longstanding obsession for Hitler and the Nazi leadership. The outcome of the world war and the destruction of the Jews in Europe apparently were linked for him. As noted earlier, Kershaw (2000) considered the Jews to be at the forefront of a "titanic struggle for supremacy . . . backed by the mightiest enemy of all, perhaps more powerful even than the Third Reich itself: international Jewry" (p. 130). Describing this battle as a "titanic struggle" appropriately describes the intensity of Hitler's pressure toward supremacy and murder that consumed and enveloped him, the Nazi leadership, and ultimately the world in war.

This understanding of the Germans' self-destructive and delusional obsession with the Jews may have seemed fantastical to many observers—as it must have seemed to many uncomprehending Jews whose heads were about to be blown off by German battalion policemen standing over them. The German attempt to annihilate this presumed ancient and eternal enemy was all-consuming, however. An obsessive, zealous, and horrific focus on the destruction of the Jewish enemy that the German leaders believed had always threatened the Aryans was considered a longstanding necessity. The apparently helpless condition of the Jews whom the Germans slaughtered meant little. The Germans saw the Jews as enemies, not as helpless victims. The torment and humiliation inflicted on the Jews before killing them expressed the German rage at the threat they believed was confronting them and their fear of it. This was a third front against an imaginary enemy that Goldhagen (1997) describes in a stark and horrifying narrative of destruction and death that defies logic and self-interest.

Jan T. Gross (2002) presents another stark description of the murder of Jews by members of their own ancestral community of Jedwabne, Poland in 1941 in his book *Neighbors: The Destruction of the Jewish Community in Jedwabne, Poland*. The killers in this case were not officials of the government but people who had lived with, and known, the Jews for many years. Gross's (2002) description brings to mind the slaughter of Jews in Kovno, Lithuania that is mentioned above. As noted above, the irrational slaughter and murderous rampage in Kovno also was perpetrated by civilians (Goldhagen, 1997, pp. 191–192).

Jedwabne was a small farming community inhabited before World War II by Jews as well as ethnic Poles. Its population of about 2,500 was composed of two thirds Jews, with the remainder being ethnic Poles, who were Catholic (Gross, 2002). From September 1939 until June 1941, the area was under the control of Soviet forces. When the ensuing war between Germany and Russia led to the flight of the Russians, Germany seized the town. As Gross (2002) indicates, the German occupation was welcomed by the local Polish population, while the Jewish population, although not very much involved in the politics of the war, had seemed to favor the Russians. This is not surprising considering that the German threat to the Jews of Europe was well known.

Soon after the arrival of German troops in the area, a series of pogroms occurred. These seemed to be incited by the Poles, who ignited longstanding fabricated stories of Jewish atrocities involving the use of Christian children's blood to make matzoh for Passover. Egged on by Polish elites, a plot apparently was hatched by local Polish leaders of Jedwabne (including the mayor) to attack and slaughter the Jews of the town. This was done on July 10, 1941. Jews were killed with clubs, knives, and other weapons. The massacre culminated with the herding of a large number of Jews into a barn and setting the structure on fire. Ultimately, although the figures are disputed, the total killed was about 1,600 people (Gross, 2002). There were only a handful of survivors.

The murderers of the Jews of Jedwabne were their "neighbors"; German authorities had allowed the incident but did not seem to incite it or participate in it. The "reasons" for the massacre remain unclear to the present. Jewish property was taken over by people in the town, but it does not seem that there could have been a great deal of material value to gain in this small rural community. Gross (2002) does not mention anything about actual grievances the Poles had about the Jews except for the antisemitic slurs that were centuries old.

An important part of the pogrom for this discussion involves the behavior of the Poles, dozens of whom participated in the slaughter, while others remained passively viewing the spectacles (Gross, 2002). Some people from surrounding communities also came to witness the murders, while others from these communities may have participated. There seemed to be a holiday type atmosphere. Jews were made to humiliate themselves and some were required to perform exercises before being killed. Others were tortured.

These behaviors are consistent with the sadism and narcissistic enjoyment that are so often associated with the irrational violence and killing of a weaker, targeted population during a genocidal action. Indeed, more easily understood or more factual reasons beyond the human propensity toward violence and murder that resulted in the sudden massacre of Jews by their ethnic Polish neighbors remain obscure. Whether the mayor and other community leaders wanted to ingratiate themselves with the Nazis is not known. The occurrence of this type of massacre suggests that the perpetrators were caught in a frenzy of rage and hatred that would be consistent with the expression of a deeply held unconscious drive toward murder, including the murder of other humans.

The massacre of the Jews of Jedwabne serves as an example of how seemingly easily the propensity to violence and murder can be activated when social pressures are brought to bear on the aggressors and the environment is ripe. Did the various issues such as old calumnies against the Jews, that are noted above, serve as a catalyst for smoldering resentments and petty grievances in an already charged environment of war? There seems to have been little to restrain these "neighbors," but there was also little that they appear to have gained as a result of their day-long frenzy.

It is hard to draw firm or broad conclusions about the ease or difficulty of the mass killings of other human beings based on these works by Grossman (1995),

Browning (1992/2017), Goldhagen (1997), and Gross (2002). The situations and circumstances are very different. Grossman's work is more general and focuses only to some degree on the World War II period. Browning and Goldhagen focus entirely on what were essentially murders of unarmed Jews. Gross focuses on the killing of Jews by their former neighbors (civilians) in a Polish community.

My general impression from these works is that killing other people does result in a sense of repugnance and some resistance in many perpetrators, but this occurs to variable degrees, and not consistently, especially when large groups or "mobs" are involved. Only about twenty percent of the German Order Police members seem to have had sufficient difficulty performing executions that they tried to avoid these killings of unarmed Jewish civilians (Browning, 1992/2017). The remaining men adjusted or, in some cases, sought the experience of being an executioner of the Jews. It does seem that, the further the German civilian population was able to remove itself physically and psychologically from the actual killing enterprise, the less these people were troubled emotionally by the killings that did occur. This also seems true based on Grossman's (1995) work on combat-related killing. There is no evidence based on Goldhagen's (1997) work that involvement in a killing enterprise as a civilian working in a military plant, for example, causes significant distress to most people.

These studies do suggest that, when distress potentially did occur for Germans who were killers of unarmed Jews (and perhaps for the Polish neighbors in Jedwabne, too), factors such as acceptance of authority, conformity, and social pressure were more influential than a sense of repugnance or guilt at the taking of others' lives, at least for the large majority of killers. The suggestion from these observations is that, while a taboo exists around the killing of other humans, it is not nearly as strong as might be imagined. The propensity toward violence and murder works to a different extent in different situations and with different people. It can be reinforced or overcome by the strong influence of leadership, culture, and social pressure.

Before proceeding to the next section, it is important to note a dispute among scholars about the work of Daniel Goldhagen (1997) that is introduced above. Several scholars have challenged Goldhagen's tone and his assertions about the involvement of "ordinary" German citizens in the Holocaust. An important question raised in the dispute is the degree to which ordinary Germans might have approached the extermination of Jews eagerly, willingly, reluctantly, indifferently, or perhaps with silent resistance and disfavor.

Browning (1992/2017) is critical of Goldhagen's tone and perceived attitude. He challenges Goldhagen on at least two "major areas of historical interpretation" (Browning, 1992/2017, p. 192). These are antisemitism's role in German history and the motivation of ordinary Germans who became killers in the Holocaust. He understands Goldhagen's notion of German citizens' "indifference" as their actual approval of Nazi policies and criticizes Goldhagen for having, in Browning's mind, a single explanation (antisemitism in German society) to account for the Holocaust (Browning, 1992/2017, p. 203).

The research efforts of Browning and Goldhagen around Reserve Police Battalion 101 (reviewed above) overlapped. Browning (1992/2017) writes, "in contrast to Goldhagen, I offered a portrayal of the battalion that was multilayered" (p. 215). He also writes that Goldhagen seems to accept a "simplistic reduction of the perpetrators' ideology, moral values, and conception of the victim to a single factor" (Browning, 1992/2017, p. 220), that being antisemitism. Browning is arguing here that Goldhagen's views are one-sided and extreme, and hence reflect poor scholarship.

Raul Hilberg (1992) is strongly supportive of Browning in this dispute. He emphasizes that "Goldhagen overstates the extent and depth of German antisemitism. At the same time, he underplays two factors that greatly weaken his basic thesis. One is that not all the shooters were Germans, the other, that not all the victims were Jews" (p. 723). Hilberg (1992) finds Goldhagen's *Willing executioners* to be "lacking in factual content and logical rigor" (p. 724).

Yehuda Bauer (1997), an Israeli historian, is critical but also complimentary of some of Goldhagen's work in *Hitler's Willing Executioners*, a book that derives from Goldhagen's dissertation. Bauer argues that Goldhagen has not fully understood German history or antisemitism, which Bauer feels was not as universally severe or as uninterruptedly present as Goldhagen seems to him to suggest in *Hitler's Willing Executioners*.

Bauer (1997) agrees that "by the outbreak of World War II the vast majority of Germans had identified with the regime and its antisemitic policies to such an extent that it was easy to recruit the murderers" (p. 350). Prior to this time, according to Bauer, the German public would not have backed policies of extermination. Bauer (1997) writes that Goldhagen has shown "considerable capabilities in extensive sections of his book" (p. 350), but he also says that Goldhagen has published "half-baked research, albeit studded with brilliant passages and observations" (p. 350).

Goldhagen (1996) himself has responded strongly to his critics. He argues that he is presenting a new perspective, one based largely on interviews and information about the perpetrators. He argues that his work has gone against the views of many of his critics and threatens existing notions of the causes of the Holocaust. He argues that, unlike researchers such as Browning, whom he judges to overemphasize various social and peer pressures, he places responsibilities on individual Germans. Goldhagen (1996) argues that

> the German perpetrators of the Holocaust believed that Jews and Jewish power must somehow be eliminated if Germany was to be secure and to prosper. The German perpetrators of the Holocaust were motivated to kill Jews principally by their belief that the extermination was necessary and just. (p. 2)

Goldhagen emphasizes that he attempts to explain the actions of the perpetrators, including their cruelty, in detail. This is not, from his perspective, a central part of the others' arguments. He notes that German perpetrators expressed joy and at times merriment around their murderous activities and torture. This is noteworthy and supportive of a central feature of this discussion—that there is a human inclination toward violence and murder that becomes manifest under given circumstances.

These criticisms of Goldhagen's work suggest caution in drawing conclusions from *Hitler's Willing Executioners*, but I do not consider them to be entirely disqualifying. The harshness of the arguments among scholars suggests that personal feelings may have been involved and must be taken into account. Most of the criticisms of Goldhagen are around accusations of overdrawn and hyperbolic interpretations, misinterpretations, or purported omissions in important aspects of his scholarly presentation, rather than around factual errors. He defends himself by emphasizing that his analysis of the intense murderous antisemitism emphasizes individual, personal responsibility of German citizens rather than a broader social perspective.

I do find some of Goldhagen's comments about German antisemitism and malice to be overly broad, but at times his descriptions of the behavior of many Germans seem to capture the importance of the progression from dehumanization to violence, murder and genocide that is a pillar of this book. He describes this apparently innate human potential in *Hitler's Willing Executioners* quite clearly. This propensity toward violence and murder, with its unrelenting focus during the latter stages of the Nazi era on genocide, torture, cruelty, and the zest for killing that produced an environment of death also is consistent with what Shallcross (2020) termed a "necrotopographic" zone of death and dying that was present throughout much of Eastern Europe.

This necrotopographic zone was especially noticeable in the concentration camps, ghettos, and pits of dead bodies in the east but could also be discerned in other places due to the high rates of suicide of Jews before their deportations to the camps, in the camps themselves, and in the high rates of suicide of Germans during the final days of the war and in the postwar period (Goeschel, 2009). Goldhagen's work captures some of these phenomena quite well and can be understood to support the view that, while centuries of antisemitism possibly were a proximate cause of the Holocaust, a deeper and often overlooked cause of the Holocaust (and probably of other genocides) was a reservoir of murderous impulses found in human beings that appears to have been activated by a variety of socio-political factors as well as increasingly severe dehumanization, as indicated earlier in this and the preceding chapter.

## Psychological Implications of Severe Trauma

This chapter is heavily devoted to external manifestations of an internal drive toward death and destruction of others that was reflected in the killing of Jews (and others) by Germans (and others). The focus has been on the physical death of victims, and in some cases, on the sadism, torture and cruelty associated with these murders. The psychological trauma and what might be called the "psychic murder" of survivors and of those who have been victims of severe dehumanization has not been emphasized, although phenomena such as the Muselmann (which is discussed in the previous chapter) suggest to several authors that a form of "mental death" in life may be caused by severe dehumanization, abuse, and trauma such as occurred in the Nazi era.

This section focuses briefly on the concept of an individual's loss of the ability to reflect on, or to represent, his or her past, present, or future due to the trauma of the Holocaust. This is a large topic that falls within the scope of other Holocaust and trauma studies. It merits greater discussion than can be offered here. An important perspective relevant to this area is found in Shallcross's (2020) discussion of necrotopograhic zones.

Laub (2003), Laub and Lee (2005), and Felman and Laub (1992) have described psychological problems that may be related to traumatic experience, such as occurred in the Holocaust. The Holocaust provided for many people a necrotopographic environment in which death or impending death was constantly confronting prisoners. Prisoners became emaciated, weakened, disease-ridden, and were often devoid of meaningful positive contact with others. They were dehumanized, tortured, and considered useless and unworthy of life. The Muselmann is an example of this severe state between life and death.

Dori Laub (2003), a psychoanalyst and Holocaust survivor, has written about what might be called "inbetween" states that result from severe trauma. He has emphasized the importance of Freud's concept of the death drive in understanding severe trauma victims from clinical perspectives. Laub & Lee (2005) emphasize that the Holocaust victim with severe trauma does not "know" what really has happened to him or her. These individuals have often lost the ability to symbolize or even to effectively communicate with themselves or others. Laub & Lee (2005) emphasize that in such individuals "narrative is flat, repetitive, stereotypical, impoverished, overflowing with rationalizations, and very self-centered; somatic preoccupations and obsessive rituals take the place of real life" (p. 320). To me, images of Holocaust survivors being liberated from concentration camps reveal individuals with stunned, unemotional, "deadened" expressions on their faces. Life seems to have been drained from them, replaced by what seems to be largely apathetic contact with life's movements around them.

In their collaborative effort, Shoshana Felman, a literary critic, and Laub (Felman & Laub, 1992), provide additional depth to the discussion around these issues. These authors approach issues of memory, testimony, and witnessing from their own perspectives. Laub's focus on the loss of personal history and the inability of Holocaust survivors to communicate with themselves and with others are two of his emphases here. He comments that the Nazi system had tried to shield its activities not only from the outside world but also from its victims' own inner worlds. Laub argues that the Nazi system of severe trauma-infliction worked to convince these dehumanized prisoners that the victimizers were correct and that prisoners were in fact guilty of the crimes of which they were accused.

Further, the Nazi system worked to convince prisoners that they could not be adequate witnesses to themselves or to others regarding what was happening to them in their confinement. The destruction of the individual's ability to witness, to remember, and to experience happened in many cases before physical death occurred. It was only years later that these traumatic events might at times be retrievable in one form or another.

The use of the Holocaust in this book as an illustration of the activation of the human impulse toward violence and murder emphasizes the importance of considering this tendency in larger social contexts, such as in genocides, riots, or wars. The works of clinical psychoanalysts, such as Laub, demonstrate the psychological effects of the propensity toward violence and murder on surviving individuals, but this only reveals part of the effect of this human propensity.

A focus only on individual clinical situations, however useful, may obscure larger social patterns. Individual patients or contexts may always present circumstances that allow or tempt one to suggest there is no need to postulate a more universal human tendency toward violence and murder if there are individual situations or clinical diagnoses (such as antisocial personality disorder or depression) that might help to explain one or more killing episodes. A more distanced view of events involving mass killings and larger groups of perpetrators allows a different perspective that may suggest less the involvement of an individual killer's psychopathology and more the phenomenon of a universally present tendency that often is most clearly activated, supported, or encouraged in a larger group setting, as seems to be true in cases of genocide or mob related riots. The example of a killing spree in *Neighbors* (Gross, 2002) noted earlier in this chapter is instructive in this way.

## Illustrations of Dehumanization and Murder of Jews in the Nazi Era

The treatment of Jews in ghettos and in concentration camps was particularly harsh. Jews in these settings were very likely to die, either because of the harsh conditions imposed on them, or because of "actions" taken by the Germans that would bring them to the crematoria. It was in these settings that the continuity between severe dehumanization and murder was most striking.

The motivation for the dehumanization and humiliation imposed on the Jews is characterized insightfully by Kovner (2001) who offers another perspective on the cruelty of the Nazis toward the Jews that is consistent with the psychological impressions of Laub presented above: "The Nazis were not content with the death of the Jews, with suffering and humiliation. They wanted the victims to believe that they were rightly despised, that their death had no meaning just as their lives were not sacred" (p. 11).

The following descriptions illustrate these and other points around dehumanization and murder. They are taken from the notes of A. W. Landau (2011), a concentration camp survivor who was liberated by British troops at Bergen-Belsen when the Third Reich collapsed. Landau (2011) was in a number of camps. The following incident from his time in the Buchenwald concentration camp is illustrative of the humiliation and torture endured by the Jews that was associated with the dehumanizing and cruel activities of the Nazis' malevolence and impulse to kill.

Because of extreme hunger, Landau had found and eaten some wild nuts. A guard ultimately became aware of this. After being lashed with a whip because of his "crime," Landau reports on what came next: "He had me taken outside the camp to a small pond and pushed me in. He then threw sticks in the water and told me to 'fetch' like a dog, using my teeth. I was in the water maybe twenty minutes retrieving the sticks. He was just humiliating me, for sport" (p. 82).

This incident again reflects the dehumanization of essentially enslaved people, with its cruelty, shaming, and humiliation, that precedes murder. Death often came quickly to inmates of concentration camps, who had or had not infringed on the rules. In this case, seeking additional food was an infraction that easily could have resulted in Landau's being shot. Humiliation served to remind him (and the perpetrator) that he was powerless to resist the will of his captors and was always at their mercy. He had no rights that are usually associated with being human or being free (such as a trial). It might have been that Landau was not killed when he broke the rules because he was "useful" and could work, at least for a period of time. He nonetheless was punished by being whipped and shamed and treated like a dog. In this case, as noted above, impending or potential death overlapped, as it often did, with severe dehumanization. It also was associated with the apparently gleeful conduct of his oppressor who reveled in his exercise of power at Landau's expense. Living or dying was not in the inmate's control; nor was it fully in control of the guard who acted impulsively and unconsciously in accord with his murderous impulses that came to the fore as a result of factors such as the longstanding dehumanization of the Jews, years of propaganda against them, social pressure to enact impulses of extreme violence, and the cruelty and isolation of the camps. The prisoner's fate resided with the whim of his oppressor, which was itself irrational.

In another incident (from another camp) Landau (2011) describes his personal reactions in Auschwitz as he observes the imminent death of new arrivals to the camp and senses that his own death is near.

> In late September, the trains began coming in right through the camps, and it seemed as if things were happening faster. Gazing through the barbed wire, we watched as people were brought from the transport and marched in a column toward the gas chambers.
> At that moment all hell broke loose, as people suddenly realized they were facing certain death. There was crying, shouting, praying...
> What I remember most was the stench and the music. There was a foul smell penetrating the camp you just couldn't avoid. The nearer you got to the crematorium, the worse the smell.... And the music was always playing—loud marching music, German music. The orchestra players were inmates, Germans,

Jews and others. There was one verse that the SS sang along with in German: 'The Jewish blood will flow into the rivers. . . .' (pp. 66–67)

The rage and hatred felt by many Germans, especially Nazis, toward Jews was intense. Their sadism and desire for vengeance against the Jews whom they believed had brought their country to ruin exceeded the bounds of usual hatred or animosity. It seemed that only death could satisfy them. They felt that all Jews in Europe, men, women, and children should suffer this fate.

Landau's recollection brought to my mind the 137th Psalm, also a call for activation of murderous impulses and a wish for revenge. In this psalm, the Jewish captives give vent to their own rage against their captors, the Babylonians of the sixth century BCE. Music is a part of the incongruity of the oppression here, too. The Jews also imagine a river and wish for the deaths of their enemies, even of their enemies' children. Here, too, it seems that only revenge and death will satisfy.

## Comment

I have argued in these pages that there is a human tendency toward violence, destruction, and murder that becomes manifest when activated by various personal and socio-political conditions. The Holocaust has been presented as an example of a model that argues for the progression from dehumanization to violence, murder and genocide when particular stressors are present (for instance, humiliation of the host nation as in the case of Germany). The model I have used avoids the unfounded assertions and speculations that Freud proposed, especially his assertion that the organism strives toward an inert state. I also have found helpful the developmental concepts of Melanie Klein (1946; 1955), which emphasize the infant's apparently innate fear of annihilation that becomes directed outward as violence toward others.

One important issue in studying the human tendency toward violence and murder is the question of how strongly resistant humans are to taking another's life. This question cannot be answered definitively through the limited study of only the Holocaust, but information available from authors such as Grossman (1995), Browning (1992/2017), Goldhagen (1997), and Hilberg (1992), who have focused a great deal on this question, directly or indirectly, suggests some tentative conclusions.

There often seems to be significant resistance to killing combatants in war or unarmed non-combatants, such as the Jews in the Holocaust. This resistance may be relatively weak, however, and can be overcome for the majority of potential killers by combinations of propaganda asserting the evils of the adversary, acceptance of the dictates of authority, social pressure, and personal concerns about the security of one's job or advancement in one's career.

The literature available about the Holocaust and survivor testimonies suggest that the human tendency toward violence and murder is continuous with, and overlaps with, severe dehumanization of the victim. The definition I offered of dehumanization in the previous chapter reflects a continuum between dehumanization and violence and murder. The human impulse toward murder is frequently accompanied by sadism, narcissistic enjoyment of the suffering of the victim, and a sense of omnipotence, as Freud (1923/1960; 1930) indicated. These reactions also may accompany severe dehumanization of the victim. In both murder and in dehumanization, perpetrators (or killers) clearly consider themselves to be the masters, and the victims, metaphorically or actually, slaves. Killing another human being is the supreme dehumanizing event that one can inflict on a victim, depriving the victim, as it does, of life, itself.

# CHAPTER 5

# The Progression from Dehumanization to Murder and Genocide in the Nazi Era

---

## Introduction

This chapter explores in more depth how increasingly severe dehumanization during the Nazi era activated the impulse toward violence and murder in Nazi persecutors that resulted in genocide. I consider dehumanization to be a process by which a powerful individual or group (the victimizers) actively deny or withdraw a second group's (the victim's) sense of human worth or personal value through various actions, attitudes, and/or behaviors. The victimizers' actions are intended to increase their own sense of power and personal worth at the expense of the victimized individual or group. Dehumanization results in the loss of the victims' sense of individual or group value, self-worth, or "personhood."

The following pages describe the specific timeline and means by which the dehumanization of the Jews was accomplished in the Nazi era and how this dehumanization overlapped with, and activated, the impulse to murder that ultimately resulted in genocide and the decimation of the Jewish population of Europe. The narrative emphasizes that Nazi Germany's attempts to dehumanize and eliminate the Jewish population of Europe were a largely successful, ideologically driven effort to demonstrate Aryan supremacy over what the Nazis believed to be the Jewish menace that threatened the Aryans' very existence. This ideological fanaticism fueled the dehumanization that activated the urge to murder and led to genocide and deaths of millions of Jews (and others). The Nazi fanaticism was such that it could not be tempered despite the wasteful utilization of resources used to murder Jews (and others) that might have been used to support Germany's military efforts.

Previous chapters have reviewed the remote and the more proximate background for the antisemitism of the Nazi era (which can be understood as systemic dehumanization) that set the stage for the hatred and genocide of the Jews at this time. This earlier review included mention of both the geopolitical situation in Germany and the writings of the Nazi and earlier rightist political figures, including Adolf Hitler.

In this chapter, I argue that dehumanization of the Jewish people had numerous components, economic, social, political, religious, familial, and personal (including the loss of control over one's individual dress and sovereignty over one's body). Dehumanization was intended not only to force Jews to leave Germany but also to increase the sense of power, worth, and supremacy of the perpetrators while decreasing the sense of personal and communal value or worth of the Jewish victims.

This chapter also includes a discussion of the final stage of the Nazi era, when dehumanization clearly turned to, and became, genocide and murder. During this time, in what has been called the "final solution," firm decisions were made and actions taken on a grand scale, intended to kill all of the Jews in Europe.

This period saw countless "executions" of Jews in concentration camps, "Jew hunts," and ideologically driven death marches that served to demonstrate the sadism and cruelty, which accompanied the human inclination toward violence and murder so strongly exemplified by the Nazi regime. The urge to exterminate Jews was uncontrollable, insistent, and irrational; it was an expression of an ideologically driven tendency toward destruction and murder. Resources devoted to killing and genocidal actions were expended in ways that otherwise could have been used to support military conflicts in which Germany was engaged, but delusion and zealotry continued nearly to the end, likely hampering the overall military effort.

## Background

When the Nazis assumed power in Germany in 1933, they became the leaders of a society with many members who desired the "elimination," coerced removal, or emigration of Jews from their country. This was the result of a long history of what Goldhagen (1997) has described as a strain of "virulent and violent 'eliminationist' antisemitism within German society" (p. 23). The German people, however, were not yet ready to accept a policy of "exterminationist" antisemitism, a term that denotes the removal of the Jewish people through state sanctioned murder, although this was an end toward which Hitler's writings in

*Mein Kampf* (1925/1999) and the vitriolic antisemitism of the time might (and did) lead in the late 1930s and 1940s (Landau 2016).

It is not clear to what degree this latter goal of extermination of all Jews in Europe would have been accepted even in the early 1940s, but certainly, as the title of Goldhagen's (1997) *Hitler's Willing Executioners: Ordinary Germans and the Holocaust* suggests, the numbers of Germans (and others in countries allied with Germany) who would accept or encourage an exterminationist approach rose greatly during this time.

The sheer volume of facilities and personnel needed to enact this exterminationist approach was staggering. Goldhagen (1997) has compiled figures on the number and types of institutions involved in the latter phases of the Nazi era when Jews were mainly confined to ghettos or various types of "camps," a designation that includes concentration camps. The number of camps (see pp. 147–148) is very large and points to a huge operation that was needed to find, guard, transport, house, and murder millions of Jews and other prisoners. The deaths and extermination of Jews in much of Europe clearly was supported, directly or indirectly, by large numbers of citizens inside and outside of Germany.

Preparing the German people for the conceptual movement from elimination to extermination required an intensive propaganda effort that reached far into the everyday lives of ordinary German citizens, from activities such as lessons in schools, to forms of entertainment, to mass media, to sporting and other cultural venues.

> As soon as they came to power, the Nazis launched a programme of subtle conditioning and indoctrination of their own people. This program was masterminded by Joseph Goebbels, the Propaganda Minister, who controlled all the communications media—radio, newspapers, film, theatre and books. It also coincided with the beginnings of the Nazification of the educational system. All new teaching appointments to state schools would soon be confined to Nazi Party members; subjects such as history, German literature and biology were revamped in accordance with Nazi ideology, particularly its racial components; and there was a growing emphasis on the glorification of militarism and the strengthening of a regenerated Germany. (Landau, 2016, p. 128)

It seems appropriate to state that the German people themselves were confined or entrapped by the extensive and unyielding misinformation about Jews that was intended to inflame public opinion against the Jews. In some sense, providing false or misleading information through propaganda is itself a form of dehumanization, since it deprives the target of the misinformation (the German citizens) of their own ability to judge and form opinions about crucial information.

Through all of this anti-Jewish activity, propaganda, and isolation from mainstream society, Jews became increasingly dehumanized and socially isolated. Goldhagen (1997) speaks of Jews having become "socially dead" to the average German. Jews were made social pariahs, a group to be denigrated, despised, shunned, and dehumanized. Social death is one product of dehumanization; people in these situations are no longer considered to be a part of the social fabric of the society. As I argue throughout this book, the severly dehumanized and socially isolated person is more likely to be further denigrated, abused, and ultimately killed.

Indeed, over time, much of German society and the German people were involved in some way in various direct or indirect processes of dehumanization that were followed by the organized slaughter and deaths of the Jewish people in Germany and its allied countries. Participation in processes of dehumanization commonly occurred along with other activities and duties of the average German's everyday life (Goldhagen, 1997).

The enforced social isolation, ghettoization, administration of various camps (such as work and death camps) was a huge administrative undertaking that required large-scale social participation, although the degree of conscious awareness or active reflection related to these activities presumably varied greatly among the population. Administrative clerks arranging the schedule of trains to Auschwitz, along with the schedules of trains to other places in the Third Reich, for example, would have been able to deny or rationalize their activities more easily than members of police battalions assigned to executioner roles at other sites in Poland.

Participation in the dehumanization and ultimate murder of the Jews was broad and deep, but not universally the same across sectors or persons. As Hilberg (1992) concluded:

> The destruction of the Jews was not centralized. No agency had been set up to deal with Jewish affairs and no fund was set aside for the destructive process. The anti-Jewish work was carried out in the civil service, the military, business and the party. All components of German organized life were drawn into this undertaking. Every agency was a contributor; every specialization was

utilized; and every stratum of society was represented in the envelopment of the victims. (p. 20)

Some participated more willingly than others, but by the time extermination was decided upon by the Nazi leaders, nearly all the German people would have realized that the Jews were considered subhuman or "less than human" by their leaders (and ultimately by many bystanders as well).

This process of dehumanization that stripped Jews of their rights as citizens, their abilities to function socially, professionally, and educationally, their freedom of movement, and their control over their own bodies happened over a relatively short period of time, about eight years, from 1933 to 1941. By the end of this period, Jews would have lost much of their self-esteem and former identities. Seen as subhuman creatures without power, without social support, and without identities of their own, their situations would allow or activate the perpetrators' sadism and enlist the perpetrators' impulses to murder that ultimately would result in genocide. The Jews' continuing dehumanization would have likely strengthened the propensity to violence in their persecutors until killing those thought to be subhuman became less objectionable. The following section describes the stages and processes that were involved in this movement in more detail.

## Periods or Stages in the Persecution and Dehumanization of the Jews during the Nazi Era

Three distinct but overlapping stages or periods of increasingly severe dehumanization of the Jews in the Nazi era can be discerned. Legislation was a preferred method to legitimize the Nazi persecution of the Jews, at least at the beginning of the Nazi era. Indeed, there was a "legal onslaught" of legislation targeting Jews once Hitler came to power (Landau, 2016). These laws included various punishments, restrictions, and requirements expected of Jews living in Nazi Germany. Some of the laws limiting Jewish activity had been instituted even before the Nazi era, and many similar laws and regulations were imposed by other countries in Europe that came under German influence during the Nazi period (Machala, 2014; MacQueen, 1998). Many of these early laws were intended to isolate Jews from the Aryan population and/or to restrict or limit Jewish participation in their own religious life and in the civic and cultural life of Germany and its protectorate and allied states.

During the first period, 1933–1938, the new laws and practices were aimed primarily at clarifying the question "Who is a Jew?" from the Aryan perspective and limiting the Jewish people's activities in religious, cultural, and professional spheres. During the second period, 1938–1941, laws and practices were aimed at restricting and channeling residential and living space allowed to Jews. Ghettos were prominent in this period. During the third period, 1941–1945, various forms of imprisonment, such as containment in labor camps and concentration camps often were used to force the Jews to work for the state, usually in its military preparations, prior to their mass murder in concentration or extermination/death camps, but also through mass shootings or "death marches."

Landau (2016) provides a useful chronology of events during the years 1933–1945. Some of the most important events reflecting the Nazis' dehumanization efforts, taken mainly from Landau, are listed below.

## First Stage: the Years 1933–1938

During this stage, the Germans increasingly controlled the external activities and involvements of the Jews in social, professional, educational, and to some degree, religious arenas. The Nazis' perceived need to deal with the Jewish question and to force their eliminationist goals were high on the agenda of Hitler and the Nazi party as they assumed power in Germany in 1933. A number of strategies, verbal, physical, and legislative, were used in this first stage and throughout the Nazi era to further these goals.

As suggested earlier, a constant verbal, media, and propaganda barrage was instituted against the Jews that was intended to emphasize their lowly status and reprehensible ethical standing in the view of the new government. This was intended to reduce the acceptance of Jews by the German people, while also demoralizing, terrorizing, and frightening them in order to force their exodus from Germany: "Constant, ubiquitous, antisemitic vituperation issued from Germany's public organs, ranging from Hitler's own speeches, to never-ending installments in Germany's radio, newspapers, magazines, and journals, to films, to public signage and verbal fusillades, to schoolbooks" (Goldhagen, 1997, p. 136). German propaganda was massive and effective in achieving its objectives, a part of which was to tarnish the equality and humanity of Jews.

Physical intimidation and violence were also used by the Nazis and their followers throughout this era, and well before the more recognized violence of Kristallnacht, the ghettos, or the camps.

> The regime perpetrated, encouraged, or tolerated violence against Jews ... at any moment even during the 1930s. It took the form sometimes of impromptu physical attacks and ritualistic degradation by local officials, and sometimes of centrally organized campaigns of violence, terror, and incarceration in concentration camps. (Goldhagen, 1997, p. 137)

This intermittent and ongoing violence against Jews, which was encouraged by governmental authorities, would have created a sense of helplessness and terror among the Jews and hastened their attempts to flee from Germany.

The Nazis wasted little time in moving an authoritarian racist agenda forward as soon as they achieved power in 1933. They approached the dehumanization of Jews (and others) in a number of ways, acting legislatively in several domains. Within months, the Dachau concentration camp was set up. The inmates included not only Jews but also communists, socialists, and homosexuals. In April 1933, a boycott of Jewish businesses and professions was announced. The Restoration of the Professional Civil Service Act, also enacted in April, resulted in the dismissal of Jews from the civil service. In the same year, following the the Law against the Overcrowding of German Schools, the process of eliminating Jewish teachers and students from public schools in Germany began. In the religious domain, kosher ritual slaughter, an important component of Jewish religious practice, was outlawed.

Still in the first half of 1933, a Nazi-organized "book-burning" was held in Berlin. Books by Jewish authors (and those of other authors considered "degenerate") were removed from libraries and publicly burned. On symbolic level, it is clear that through the burning of books the Nazis wished to control information and suppress suspect opinions, especially those of intellectuals and subversives whom they considered enemies.

Later in 1933, the hereditary farm law banned Jews from owning land. In the same year, Jews were banned "from all aspects of German cultural and sporting life" through a law that would affect Jewish participation in sports, the arts, literature, and the press (Landau, 2016). Other early acts that reflected the desire of the Nazis to isolate and condemn the Jews included restrictions of the use of public facilities, such as swimming pools and public parks. Goldstein (2012) reports that forty-two anti-Jewish measures were enacted in 1933 and another nineteen were enacted in 1934.

These early acts occurring at the outset of the Nazi era demonstrated the Nazis' intent to dehumanize Jews in several domains, and to control and restrict Jewish participation in the economic, cultural, and professional life of Germany while also restricting the Jewish people's own religious practices. They reflected the intent of the German government to isolate Jews and to restrict their own and German citizens' involvement with one another, a practice that would make it easier for average Germans to distance themselves psychologically from the fate of the Jews (Landau, 2016). All of this was consistent with Hitler's emphasis on the importance of separating members of the Aryan race from members of what he considered the subhuman Jewish race because of the fear of contamination of the Aryans by the Jews (A. Hitler, *Mein Kampf* extract, in Landau, 2016). Burning books written by Jews, for example, suggests the importance in the Nazis' eyes of limiting corrosive information propagated by the Jews in order to avoid being contaminated by them. As Goldhagen (1997) says, the Jews were expected to become "socially dead" to the larger Aryan society.

Further restrictions and prohibitions consistent with the Nazi party platform were enacted in the well-known Nuremberg Laws of 1935 (Landau, 2016) These laws included 1) the Reich Citizenship Law "that removed Jewish equality before the law . . .," and 2) the Law for the Protection of German Blood and Honour, "which prohibits marriage or sexual relations between Jews and non-Jews" (p. 350). Later, in November 1935, under a supplement to the Reich Citizenship Law, Jews were disqualified from German citizenship.

The Nuremberg Laws thereby established that Jewish people could not be citizens and that they did not have the rights of citizenship. Jews also could not intermarry with Germans, an apparent reference to the feared contamination of Aryan blood by the blood of the Jews. Through the Nuremberg laws, as Hitler had emphasized in *Mein Kampf*, Jews were defined in racial terms, a condition that was further determined on the basis of the number of Jewish grandparents a person had. A person was considered a Jew if he or she had three or more Jewish grandparents (Landau, 2016).

The Nazis' multifarious dehumanization of Jews continued through this period and spread to other countries, often building on the groundwork laid by the antisemitism of earlier times. A number of pogroms occurred in Poland in 1936, apparently instigated by a Polish cardinal who condemned usury and fraud attributed to Jews by Christian clergy (and others) that is reminiscent of the antisemitic calumnies of earlier periods that focused on religion rather than race. It may be that "scientific racism," a popular designation among Nazis and their sympathizers in the 1930s and 1940s (and earlier), was a superfluous label for the expression of the virulent antisemitism spawned in part by the Nazis that was present in Eastern Europe at this time and before. Finally, in 1937, the Buchenwald concentration camp was created.

By the end of this stage (roughly 1938), it had become clear that Jews were to be shunned socially and excluded from all forms of civil and community life in Germany. The population of Jews in Germany before the Nazi era was only about 550,000 or one percent of the population (Landau, 2016). Half of these people emigrated because of the early conditions imposed by the Nazi government. For those who had not left, or for those who could not leave because of economic or other reasons, it was clear that Jews were not even second-class citizens at this point; they were considered aliens and were living in a hostile country whose leadership could not be counted on to protect them from violence and that viewed them as vermin, ready to infect the Aryan race. These Jews of Germany were, in fact, stateless.

## Second Stage: the Years 1938–1941

During this stage, the restrictions, limitations, and social isolation of the first stage increased as the Germans came to control where the Jews could live and ultimately how much space, food, electricity, medical care, and other necessities they would receive (Landau, 2016). The first ghettos were established. In this period, also, the German state expanded, as Hitler had promised. Further persecution of the Jews, socially and economically, took place; and the Nazis fomented the Kristallnacht riot (Goldhagen, 1997).

Firstly, Germany expanded into what would be called "Greater Germany" through the incorporation of Austria (the Anschluss) and the Czech Sudetenland. These acquisitions increased German territory and began to fulfill Hitler's goal of acquiring more land (living space) for people of the Aryan race. Secondly, certain amounts of personal property of Jews in Germany now required registration, an indication that property owned by Jews might ultimately be confiscated or appropriated. Third, after the assassination of a German embassy official in France by Herschel Grynszpan, a young Polish Jew who was angered by the forced deportation of his parents from Germany in November 1938, the Nazis responded with "collective punishment." During Kristallnacht, large-scale rioting, destruction, and violence against Jews and Jewish property across Germany was instituted by government agents (Goldhagen, 1997; Landau, 2016). Jewish property—businesses, religious buildings, such as synagogues, and artifacts—was vandalized, looted, and destroyed. Scores of Jews were killed and thousands were sent to concentration camps.

The German authorities blamed the Jews collectively for the actions of the one Jew who had assassinated the embassy official. All Jews in Germany were considered responsible, and the Jewish community was required to pay for repairs to their own property. They were also required to pay a collective reparation fee to the state. Worldwide outcries against the German state made no apparent difference in Nazi policies. Kristallnacht served as a warning of Nazi Germany's determination to deal harshly with Jews as a collective, rather than as individuals. This was another form of dehumanization, a loss of individuality.

Kristallnacht reflected a dramatic escalation in state-sponsored violence against Jews. It also reflected the early use of concentration camps to imprison significant numbers of Jews. After Kristallnacht, it became impossible for Jews to experience a sense of safety or to maintain their property or economic livelihoods in Germany. It was clear that they would no longer be able to express their religious beliefs freely or openly.

Another important event that emphasized the hopeless condition of the Jews and their lack of tangible support in the world occurred in 1938. President Franklin D. Roosevelt convened a conference in Evian, France in July of that year that was attended by representatives of thirty-nine governments (Landau, 2016). The stated goal of the conference was to address problems of Jewish refugees, although the United States wished to encourage other nations to accept increased numbers of Jewish emigrants from Germany.

This effort was a failure, however. A small number of countries at the conference agreed to only token increases in immigration. Furthermore, in October 1938, the Evian Committee sent a memorandum to the German Foreign Office indicating that the Evian conferees did not challenge the right of Germany to govern its own subjects in accordance with accepted standards of state sovereignty. This statement and the failure of Evian conferee states to accept more immigrants may have emboldened Hitler. In any case, Kristallnacht, the event that unleashed previously unseen violence against the Jews, occurred the month after the Evian Conference.

In the next few years, Germany increased its emphasis on Jewish emigration but had little success. As war seemed inevitable, Hitler delivered a chilling speech in the Reichstag in which he threatened to annihilate Europe's Jews "if the international Jewish financiers in and outside Europe should succeed in plunging the nations once more into a world war . . ." (Hitler, 1939, as cited in Landau, 2016, p. 158). Hitler's statement warning about world war and the annihilation of the Jewish people suggested that conflict, violence, and terror were about to increase. In Hitler's mind (or at least through his statements), the Jews continued to be responsible for much of the misery of the world that he, himself, was about to increase in horrifyingly violent dimensions.

The Molotov-Ribbentrop non-aggression pact between Germany and the Soviet Union in 1939 divided much of Poland between these two countries and provided additional land for each. Hitler was not satisfied with what he had obtained, however, and later pushed eastward into Russia. Many more Jews came under German control with Hitler's eastward thrust into the Pale of Settlement where about three million, generally poor, Jews lived. Emigration of significant numbers of Jews, the lynchpin of the Nazi eliminationist strategy to deal with the removal of the Jews, stalled. There was little prospect for emigration to inhospitable and/or unwelcoming environments, such as Madagascar, Palestine, or South American nations that had been previously discussed as a means of removing the Jews from the Aryan presence.

The beginning of the settlement of Jews into ghettos occurred in 1939. The ghettos were temporary sites in cities that housed large numbers of Jews who were forced into them, often being required to sell their own homes to local residents at enormous losses. The loss of residence was another source of dehumanization and humiliation, as well as of anxiety about safety. Jews in ghettos were confined and under the complete power of the German forces. The ghettos became filthy, unsanitary, and disease-ridden environments, as Emmanuel Ringelblum describes in his account from the Warsaw ghetto (Sloan, 1974). Forced labor was common. Rations, as reported by Ringelblum in the Warsaw ghetto, were restricted to about 800 calories per person per day (Sloan, 1974). Malnutrition, disease, and death were common. When people were defiant or unable to work, they were often summarily shot in another example of how dehumanization and helplessness led to murder and death of the weak or the noncompliant. Ghettos often were necrotopographic zones, places where death was omnipresent, as Shallcross (2020) has indicated.

Ultimately, hundreds of ghettos (including those in Łódź and Warsaw) were established, as noted earlier. The Warsaw ghetto, for example, was the largest ghetto in Nazi-occupied lands. It grew to contain about 500,000 people, but through disease, overwork, murder, and deportations, the final population was about ten percent of this number (Landau, 2016). Since the Nazis had openly stated their intention to eliminate all Jews in Europe, and other countries were now accepting only very small numbers of refugees, the Nazis decided to solve the Jewish question through a "final solution" that was formulated definitively in 1941. This "final solution" to the Jewish problem involved mass murder on a horrific scale.

Ghettoization facilitated the murder of large numbers of Jews since it allowed them to be maintained, monitored, and controlled in designated areas, making it easier to deport them to the "east" where they ultimately would be overworked and/or killed. German fears of a hostile force that would retard the German military advancement also were eased by forcing Jews into ghettos.

The cultural, social, economic, and religiously dehumanizing steps of earlier years progressed further during these ghetto years. Jews were restricted in social contacts among themselves and with non-Jews; they were deprived of adequate housing, education, medical care, and food supplies. Dehumanization came to affect Jewish family life, personal identity, and dress. Depending on location, Jews were required to wear identifying armbands or a star on their coats in this period, thus forcing them to identify themselves publicly as Jews in a derogatory manner. In 1938, it became compulsory to add the name "Israel" for men or "Sara" for women "to their existing names and, on pain of imprisonment, to use those names in all official matters" (Kershaw, 2000, p. 131). Jews also were required to have their passports stamped with a "J."

As indicated earlier, Jews in ghettos were doomed to a sometimes slow death if they were able to survive these harsh and dehumanizing conditions at all or to a rapid death by shooting if they attempted to escape the ghetto or defied their oppressors in other ways. Later, beginning in 1941/1942, death came not only in the ghetto itself but through "actions" or deportations of increasing numbers of prisoners who were loaded onto trains and transported to the east for further hard work, starvation, humiliation, and murder in concentration camps. The illustrations provided later in this chapter, as well as those in previous chapters, show grim images of life in ghettos and camps.

## Third Stage: the Years 1941–1945

This was the stage in which the Germans controlled not only what Jews were permitted to do (their activities) and where they could live (mostly in ghettos or camps), but also where and when each of them would die. Concentration camps of various types were characteristic of this stage. There were several types of concentration camps (when the term is used generically) (Pingel, 1990). These included labor camps, transit camps, prisoner-of-war camps, and extermination camps (such as Auschwitz-Birkenau).

There were other means of extermination employed by the Nazis and their allies in addition to, or before, the widespread use of the concentration camps. These included organized death squads, the Einsatzgruppen, that accompanied the German military in its eastward expansion and executed Jews along the way; death squads of the Order Police described in an earlier chapter; "Jew hunts" for those Jews who were hidden or who had not yet been apprehended through the aforementioned approaches; and "death marches" of Jews toward the end of the war during which they were being moved to ostensibly more secure concentration camps as Allied forces approached formerly secure camps.

Death was the intended outcome for all Jews. Some Jews, usually younger able-bodied men, prolonged their lives in concentration camps through work the Germans needed for the war effort. When these men (and older male teenagers) were no longer able to work effectively, they were killed. These final years of the Nazi era were characterized by dehumanization, horrendous violence, massacres, torture, and death for millions of Jews and others who suffered at the hands of what must be considered a crazed and fanatical regime.

Hitler's ideological fanaticism required the extermination of all Jews in Europe. As noted earlier, this commitment may have taken precedence even over Nazi Germany's efforts in the conduct of war. As Kassow (2018) indicates, this was a regime that emphasized ideology and racist dogma above the needs of its own population and its own war effort. Landau (2016) argues the same point when he writes,

> Ultimately, the destruction of the Jews would be so intrinsically desired by the Nazi state that even when it was clear to all but the most fanatical and self-deluded that Germany was heading, inescapably, for military defeat, her anti-Jewish policy would be carried out with even more rigour and determination. What is even more remarkable and noteworthy is that this policy continued to be enacted with ruthless efficiency even though it often worked directly against the German war interest. (p. 126)

It seems odd but nonetheless true in the minds of Nazi leaders, that any living Jew was a threat to the Aryan race.

Gutman (1988) argues the same point. The harsh anti-Jewish policies of the Nazi regime continued even when they were of no value to the regime or to Germany itself, and even when they were at times detrimental to its war effort. "Hitler believed, or had convinced himself, that the Jews were the instigators of war, and he often repeated this senseless charge in his public speeches and within the intimate circle of his cohorts" (Gutman, 1988, p. 369). In the context of the discussion in this book, violence was set; the propensity to murder could not be controlled. Gutman (1988) notes that: "In the 'final solution' phase of the Jewish problem, people who were working under slave conditions for the Nazi war effort were murdered and at a time when the third Reich was faced with a constantly growing labor shortage" (pp. 365–366). Murder of Jews, as a "final solution," took precedence over other wartime tasks.

The extent to which the annihilation of Jews remained a crucial enterprise for Nazi Germany in its final years can be understood further by considering where the Nazi regime placed its resources. By late 1941, when the "final solution" was formally decided upon, and by early 1942, when details of the project were made into a state sponsored program of genocide at the Wannsee conference in Germany, ghettoization was actively in progress. Jews ultimately died in ghettos in significant numbers through overwork, starvation, ad hoc executions, and inadequate medical care. By the war's end, as indicated above, large numbers of Jews also would be killed by the Einsatzgruppen, the forces of the Order Police, the "Jew hunts," and the "death marches" as prisoners were ordered out of camps that were in danger of being overrun by the Allied forces and made to march to other concentration camps or to transportation that would take them to other camps. Many of these half-dead prisoners died along the way, often they were shot if they fell behind.

Goldhagen (1997) argues that sparing German forces the psychologically odious task of directly shooting Jews was an important motive behind the extensive camp system the Nazis came to employ. Extermination in gas chambers and crematoria brought greater efficiency to the genocidal endeavor, but the harsh treatment, cruelty, and murder of prisoners might also have been self-defeating.

It is hard to conceive of an effective work force with diseased and half-starved men in concentration camps, or a work force largely devoid of women (who generally were gassed on arrival to concentration camps). Better treatment and the greater use of women might have resulted in higher productivity, but this also would have kept more Jews alive longer. Goldhagen (1997) says that

> the priority given to the extermination of the Jews, both by Hitler and the Nazi leadership ... was so great that the Germans willfully destroyed irreplaceable and desperately needed Jewish labor and production, and thereby further imperiled their prospect of military victory. (p. 158)

From this perspective, it was better to have a dead Jew than an adequately fed Jew who worked effectively for the Nazi war effort.

Framing these issues differently, it seems that these efforts, the construction and maintenance of an extensive system of camps, the emphasis on prisoners' work while starving and mistreating them, and the murder and rape of women prisoners were consistent with the argument advanced here. When dehumanization was no longer sufficient to meet the Nazi's ideological goals, and their sadism was not balanced by accepted mores of civilized societies or conscience, the Nazi tormentors' fanaticism was further activated. The result was the murder of countless people, a horrendous action that was accompanied by great cruelty and inefficiency that, at times, interfered with what would have benefitted the Nazi war machine and their own war effort.

The same question about prioritization and perceived importance of resources can be raised about "death marches" from concentration camps toward the end of the war. The apparent purpose of the death marches was to force those concentration camp victims who were able to endure harsh conditions to relocate to more secure camps, where their forced labor and threatened existence would continue for a time. Yet, as Goldhagen (1997) points out, the marches were senseless and aimless. They often seemed to follow no specific route. They seemed to have been an end in themselves, a continuation of the starvation, cruelty, and ultimate death of the camp prisoners. "The fidelity of the Germans to their genocidal enterprise was so great as seeming to defy comprehension" (Goldhagen, 1997, p. 367). The marches did not serve any real purpose short of the perpetuation of the genocide in which they were embedded. The prisoners were too weak, too frail, and too sick to contribute meaningfully to labor for the war effort that was clearly coming to an end. Jews were intended to die. There was no utilitarian purpose to the death marches, save for the ongoing punishment and death of the victims. Productive work was a fantasy in which few, Jewish victims or German perpetrators, believed.

These final years of Nazi rule (and of the Jewish experience in Eastern Europe at that time) were characterized by mass killings, forced deportations to concentration camps, and suffocation in gas chambers after which Jewish corpses were cremated as soon as their mouths were checked and gold was extracted from their teeth. Overall, six million European Jews were killed during the Holocaust. This was two thirds of the Jewish population in Nazi-controlled areas (Dawidowicz, 1989), over one half of the Jews in all of Europe, and one third of the Jewish population in the world (Landau, 2016). To a significant degree, Hitler's speech to the Reichstag six years earlier that threatened world war and the annihilation of the Jewish people in Europe had come true even if his attribution of blame for these events onto the Jewish people seems delusional and without merit (Landau, 2016).

## The Impact of Various Forms of Dehumanization on Jews and Jewish Life in the Nazi Era

In this chapter, I have described the dehumanization of Jews in the Nazi era by emphasizing several domains in their lives (economic, educational, cultural, religious, and bodily spheres) that were restricted and/or altered for Jews during this time. My treatment of the subject has been based on three chronological stages from 1933–1945.

Common elements in most of these restrictive or altering practices included limited social interchange with non-Jews, and social isolation and ostracism from normal social life as practiced in the society as a whole. These efforts dehumanized Jews and made them, in Goldhagen's (1997) words, "socially dead" to members of the larger German society. A brief review and further elaboration of some of these important dehumanizing practices imposed by the Nazis follows.

### Furtherance of Traditional Antisemitism in Germany

The Nazi leadership sought to dehumanize Jews through ongoing efforts to stigmatize them with well-known prejudices and vile comparisons to animals such as "vermin." The Nazis emphasized and reinforced already prevalent notions of an evil Jewish conspiracy and Jewish complicity in much of the world's misfortunes over the centuries before the Nazi era. A major emphasis in this area was the notion of Jews being part of a worldwide nefarious financial network. Characterizations of Jews as Christ killers, perpetrators of the murder of Christian children whose blood was used in Jewish religious rites, and as fomenters of worldwide social and economic ills were emphasized. Hitler himself said that the Nazi hatred of Jews was due not to religion but to their race, a difficult-to-describe and vague designation that nonetheless served to pit the Jewish Semite against members of what Hitler (and many others) felt was a superior Aryan race.

### Withdrawal and Denial of German Citizenship

Under the Nuremberg Laws passed in 1935, Jews were stripped of their German citizenship and its rights and protections (Dean, 2002). Ultimately, they were required to wear the yellow star of David badges to stigmatize them and distinguish them from non-Jews. They were not allowed to intermarry, or to have sexual relations, with members of the Aryan population since such behavior was believed by Nazi leaders to risk contamination of the Aryan race by the subhuman Jewish race. These laws were a clear message of exclusion and of dehumanization.

## Business, Commerce, Economics; Professions

One of the first acts organized by the Nazis on assuming power in 1933 was a boycott of Jewish owned businesses (Landau, 2016). The Jews were considered unfit to engage in trade or conduct business with Aryans. Jews who were physicians were considered inappropriate to treat Aryans medically. Jewish lawyers were not allowed to provide legal services for Aryans. Ultimately, Jews were not allowed to be trained in these professions, or to be licensed and to take entrance exams for them. Through these efforts, the Nazi leadership emphasized its commitment to keep the Jewish and non-Jewish (Aryan) populations separate, to isolate members of the Jewish population, and to emphasize the lower status of Jews compared to Aryans (Landau, 2016). Jewish businesses suffered greatly because of Nazi policies and were sold at below-market value or were later appropriated by the state. The Jews' telephone usage, use of public transport, and times during which they were allowed to use public facilities were restricted.

## Religion

Although Hitler emphasized that his antipathy toward Jews was based on race and not on religion, Nazi suppression of Jewish religious practices and destruction of Jewish religious objects and synagogues made it clear that the Nazis considered Judaism to be an inferior religion, one that might be chosen by a subhuman race. Kristallnacht emphasized the Nazi vilification of Judaism, exemplified through the destruction of synagogues and religious objects (as well as other property) (Landau, 2016; Machala, 2014).

The practice of religion became nearly impossible over time. This was true in both ghetto and camp environments. Kovner (2001), for example, reports on one situation in which some German soldiers were "tormenting elderly Jews in the streets" of the ghetto (p. 45). The soldiers made one of the old men "spread out a Torah scroll in the roadway and forced the Jews to urinate on its pages. Anyone who hesitated was hit across the head with a rifle butt" (Kovner, 2001, p. 45).

Religious beliefs and the practice of religion are important aspects of how people define who they are and how they relate to their worlds. The debasement of a central religious artifact and the ridicule of the elderly Jew indicate an attempt to sadistically dehumanize the Jew and his religion. The powerful German soldier essentially says to the Jew that the Jew's value and worth, and the value and worth of his belief system, are nonexistent. The German, towering over the Jew and beating the Jew with a rifle butt, is who is most important. The soldier is telling the Jew that the Jew must have a new value system, one in which there is a master, the German, and a slave, the elderly Jew, with essentially a new religion, the belief in Aryan supremacy that defiles or "pisses on" the Jews and their traditional belief system.

## Property Ownership, Property Rights, and Living Situation

Over time, Jews were required to register and then surrender or sell their property, either to government authorities or to German citizens. The compensation they received in these cases was invariably below actual value, but there was no choice when they were forced to evacuate their own homes, emigrate, or move into ghettos (Sloan, 1974). Later deportations to concentration camps involved a total loss of property that was expropriated by the state. The humiliation, cruelty, deprivation, and violence in the ghetto and concentration camps were almost unimaginable. Several Jewish writers (for example, see Kovner, 2001; Kassow, 2018; Landau, 2011; Levi, 1996; Sloan, 1974; Des Pres, 1976; Wiesel, 1958/2006) describe the dehumanizing conditions in the ghettos and concentration camps.

## Education

The Nazi government was intent on promulgating its ideology at all levels of education and its rise to power "coincided with the beginnings of the Nazification of the educational system" (Landau, 2016, p. 128). Public schools promulgated Nazi views throughout the Nazi era, as described in more detail in the next chapter. Hitler Youth groups indoctrinated youngsters with Nazi propaganda (Landau, 2016). The restrictions of Jews from higher education, professional licensure, and professional practice is described above.

## Arts, Culture, Literature, Sports

On coming to power, the Nazis launched a propaganda program intended to indoctrinate their own people in what can be considered a form of dehumanization since it withheld and restricted the free exchange of ideas and views. The Nazis came to control all of the communications media in the state, including radio, newspapers, and film (Landau, 2016). The burning of books written by Jews and other so-called "degenerates" that was organized by the Nazis in 1933 was an example of the Nazis' desire to ultimately control all information and all forms of art and communication in German society.

The writers of banned or burned books, many of whom were Jews and/or intellectuals, were considered potential enemies of the Aryan people, as they supposedly reflected what the German authorities considered degenerate ideas. The burning of books literally dehumanizes citizens, Jewish or not, by depriving people of divergent perspectives, while also carrying much symbolism around the denigation of knowledge, the advocacy of ideas, and freedom of expression, all forms of intellectual endeavor that were suspect to the Nazi regime that tolerated no dissent.

Burning books as a form of thought control and disapproval of unacceptable messages was not introduced historically by the Nazis, and its ominous portent of reducing the availability of books and their contents for the future of the culture was appreciated well before the Nazi era. The German Jewish Romantic poet, Heinrich Heine (1797–1856), for example, wrote in an early play, *Almansor*, that "where they burn books, they will ultimately burn people" (United States Holocaust Memorial Museum Encyclopedia, n.d.).

The Nazis were especially distrustful of psychoanalysis. During the book burning of 1933, they destroyed works of Sigmund Freud, who by then had become well known in German intellectual circles. Freud, a Jew, reportedly commented, "What progress we are making. In the Middle Ages they would have burned me. Now they are content with burning my books" (Burton, 2015). In fact, five years later, in 1938, Freud had to flee Austria for England after the German Anschluss. He barely escaped concentration camps and being burned in a crematorium. It seems that Heinrich Heine, writing a century before, had been correct, and Freud, writing before the Holocaust itself, had been too optimistic.

## Family Life and Relationships

Witness/survivor accounts of the Holocaust inevitably describe the loss of family members and disrupted family relationships that accompanied the persecution of Jews in the Nazi era. Confused, strained, and severed relationships were common. There was enormous grief over lost family members. Familial structures and identifications are important aspects of one's sense of oneself, his or her place in the world, and the meaning people attach to their lives. Ghetto and camp environments challenged and disrupted these core areas of voluntary identification, thus controlling and further dehumanizing the Jewish population.

Holocaust survivor Elie Wiesel (1958/2006) describes his family's brief residence in a ghetto prior to transport from their home in Transylvania to the Birkenau concentration camp in 1944. He describes the anxiety of the frightened passengers on the packed train during their transport, and the apparently hysterical or psychotic reaction of one of the women.

On arriving at the camp, he and his father were told by an inmate to lie about their ages so that they would not automatically be killed as being too young or too old to be considered useful to the Nazi work effort. The now dehumanized father and son, deprived of their true ages, became forty years of age (instead of fifty) for Wiesel's father and eighteen years of age (instead of fifteen) for Wiesel himself. This saved them, although they were separated from Wiesel's mother and three sisters, who were promptly taken toward the crematoria. Somehow, the older two sisters survived, but Wiesel's mother and youngest sister did not. In general, women, children, and the elderly were killed on arrival at Auschwitz since they were felt to be useless for the hard work to follow.

Wiesel (1958/2006) speaks elsewhere of the family separations that were a part of the horrors of the Nazi era. He asks:

> Was there a way to describe the last journey in sealed cattle cars, the last voyage toward the unknown? ... Or the countless separations on a single fiery night, the tearing apart of entire families, entire communities? Or, incredibly, the vanishing of a beautiful, well-behaved little Jewish girl with golden hair and a sad smile, murdered with her mother the very night of their arrival? How was one to speak of them without trembling and a heart broken for all eternity? (p. ix)

He is speaking here years later of Tzipora, his younger sister, a child who was clearly a special light to him. *Night* is dedicated to his parents and to Tzipora.

Wiesel (1958/2006) later describes his first night at Auschwitz:

> Never shall I forget that smoke.
> Never shall I forget the faces of the children whose bodies I saw transformed into smoke under a silent sky.
> Never shall I forget those flames that consumed my faith forever.

> Never shall I forget the nocturnal silence that deprived me for all eternity of the desire to live.
> Never shall I forget those moments that murdered my God and my soul and turned my dreams to ashes.... (p. 34)

Wiesel writes here about indescribable trauma and the forever loss of a certain joy and faith in life, as well as a desire to live. His sense of being a part of humanity has been shaken.

Cohen (2006) also describes family life, but in a ghetto in Kovno, Lithuania. She talks about the heart-wrenching experiences of family breakup and "selection" in which some individuals in the ghetto were designated for deportation to an unknown location that probably would mean death in a concentration camp. Individual family members, as noted above—usually males who were neither too young nor too old to work—might remain alive for a period of time because they were "useful" for work that must be done for the war effort. There was no consideration of family ties in the "selection." Cohen (2006) goes on to state,

> Therefore, it was here at the 'selection' that the family was divided into those who were considered 'useful' and 'useless.' ... The family as a unit was physically destroyed here, and each member was given a new identity and fate, not according to their family name, talents, or personalities, but according to their perceived temporary "usefulness." (p. 274)

The process described here is reminiscent of the situation in the pre-Civil War America where slave families were torn apart by their owners to further the economic needs of the slave holders. The dehumanization and breakup of families in the Nazi era also was based on the usefulness of the slave, or victim, to the owner or the Nazi regime.

## Personal Appearance, Dress, Control of One's Own Body, Identification of Self

There were numerous requirements imposed by Nazi Germany or its affiliated states that reflected the desire of the oppressor to identify and control the Jew's body. This was a way to monitor and single out the Jew from other citizens, to essentially dehumanize Jews who no longer had the freedom to express themselves through their dress or their bodies as they wished.

Power, therefore, was in the hands of those who could oversee and determine the identification of others. Yellow star of David badges were required to be worn by Jews in Germany soon after Kristallnacht. Variations on the theme were instituted in conquered and allied territories. Jews taken into concentration camps had designating numbers tattooed on their arms, thus dehumanizing them by depriving them of individual name identities and substituting numbers as identifiers, much as would be the case for domestic animals (that is, non-humans or subhumans).

In some camps and ghettos, pregnancy was outlawed. Women found to be pregnant in ghettos might be shot, apparently because caring for an infant would consume time needed for work on government military preparations. As noted earlier, women, children, and the elderly were commonly killed in gas chambers immediately on arrival to concentration camps, under the assumption that they would contribute little to the work activities of the camps. As we have seen in Wiesel's account, older teenage boys and men through middle age were spared initial execution in such situations. They would be kept alive to provide the labor needed for the war effort until fatigue, illness, demoralization, or starvation from inadequate rations made them "useless." They, too, would then be murdered.

## The Progression from Increasingly Severe Dehumanization to Murder

Dehumanization involves a denial of an individual's or a victim group's humanity (Haslam, 2006; Haslam et. al., 2013; Haslam & Loughnan, 2014). The concept of dehumanization, as used in this book, emphasizes that the individual or victim group, in this case the Jews of Europe, is considered a subhuman group or, in Hitler's assertion, a subhuman race. Dehumanized individuals and groups may be treated with impunity because the usual rules of social and human interaction are considered by the victimizers to no longer apply to them (Smith, 2011; 2020). Dehumanization, then, either activates an innate human predisposition to murder—in this case, the murder of the dehumanized and despised group—or is a link in a chain from progressive dehumanization and denigration of the Other to murder that is "permissible" since the Other is considered dangerous, is no longer human or not really human, or does not have essential moral or ethical qualities that define the essence of what it means to be human. Dehumanization in this latter case therefore reflects the innate desire to kill others that usually is restrained by a variety of cultural and personal inhibitions (such as social support for the victim), which must be overcome in order for the murders to proceed. It seems obvious, but nonetheless important to emphasize, that murder, notably in situations of genocide, riots, or massive social unrest, is an extreme and final form of dehumanization, taking from victims the last shred of their living humanity.

As Landau (2016) points out, the series of antisemitic laws and practices instituted by the Nazis when they assumed power in 1933 were viewed by most Germans either with indifference or with rejection. The Kristallnacht rioting and destruction in 1938 also were condemned by the German population as a whole (Landau, 2016). Over time, however, Nazi propaganda efforts to dehumanize the Jews in the eyes of the Germans became more successful. The isolation of Jews, unending negative propaganda, segregation from the mainstream population, and the restrictions on normal communications and interactions between Jews and non-Jews are likely to have been strongly influential in their loss of support from the German population. Forced placement in ghettos and concentration camps were extreme forms of social isolation and ostracism in which usual social controls were limited or not present at all. Severe dehumanization, murder, and death were in some sense horrific replacements for civilized interactions.

As Landau (2016) also notes:

> In the end the Nazis successfully quarantined their victims by cutting the normal channels of social interaction and by constructing a wall of isolation behind which the Jewish community could be slaughtered with most of the non-Jewish population reduced either to unawareness or indifference. (p. 226)

Many Jews, especially those who had been starved, overworked, disease-ridden, tortured, beaten, and/or reduced to near-skeleton status in ghettos or concentration camps did indeed appear ghastly, dehumanized, and subhuman (Goldhagen, 1997). The average German citizen, having been isolated and segregated from Jews for years, seemed ready to either accept, tolerate, or endorse the dehumanization of Jews that culminated in mass murder over the last several years of the Nazi era.

The extermination of the Jew—of all Jews in Europe at least—was a prime objective of the Nazi leadership. As noted earlier, and emphasized here, it was perhaps more important than the success in the war effort itself. As Goldhagen (1997) argues: "Annihilating European Jewry became, with the war and at times even of higher priority than the war, the central mission of the German juggernaut" (p. 158). As the war became more desperate, one would think that all resources, including Jewish labor, would be devoted to it, but as Goldhagen (1997) goes on to write:

> The Germans willfully destroyed irreplaceable and desperately needed Jewish labor and production, and thereby further imperiled their prospects of military victory. The destruction of the Jews, once it had become achievable, took priority even over safeguarding Nazism's very existence. (p. 158)

The Nazi fanaticism in dehumanizing and sadistically torturing the Jews who could not possibly have posed a realistic threat to them becomes even more striking in light of these comments. This zealotry, singlemindedness, and obsessive pursuit of killing and death must certainly have reflected a severe manifestation of the human urge toward violence and murder that is being discussed here.

The Nazi ideology of Aryan supremacy was a delusional system that activated the human propensity to violence and murder and drove Hitler and the Nazi party throughout the Nazi era and before it. This was the delusional system expressed in *Mein Kampf* (1925/1999) that helped bring ruin to much of the world in the 1940s. The Jews were, for Hitler, a subhuman race worthy only of dehumanization and death. They were the universal devils who created all that was evil in the world, according to his worldview. Hitler had overseen the slaughter of six million Jews but, at his death, he felt the work was unfinished.

In Hitler's final political testament, written (or dictated) on April 29, 1945, one day before he killed himself in his bunker in Berlin, he continued to uphold the concept of the supremacy of race and to blame the Jews for the world war. Hitler (1945) exhorts his followers: "Above all I charge the leaders of the nation and those under them to scrupulous observance of the laws of race and to merciless opposition to the universal poisoner of all peoples, international Jewry." These themes—race and antisemitism—had been crucial to Hitler's delusional belief system from before the onset of the Nazi era in 1933 and were still crucial for him when it ended in 1945.

CHAPTER 6

# Dehumanization of School-Aged Children in Nazi Germany

---

## Introduction

An important insight conveyed through the material presented in this book is that dehumanization and the propensity to violence and murder existed on a continuum in the Nazi era. Increasingly severe dehumanization seems to have laid the groundwork for the genocide known as the "final solution" in which six million Jews were killed.

Dehumanization of Jews, in a literal sense, can be said to have begun before birth and to have lasted beyond their physical deaths. Almost all of the Jews killed in the "final solution" of 1942–1945 were murdered in such a manner that their remains were disregarded or disrespected and not treated according to ritual law. They were shot and buried or left in open pits where their bodies would not be recognizable. Alternatively, they were gassed and burned in crematoria, where their ashes were mixed with those of others who had been killed in a similar manner. These ashes were then disposed of unceremoniously.

If death was the endpoint on a continuum from dehumanization to death for Jews in the Nazi era, what was the beginning of this continuum? When, in the individual life cycle, did dehumanization of Jews in Nazi Germany begin?

In some sense, the dehumanization and murder of Jews began at or before an infant's birth. Preceding chapters that focused on dehumanization and the sequence of processes leading to murder illustrated the various personal, social, occupational, civic and religious burdens and restrictions placed on Jews over time. These burdens and restrictions would have affected Jewish children and youth to varying degrees. Restrictions on the use of public transportation would be an example of a restriction that affected parents and their children. Loss of professional licensure, restrictions on the use of public facilities, such as parks, or closures and restrictions on businesses under pressure from Nazi authorities would have affected both Jewish parents and their children financially and/or socially.

Pictures in texts of preschool-aged Jewish children wearing Jewish stars sewn into their outer garments are common and reflect the emphasis Nazi Germany placed on dehumanization of Jews across the life cycle (see Pitch, 2015). Accounts of threats to automatically kill mothers found to be pregnant in ghettos or concentration camps is another example of sadism that affected mothers and their unborn children (Des Pres, 1976). In this case, Nazi arguments around the automatic murder of pregnant mothers centered on the loss of the mother's ability to work for the Nazi cause when pregnant or when caring for her child and the infant's own "uselessness" to the Nazi war effort. Mothers (and fathers) faced with this threat often chose to abort their unborn children out of necessity to save the mother's life (Cohen, 2006).

These situations reveal the dehumanization and death inflicted from (or before) birth on the infant and child who existed as a part of a family or a maternal-child grouping. In these cases, the child's dehumanization and death generally were associated with that of the parent or family. Most children in Nazi Germany attended public schools, and it is in these settings that we can see the early dehumanization of Jewish children in their own child-centered social environments. Emigration or deportation and death for these children in concentration camps was the ultimate outcome, as was true for their parents.

This chapter focuses specifically on the plight of Jewish children in schools in Nazi Germany. Dehumanization, ridicule, and shaming of Jewish children was widespread in public schools in Germany during the Nazi era. Humiliation of Jewish children was intended not only to demoralize them (and their families) in order to force their emigration but also to enhance the notion of Aryan superiority in non-Jewish children and to suppress any questioning of Nazi ideology that potentially might have occurred.

This chapter will provide background information on the dehumanization and humiliation inflicted on Jewish children in Nazi-era German schools. Illustrations of practices used to dehumanize and bully Jewish children, and the likely outcome of these efforts on the later attitudes and beliefs of German children, will be emphasized. Psychological aspects of dehumanization and the potentially harmful effects on the child being dehumanized and considered "different" from others in the school setting will be discussed.

Bullying is considered here to be an example of dehumanization that conveys some of the difficulties encountered by Jewish youth in the Nazi era.

The outcome of bullied youth will be considered in this chapter, given the limited empirical literature on the outcome of dehumanization in youth generally and the far more extensive literature on bullying that is available. It must be recognized, however, that, while bullying is a form of dehumanization, the situation of Jewish children in German schools reflected a broader form of dehumanization than bullying alone, one that was racially based and that affected not only these youths themselves but also their families.

## Background

Hitler and the Nazi government believed strongly in the value of education for German children. This "value" was very strictly delimited, however. Indoctrination in notions of Aryan superiority were primary.

> *The crown of the folkish state's entire work of education and training must be to burn the racial sense and racial feeling into the instinct and the intellect, the heart and brain of the youth entrusted to it. No boy and no girl must leave school without having been led to an ultimate realization of the necessity and essence of blood purity.* (Hitler, 1925/1999, p. 427, italics in the original)

Physical fitness and health were emphasized. An individual's character was also important because it was crucial to produce determined soldiers for war. Intellect, science, and scholarship were less important. In *Mein Kampf* (1925/1999), Hitler says,

> *The folkish state must not adjust its entire educational work primarily to the inoculation of mere knowledge, but to the breeding of absolutely healthy bodies. The training of mental abilities is only secondary. And here again, first place must be taken by the development of character, especially the promotion of will-power and determination, combined with the training of joy in responsibility, and only in last place comes scientific schooling.* (p. 408, italics in the original)

The educational goals for boys and girls were different. Hitler (1925/1999) wrote:

> Analogous to the education of the boy, the folkish state can conduct the education of the girl from the same viewpoint. There, too, the chief emphasis must be laid on physical training, and only subsequently on the promotion of spiritual and finally intellectual values. The goal of female education must invariably be the future mother. (p. 414)

There was no place in Hitler's views of education for Jewish children, who, along with their parents, were to be eliminated from German soil. Jews were coerced and encouraged to emigrate as soon as possible. As Pine (2010) indicates, "The Third Reich did not have a clear and coherent concept of education beyond indoctrination. Political attitudes played a central role in the shaping of Nazi education policy. Education was linked with racial values" (p. 140). Large-scale Jewish emigration from Germany did in fact occur during the first years of the Nazi era (prior to Kristallnacht in 1938) when almost one-third of the roughly 550,000 Jews in Germany, at the start of the Nazi era, emigrated (Landau, 2016).

Jewish children remaining in Germany or those living and going to school in Germany prior to their emigration were subjected to dehumanization and humiliation, consistent with general Nazi practice as envisioned in the Law against the Overcrowding of German Schools, an early law enacted on April 25, 1933 that began the removal of Jewish teachers and Jewish pupils from German public schools (Landau, 2016). Given that a central tenet of the Nazi party's governance and ideology held that there was no acceptable place for Jews in Germany, the public schools became an important vehicle through which to express these beliefs. Jewish youth paid the price for their non-Aryan status while Aryan children, in contrast, were encouraged to recognize and take pride in their alleged superiority. Frequently, this comparison involved dehumanization and humiliation of the emotionally defenseless Jewish child and adolescent in the classroom setting.

## Jewish Children in German Schools

Life changed dramatically for Jewish children attending German public schools after the Law against the Overcrowding of German Schools was enacted (Landau, 2016; Evans, 2005). Dehumanizing practices were instituted that essentially forced the drastic reduction of Jewish students, many of whom emigrated from Germany with their families. Other children and youth whose families decided to stay, or attempt to stay, in Germany transferred to Jewish schools, which provided education for about fourteen percent of Jewish youth in 1932, and for about sixty percent of Jewish youth in 1937 (Kaplan, 1997).

In 1933, there were about 60,000 Jewish children from seven (when formal schooling began) to fourteen years of age (when schooling was no longer compulsory) who were enrolled in German schools. Other youth were enrolled in secondary schools. Emigration and policies of dehumanization and harassment lowered the number of Jews between six and twenty-five years of age from 117,000 in 1933 to 60,000 in 1938. It would, of course, go down further from there. As Evans (2005) indicates, "the hostility of fanatical Nazi teachers, and increasingly, Hitler Youth activists in the schools had a powerful effect in driving Jewish children out" (p. 561). The Hitler Youth was the Nazi party's officially sanctioned youth organization for boys from fourteen to eighteen years of age. There was also a related program for younger boys aged ten to fourteen.

While experiences differed based on locale, personnel, and commitment to Nazi ideology, dehumanization, harassment, and concerns about safety were constant troubles for many Jewish children and families. Evans (2005) indicates that in some schools Jewish children were forced to sit on special benches; were banned from German lessons; were given poor marks on school work that was done well; heard teachers describing Jews as criminals or traitors; and were not allowed to participate in ceremonies, festivals, concerts, or plays.

Nazi ideology and the personality cult of Adolf Hitler came to dominate the schools. At least one picture of Hitler was apparently present in every school. "Heil Hitler" was a salute forced on the children upon coming to school each day, and patriotic Nazi songs and essays extolling the virtues of the Nazi regime were expected.

Jewish children were continually ostracized, directly or indirectly. They did not (could not) wear Aryan uniforms and were not allowed to swim in pools with other German children. Kaplan (1997) reports that all students were expected to repeat Nazi dogmas in essays whose themes would have been denigrating and humiliating to the Jewish child.

Issues around identity were prominent. Family disputes between parents about whether children should remain or be taken out of the schools occurred. Through their humiliating ordeals, some children apparently came to be prouder of their Jewish identities; others wanted to become Nazis; others learned for the first time that their Judaism or Jewishness was denigrated by classmates and teachers (Kaplan, 1997). Friendships were quickly terminated since associating with Jews or coming to their homes was discouraged. Physical fights broke out. Kaplan (1997) reports on an incident in which a Jewish girl was accosted on the street and a "ticket to Jerusalem" was forced on her by a group of German boys who reflected the goals of their parents and the larger society.

As Kaplan (1997) says, the public school experience for Jewish children in the Nazi period "ranged from hostility to humiliation to ostracism. Going to school could be like running the gauntlet, physically and psychologically" (p. 49). The dehumanized Jewish child was isolated and denigrated. By the time when even the Jewish private schools were closed in 1942 (or before), the pattern was clear. Deportation and ultimate death were ensured for those who had not gotten out of Germany in time.

To summarize, important dates and processes in the increasingly severe dehumanization of Jewish youth in German schools are as follows.

- Hitler (1925/1999) states in *Mein Kampf* that the defining principle of education for German youth is racial indoctrination according to Nazi principles. This view is acted upon several years later when the Nazis assume control of the German government.
- Hitler is appointed Chancellor of Germany in January 1933. In subsequent months, a series of laws is enacted that is intended to implement Nazi ideology. The Law against the Overcrowding of German Schools, passed April 25, 1933, begins the reduction and elimination of Jewish youth and educators from public schools (Landau, 2016).
- Dehumanizing practices inflicted on Jewish students, such as social isolation, humiliation, and ridicule, become increasingly severe over the course of the next several years; these practices are perpetrated by German teachers and other students, who come increasingly to accept and express Nazi ideology. Many Jewish students leave German public schools in the years 1933–1938. Emigration and increased attendance in Jewish schools as a result of their dehumanizing experiences in public schools account for this vast decrease in Jewish enrollment in German public schools.
- Jewish children are barred from attending public schools entirely in 1938 (Kaplan, 1997).
- Jewish private schools are officially closed in 1942 (Kaplan, 1997). Any remaining children and families faced deportation and death in camps.

Grunberger (1995) reports that the attitude of the German public (the bystanders) to what was happening to the Jewish population around them in the Nazi period was one of indifference. He provides an anecdote that describes on a number of levels the dehumanized condition of young Jewish children in this period. Grunberger (1995) speaks of teachers' practices at Jewish kindergartens in Berlin "of letting their charges spend their playtime among tombstones: the communal cemetery was the only patch of green from which wearers of the Yellow Star were not debarred" (pp. 460–461).

Grunberger (1995) points out that this image of young kindergarten children who are able to play only in a cemetery is "almost poetically symptomatic of the Jews' terminal condition" in Nazi Germany at that time (pp. 460–461). It is an image filled with sadness and an ominous portent of the future when these youngsters, now allowed to play only among the dead, will be required to emigrate or die, themselves, in a concentration camp without grassy areas where their bodies will be cremated and disposed of unceremoniously.

The dehumanization of Jewish youth was clearly difficult and at times dangerous for them. As indicated in the conceptualization of dehumanization offered earlier, however, there also were apparent personal or social benefits to the perpetrators (victimizers) of the Jews, at least in the short term. Victimizers who dehumanized Jewish students intended that their actions not only deny their victim's sense of personal value or self-worth but also enhance their own (the victimizers') power and feelings of self- worth and value.

Teachers who were Nazis or Nazi-supporters, or the non-Jewish students who victimized Jewish youth, probably felt an increase in their own personal or social standing with other Aryan teachers or students in the schools when they successfully diminished the sense of value or self-worth of the Jewish students. Victimizing Jewish students in the ways noted earlier (for example, not allowing them to use the swimming pool with Aryan students) would have confirmed for them (and for the Jewish students) the importance of Aryan power and the inferior status of the Jews in comparison to the Aryans who controlled, in a practical way, the universe they were inhabiting at that time. Power and commitment to the Nazi cause would then have almost assuredly increased in the minds of the Aryan students, while a sense of power and self-worth would have diminished in the Jewish students' assessment of themselves. It is likely that this type of power would have increased the commitment of these non-Jewish students and teachers to the Nazi party that so strongly emphasized Aryan superiority and would have confirmed in the minds of the non-Jewish students the inferiority and "crimes" of the Jews. Dehumanization of the Jews was, therefore, a propaganda tool for the Nazi regime and a means of gaining support from the German population.

Nazi Germany's policies of dehumanization and isolation were clearly effective in forcing Jewish youth to enroll in Jewish schools or to emigrate with their families when they could. As indicated above, the efficacy of these policies on the opinions of German youth also seems to have been noteworthy, at least in fostering their antisemitism. Voigtlander and Voth (2015), using survey data, provide additional supportive evidence for this assertion. These researchers studied antisemitic attitudes of Germans who were youths born during the Nazi era (1933–1945) and compared their attitudes about Jews with the attitudes of those who had been born either before or after the Nazi era. Many of the youths born during the Nazi era would have gone to school during these years. The respondents were surveyed in 1996 and 2006. There was a total of 5,300 individuals in the two waves of the survey.

The research indicated that the individuals who were born during the Nazi era, and most likely were educated during this time, were more likely to have antisemitic views than people born either before or after the Nazi era. In considering the responses to their survey questions, Voigtlander and Voth (2015) also compared data from different regions in Germany and took into account other sources of propaganda to which people at that time might have been exposed, such as access to, or involvement with, radios, print sources of information, and cinemas. These latter variables did not increase the predictive power for the rise in antisemitism in the Nazi era. The most important factors contributing to the rise in antisemitism, according to Voigtlander and Voth (2015), was the indoctrination in schools or through Nazi-era youth organizations. This indoctrination was especially effective when it was built on preexisting antisemitic attitudes that were present in different regions.

## Additional Psychological Impact of Dehumanization on Jews in German Schools

The emphasis of this chapter has been on the dehumanization of Jewish youth in public schools in the Nazi era. While the various forms of dehumanization in this setting were not associated with imminent death, concentration camps, or ghettos, even these relatively "milder" forms of dehumanization seem likely to have had a negative impact on the youth. Much of the available research literature on outcome or consequences of dehumanization involves individuals older than the grade-school and high-school-aged students mentioned here. As noted above, some of the dehumanizing behaviors Jewish youth experienced can be understood in the context of "bullying" behaviors; research outcomes in this context are worthy of mention here, especially given the limited literature on dehumanization in youth generally.

Van Noorden et al. (2014, p. 323) defined bullying in a fairly comprehensive manner using earlier studies that had been done. They contend that bullying is

> a subtype of aggressive behavior, in which an individual or group of individuals attacks, humiliates, and/or excludes a relatively powerless person repeatedly and over time, with forms of bullying being physical, verbal, relational (gossip and social exclusion), and cyber bullying. (Van Noorden et al., 2014, pp. 323–24)

Of course, cyber bullying would not have been an issue during the Nazi era, but physical attacks, humiliation, and exclusion were all perpetrated against Jews (who were powerless) in public schools in the Nazi era.

The definition of dehumanization I have offered earlier emphasizes potential psychological consequences and motivations for dehumanization in victims and victimizers. Van Noorden et al.'s (2014) definition of bullying does include relational forms of bullying, such as social exclusion, that are important aspects of dehumanization as considered in this book. It does not explicitly include the effects of bullying on the child's sense of self-worth and personal value that are included in my approach to dehumanization.

Bullying and other relatively milder forms of dehumanization found in German schools in the Nazi era (compared to experiences in ghettos or concentration camps) have additional characteristics that are consistent with the definition of dehumanization I offered earlier. Bullying can be considered a form of dehumanization that involves the victimizer's refusal to recognize the victim's worth, value, or sense of personhood. Similar to other forms of dehumanization, bullying involves an attempt by the victimizer to gain power or social recognition at the expense of the victim's sense of self-worth, personal or social status. Bullying occurs throughout the life cycle but has perhaps received most attention in youth and in school settings (DeLara, 2019).

Bullying, in many school settings, differs from the bullying (or dehumanization) Jewish youth experienced in German schools in important ways, however. Bullying often is thought to occur mainly between fellow students, sometimes between those of different ages or different grade levels, even though in some cases it can be instituted by others, such as teachers. The bullying experienced by Jewish youth in German schools was strongly influenced by teachers, who would criticize, mock, or diminish the value of Jewish students. Hence, these teachers and German students were co-conspirators in the bullying and dehumanization of Jewish youth. In addition, while most societies give at least lip service (or more stringent disapproval) to bullying, the structure of the Nazi regime strongly supported dehumanization of Jewish people regardless of age. Jewish youth would have felt the burden of dehumanization from other students, teachers, administrators, and the Nazi leaders of the society. They would have had no sense of security or protection provided by authority figures inside or outside the school setting, given the antipathy expressed toward them throughout the society.

Bullying in many situations in diverse school settings does have racial or religious components, but these too are generally disapproved of, at least overtly, by school authorities or the society. Jewish youth in German schools were openly denigrated and dehumanized because of their race, which was probably the greatest stimulus to the dehumanization they experienced. Additionally, while students in many school settings might try to address the suspected reasons for their having been bullied by, for example, improving their athletic performance to gain the bully's respect or friendship, there was nothing Jewish youth could do to erase or diminish the ridicule they experienced since their racial characteristics were considered innate.

Insights into the psychological experiences and outcome of Jewish youth in German schools during the Nazi era of necessity come almost exclusively from anecdotal or observational information, such as that described above. There are numerous empirical studies, however, that speak to the outcome of bullied youth. Information from these studies, in addition to the smaller number of studies that focus on the outcome of dehumanized individuals more generally, provide additional clues about what the outcome of dehumanization on Jewish youth in German schools might have been. The following discusses a number of studies involving these groups.

DeLara (2019) studied the long-term effects of childhood and adolescent bullying on seventy-two young adults (eighteen to twenty nine years of age at the time of the study) in the United States, who experienced alleged bullying when they were in kindergarten through twelfth grade. About one quarter of these young adults were from minority groups; seventy-nine percent were female; and most were Caucasian. A variety of bullying experiences occurred; perpetrators included other students, educators. and coaches. Using a qualitative approach, the subjects reported long-term physical, psychological, and social effects that they attributed to the bullying. Mental health problems included anxiety, depression, and shame. Eating disorders, issues around weight and body image were found.

Although the study was retrospective and details around the alleged bullying were not confirmed, the study does provide evidence that, at least in the perception of these young adults, the effects of bullying may be long lasting and interfere with adaptive functioning years later. It is important to note that relationships and issues of trust were of concern to young adults in this study (DeLara, 2019). This is an important theme in studies of bullying, as it would be for studies of dehumanization, and for the implications of extreme dehumanization had it been possible to study the outcome in Jewish youth who attended German schools during the Nazi era. As DeLara (2019) says, "A number of seminal research studies substantiate that inclusion is a basic human need for survival and that exclusion results in mental health issues" (p. 2382).

Haslam and Loughnan (2014) reviewed the literature on dehumanization specifically. They divided their discussion into four categories: the reduction of prosocial behavior toward the dehumanized individual; increased antisocial behavior toward the dehumanized individual; the implications of moral evaluation for the dehumanized individual; and the functional consequences of dehumanization for the perpetrator and the target. Haslam and Loughnan's (2014) review is consistent with this chapter's discussion of Jewish youth in German schools in which aggressive behavior toward Jewish youth seems to have been a part of the dehumanization experienced by these youth who were isolated and denigrated in their classrooms by teachers and other students alike.

Haslam and Loughnan's (2014) review also indicates that dehumanization is associated with the perception of lower moral standards in dehumanized groups compared with those who are in the ingroup and have not been dehumanized. This impression also is consistent with the discussion of Jewish youth in German schools who, in accord with the prevailing Nazi ideology, were felt to be morally inferior to German youth. Students who are dehumanized would be vulnerable to violent and aggressive behavior toward them that, in some cases, might be justified by the victimizer group because of the alleged "moral inferiority" of the victim. This is an example not only of dehumanization but of the expression of a subtler and less severe form of the human propensity toward violence and murder that is postulated in this book to exist on a continuum that overlaps with dehumanization.

In another research, Bastian and Haslam (2011) studied the effects of "milder" forms of dehumanization resulting from what have been called "microaggressions" or "micromaltreatments" (p. 301). These researchers developed a series of vignettes to reflect subtle forms of maltreatment that might occur in everyday life. Examples of reactions to what are perceived as mild interpersonal maltreatments include feeling betrayed, or denied autonomy, or feeling that one's identity has been disrespected, or that one has been invalidated as a person (Bastian & Haslam, 2011, p. 303). In one vignette, a person who has good computer knowledge is instructed in basic computer fundamentals when he or she asks a friend for help in getting started on an advanced computer program. This assumption of a lack of computer knowledge attributed to the person who has asked for help may be considered condescending or a sign of disrespect or invalidation by the person seeking help, although other explanations also are possible.

Bastian and Haslam (2011) asked their research subjects (older adolescents and adults) to consider whether they would have felt dehumanized, that is, whether they would have experienced challenges or threats to their "personhood" (their identities or status, for example), when considering themselves as characters in these vignettes. Based on their previous work (cited in chapter three), they observed the participants reporting two forms of dehumanization that derive from what they have termed "human uniqueness" and "human nature."

The perception that one's uniqueness as a person has been denied may be associated with a personal sense of incompetence, lack of intelligence, or lack of sophistication. Negative evaluations of oneself, guilt, and shame may accompany dehumanization of this type. Denial of what the authors term "human nature" involves more severe forms of dehumanization (Bastian & Haslam, 2011). Examples in this case include feelings of being treated as an object, as a means to an end, or lacking in the capacity for feeling. A person who experiences dehumanization in this way may react as if his or her identity has been challenged.

Research subjects were asked to rate their emotional and cognitive reactions to these vignettes. When they felt that their status was not recognized as being equal to others, as in the human uniqueness dimension, shame and guilt were potential reactions. When they felt that their basic existence as a person was not recognized, as in the human nature dimension, "cognitive deconstructive states" such as feelings of numbness, cognitive inflexibility, and what seems to be confusion or lack of meaningful thoughts and anger were reported (Bastian & Haslam, 2011, p. 297).

The experiences of Jewish children and youth in German schools during the Nazi era may possibly correspond to some of these lesser forms of microaggression or more subtle forms of dehumanization Bastian and Haslam (2011) have studied. Examples might be experiences of being disregarded by a teacher who calls on another student in preference to the Jewish student or sensing that another non-Jewish student is avoiding contact with this Jewish student because he or she is Jewish.

Other dehumanizing experiences of Jewish students would fall somewhere between these milder experiences and harsher forms of dehumanization described in earlier chapters that ranged from having to wear a yellow star in public, not being allowed on public streets after a certain hour, and being forced to vacate one's home or live in a ghetto. The perceived severity of these or many other dehumanizing experiences would depend very much on the victim's own reactions and assessment.

As Bastian and Haslam (2011) indicate, there is "evidence that targets of a range of everyday interpersonal maltreatments experience some degree of dehumanization when these behaviors undermine fundamental aspects of their personhood" or their "humanity" (p. 301). The evidence does not prove that these milder forms of maltreatment resulting in dehumanization necessarily lead to more severe forms of dehumanization in a causal manner, but it would not be surprising if they did. Furthermore, it seems clear that these milder forms of microaggression associated with dehumanization experiences may cause varying degrees of psychological distress in their own right. Finally, reactions to the bullying that DeLara (2019) studied and to the microaggressions that Bastian and Haslam (2011) discuss may bear considerable resemblance to the distress experienced by bullied and dehumanized Jewish youth in Nazi schools, although empirical studies are not available to confirm this.

## Summary

Jewish youth suffered greatly during the Nazi era. They were dehumanized, ridiculed, and demeaned in German public schools by teachers and students. Many left the public schools and spent time in Jewish religious schools; others, who were able to do so, emigrated. Those unable to avail themselves of these options faced further dehumanization through ongoing restrictions on Jews and then deportation and death in concentration camps.

# CHAPTER 7

# Medical Implementation of Aryan Ideology: Sterilization, Euthanasia, Experimentation

## Introduction

Preceding chapters of this book have focused on dehumanizing practices and the ultimate murder of Jews and other groups in the Nazi era that occurred mainly because of alleged racial inferiority. The Nazi emphasis on racial superiority also led it to advocate for the dehumanization and death of even some "Aryan" citizens whose handicapping medical or mental conditions did not live up to the notion of Aryan supremacy.

Medical procedures ranging from forced sterilization of those whom Nazi authorities considered defective to secretive and coerced "euthanasia" of mentally and physically ill children and adults or criminals, to forced medical experimentation on children and adults in concentration camps, to the medically induced extermination of Jews, whom the Nazis considered the ultimate enemy of the Aryan people, were all a part of the emphasis on Aryan purity that often led to dehumanization and death.

Many (if not most) of these procedures involved physicians who were attracted to the Nazi ideology because of its emphasis on what was thought to be a biological (genetic) and anthropological basis for racial differences among groups, and the importance of "healing" the society rather than just the individual (Lifton, 2000). These doctors and other medical personnel used their professional knowledge in what they considered to be an attempt to strengthen and perfect the Aryan race by eliminating Jews and others who were considered defective, harmful, or "useless" to the state.

In this chapter, I initially review aspects of Nazi ideology that encouraged dehumanization and/or murder of those who were perceived to be enemies of the state, or burdens to it. The following sections will describe the introduction of medical procedures or experiments that were inflicted on individuals in medical and non-medical victim groups during the Nazi era. Some of the procedures or experiments performed on these individuals, and the dehumanization and death that accompanied them, are noted. The role of physicians and medical personnel in the coercive, cruel and unethical procedures and experiments performed during the Nazi era will be discussed. Psychological approaches to prevent the emergence of their own potential guilt and the motivations of doctors who willingly provided the medical expertise that supported the torturous and lethal products of a dehumanizing Nazi ideology will be included in this discussion. Comments on how these medical personnel went from "healers" to "killers" during this time period will be offered (Lifton, 2000). The final section will discuss the dehumanization of victims, families, and society that occurred as the Nazis pursued their vision of an ideal Aryan civilization. The relationship between severe dehumanization and murder will be highlighted throughout.

## Nazi Ideology and Its Contributions to Dehumanization and Death of Jews and Others, Including German Citizens who were Disabled

Adolf Hitler's preoccupation with the issue of race can be traced from his early writings in *Mein Kampf* (1925/1999) to his final political statement in 1945 (Hitler, 1945). Hitler's and the Nazis' notions of race provided the genesis for a great deal of the carnage that occurred in the Nazi era. Threats to the purity, quality, or overall population of the Aryan race, through perceived financial injustices, mental or physical weaknesses of members of the Aryan race itself, war casualties, and/or through intermarriage were all addressed during his reign, at times through brutal medically assisted means.

Hitler's (1925/1999) hatred for the Jews and his view that Jews posed an existential threat to the Aryan people are well known and have been discussed in previous chapters. In *Mein Kampf*, Hitler (1925/1999) makes explicit his fear of Jewish dominance when he writes: "The mightiest counterpart to the Aryan is represented by the Jew" (p. 300). Hitler condemns the Jews along racial, financial, social, and political lines, but he also accuses the Jews of what he believes to be their negative relationships with Aryan women, which would pose a direct threat to the integrity of the Aryan race.

Hitler argued that the Aryan people were obliged not only to maintain racial purity but also to propagate and increase their numbers. He cautioned against sexual liaisons and marriages with non-Aryans since these would defile the race and limit its potential. He seemed to especially fear relationships between Jewish men and gentile German women, although intermarriage between Jews and Germans, while present in German society at the time, was not a large percentage of marriages overall (Lowenstein, 2005). Hitler (1925/1999) writes, "With satanic joy in his face, the black-haired Jewish youth lurks in wait for the unsuspecting girl whom he defiles with his blood, thus stealing her from her people" (p. 325). For Hitler, the conniving Jew is the culprit. Hitler seems to deny any possibility that the gentile woman might have been complicit.

The Aryan blood, for Hitler, was threatened not only by contacts with Jews, but also if particular medical, psychological, or physical disabilities that could occur in Aryans themselves were propagated. Individuals with severe disabilities (Aryans and non-Aryans) used resources that might otherwise be employed to further a healthy Aryan race. Aryan blood, for Hitler, must remain "pure." In the following passage from *Mein Kampf*, Hitler (1925/1999) emphasizes the need for "purity" of Aryan blood: *"No, there is only one holiest human right, and this right is at the same time the holiest obligation, to wit: to see to it that the blood is preserved pure and, by preserving the best humanity, to create the possibility of a nobler development of these beings"* (p. 402, italics in the original). Hitler suggests here that all efforts must be expended to stop racial mixing and intermarriage.

Hitler emphasized that it was the Aryans' duty to raise healthy children in order to support and propagate the race. The child or adult who was severely disabled, even if of Aryan blood, posed a threat to the future of the Aryan people and diminished the potential for what Hitler believed to be the superior Aryan race. The individual with a severe disability, in Hitler's way of thinking, was less than the "ideal" Aryan and in this sense was less worthy than the healthy Aryan. Hitler thus lessens the value of disabled individuals, dehumumanizes them, and lays the groundwork for their elimination.

In *Mein Kampf*, Hitler (1925/1999) sets the stage for later programs of forced sterilization and euthanasia when he writes sarcastically that society considers it a "crime" if individuals having various illnesses or problems are not allowed to procreate but does not support other (presumably healthy) Aryan women who might be available to produce healthy Aryan children. He writes,

> The prevention of the procreative faculty in sufferers from syphilis, tuberculosis, hereditary diseases, cripples, and cretins is a crime, while the actual suppression of the procreative faculty

in millions of the very best people is not regarded as anything bad and does not offend against the morals of this hypocritical society.... (Hitler, 1925/1999, p. 402)

As described later, the Nazi state would not only take steps to limit the number of severely ill and disabled individuals but also subsidize the creation of large Aryan families.

Hitler (1925/1999) is clear: The volkish state

> *must set race in the center of all life. It must take care to keep it pure. It must declare the child to be the most precious treasure of the people. It must see to it that only the healthy beget children.... And conversely it must be considered reprehensible: to withhold healthy children from the nation.... It must declare unfit for propagation all who are in any way visibly sick or who have inherited a disease and can therefore pass it on, and put this into actual practice.* (pp. 403–404, italics in the original)

This is the same theme. Birth of healthy Aryan children is to be desired; and birth of children who are not likely to be mentally and physically healthy (by standards of the state's representatives) is to be decried, even if the parents are of indisputable Aryan stock.

These few passages make clear Hitler's message, which attaches paramount importance to maintaining racial purity and restricting procreation to those who are considered healthy Aryans. The lengths to which he would go to enforce this dogma and to sterilize or euthanize the "defective" are not stated and were perhaps not yet formulated in detail at the time *Mein Kampf* was written. The Nazis' use of barbaric and cruel tactics, in their attempts to eliminate or exterminate the perceived Jewish threat to the Aryan race, suggest that other groups considered undesirable by Nazi leaders also would not fare well.

As with other dehumanizing procedures during the Nazi era, the pronouncements made by Hitler and other Nazi leaders required for their enactment large numbers of German people who either supported the Nazi ideology, or at least accepted it, or did not actively defy it. Physicians were among the most important groups that would put the Nazi ideology of the superiority of the Aryan race and its supposed biological basis into concrete action. Many physicians agreed with Hitler and the Nazi leadership that race was a distinct and valuable categorization of people, that race was biologically based, and that the Aryan race was superior to other races. In addition, significant numbers of physicians in

Germany, after World War I, were Jews, and there seems to have been resentment and competition with these Jewish doctors for patients among some non-Jewish German physicians (Lifton, 2000).

Hitler noted that physicians and medical experts were well positioned to enact the vision of Aryan supremacy due to their biological and medical knowledge. As Lifton (2000) says, "While a few doctors resisted and large numbers had little sympathy for the Nazis, *as a profession* German physicians offered themselves to the regime" (pp. 43–44). Doctors used "their intellectual authority to justify and carry out medicalized killing. Doctors promoted the idea that collective German existence was a medical matter . . ." (Lifton, 2000, pp. 43–44). Sterilization, and then what Lifton (2000) terms "direct medical killing," was conducted or supervised by doctors who participated willingly and actively in attempting to secure the Nazi vision of racial purity as they forsook their ethical responsibilities, a subject discussed further below.

Perper and Cina (2010) report that "forty-five percent of German physicians became members of the Nazi party and, as officers in the SS, were active participants in the killing of the 'unfit' and 'undesirable racial pollutants'" (p. 57). Pross (1991) emphasizes that physician participation in the Nazi party was the highest of all the professions. While this high percentage of physicians in the Nazi party may be due in part to a desire for career stability or advancement, the active involvement of physicians in the various killing protocols developed by the Nazis over time suggests the personal commitment of many physicians as well.

Grodin et al. (2018) summarize important themes that Nazi physicians endorsed to varying degrees as they came to work with the Nazi leaders in "cleansing the state," which, rather than the individual, became the "primary patient" (p. 53). Ghettoization, isolation, and extermination of other peoples, such as Jews, became the "treatment" necessary to ensure the health of the state.

Programs of increasingly severe medical interventions in the lives of those considered undesirable elements in German society were not targeted initially toward Jews, nor toward medicalized killing. As with the process of dehumanization of Jews described in earlier chapters, increasingly severe or lethal actions taken against the physically and mentally disabled members of the society occurred over time and culminated in the enactment of medically supervised mass murders in the extermination camps. In this latter phase, Jews became the predominant victims, although as a group they had no characteristic psychological or physical disabilities. They were considered undesirable elements of the society solely because they were Jews.

Medical efforts to rid the society of what were considered undesirable or potentially undesirable persons was part of a program of "negative eugenics" that was intended to eliminate hereditary dispositions of individuals who might produce children and adults that would become a burden to the society. Negative eugenics involved physicians in activities intended to protect and revitalize "the genetic health of the *Volk*" (Lifton, 2000, p. 42). Programs of "positive eugenics" also existed. These included efforts to encourage large families and beneficial health practices among Aryan couples (Lifton, 2000). In one such program, welfare assistance was provided to families of SS members to promote racially desirable children; this program supported both married and unmarried mothers who had Aryan children. The German notion of "positive eugenics" also allowed the kidnapping of children from occupied areas who met "Nordic criteria" (and were sometimes fathered by German troops) in order to expand the Aryan population.

## Negative Eugenics. Sterilization and Euthanasia; Transition to Genocide; Medical Experimentation

The first Nazi attempt to prevent the birth of people who were considered unlikely to conform to the Aryan ideal was a program of forced sterilization. Although sterilization of patients considered "unfit" was approved but not required during the latter days of the Weimar Republic, "compulsory sterilization" of patients who were "unfit" became the policy of the government after Hitler assumed power in 1933 (Grodin et al., 2018, p. 54). The Law for the Prevention of Genetically Diseased Offspring required the compulsory sterilization of people with any of the following categories of disease: hereditary or congenital feeble-mindedness, schizophrenia, bipolar disease, hereditary epilepsy, Huntington's disease, chorea, hereditary blindness, hereditary deafness, malformation, and severe alcoholism. Three-member courts (with two physician members) made decisions regarding sterilization. Grodin et al. (2018) report that, between 1933 and 1939, coercive sterilization was performed on 360,000 to 375,000 individuals, although Hilberg's (1992) figures are somewhat higher at 400,000.

The next group of "patients" to undergo compulsory medical procedures intended to reduce the number of "unfit" Germans was a group placed into a program of euthanasia, or what Lifton (2000) terms, "direct medical killing" (p. 45). Euthanasia, as practiced in Nazi Germany, was vastly from medical procedures employed in some countries that involve individuals with terminal or irreversible illnesses whose lives are ended through medical means in order to relieve great pain and suffering or to prevent loss of autonomy as their conditions worsen. Grodin et al. (2018) indicate that "in the Third Reich, 'euthanasia' was a program of State-sponsored medicalized mass murder" intended to promote "racial hygiene" and purify the *Volk* "by eliminating the 'unfit'" (p. 54). A program of negative euthanasia involving children and adults became official policy in 1939, although medically induced "euthanasia" of those considered medically unfit had been ongoing well before this time (Grodin et al., 2018). The physically or mentally ill or disabled persons whose lives were likely to be taken seem to have had little or nothing to say about the matter, even if they knew their fate was being considered and even if they were able to communicate effectively.

These individuals had been dehumanized as a result of their condition by medical representatives of the Nazi leadership who, in most cases, seem to have found them "unfit," that is, unworthy of life in an Aryan world. Almost all reviews of these cases appear to have resulted in decisions to kill the medically or developmentally disabled person who, along with his or her family, does not seem to have been consulted about the judgment or offered the opportunity to challenge it. The perceived uselessness of people with severe disabilities would have been an important part of their dehumanization and subsequent killing.

The Nazi leaders were conscious of the potential for negative parental and family reactions when children or relatives in institutions were killed secretly, and duplicity was commonly involved in describing what had happened to a murdered family member. Families apparently did not know decisions of this sort were being discussed, another example of dehumanization—in this case of family members and of the involved patient, whose judgments were neither sought nor desired. Secretive killing of disabled children was recognized to be controversial but, ultimately, the perceived importance of maintaining and improving the racial hygiene of the Aryan people was more important to Nazi leaders and representatives than the wishes of family members, who were, as earlier quotes of Hitler indicate, expected to sacrifice their attachments and personal needs for those of the larger Aryan group (Hitler, 1925/1999).

The term often used by Nazi leaders and others to justify these killings of the "unfit" was *lebensunwertes Leben* ("life unworthy of living"). The Nazi program of state-sanctioned (and sponsored) killing assumed that the government had the authority to make judgments about the value of the individual lives of its citizens. This was a striking example of dehumanization of the individual, diminution in the value of individual life, and support for the notion that the state may do as it feels justified to support its own aspirations and ideology. In situations such as these, social and racial Darwinism was often invoked (incorrectly) as another (or allied) justification for the killings: the children and adults who were considered "unfit" for life allegedly consumed resources needed for others who were felt to be more productive socially.

The euthanasia program officially began in 1939, around the beginning of World War II when it was thought there would be less scrutiny of the Nazi actions. Hitler also believed that the effort would be more acceptable to the public during war when public attention would be directed, and resources would be required, for the needs of soldiers. The program began initially with infants and young children, and later included adults (Perper & Cina, 2010).

Infants and young children considered candidates for this program of negative euthanasia were referred to a Reich Committee for the Scientific Registration of Serious Hereditary and Congenital Diseases that was expected to maintain a registry of those under three years of age who had physical deformations, brain damage, and hereditary diseases. Physicians made the decision whether a child should live or die based on a questionnaire filled out on referral. No further examination was performed. Infants and children were cruelly killed by gradual starvation or the administration of increasing dosages of sedative medication. "In the end, 70,000 German children thought to be abnormal were forcefully taken from their homes, institutionalized and eventually killed. . . . The bodies were burned en masse and commingled ashes were sent to the families" (Perper & Cina, 2010, p. 59).

The subsequent expansion of the "euthanasia" program to include adults was explained, in part, as the response to the need to free hospital space for wounded soldiers returning from war (Grodin et al., 2018). The killing program for adults was given the name "Aktion T4" after Tiergartenstrasse 4, the address of the offices housing the program in Berlin (Grodin et al., 2018, p. 55). This designation was consistent with Hitler's desire to keep programs that might be controversial relatively secret and removed from public scrutiny. A name that does not indicate the nature of the program is consistent with this goal.

A medicalized structure was created for the T4 program. Adult patients with particular diseases, those considered mentally ill, or patients who had been in an institution for five years or more were to be reported to the Reich Health Ministry. The list of patients to be reported included patients with

> schizophrenia, manic-depressive disorder, epilepsy, senility, paralysis, syphilis, retardation, encephalitis, Huntington's chorea and other neurological conditions . . . the criminally insane . . . patients who did not have German citizenship, or were not of German descent, including Jews, blacks, and Gypsies were to be reported as well. (Perper & Cina, 2010, p. 57)

On the basis of the questionnaires that were completed, "a panel of three 'medical experts' was asked to judge whether the patient needed 'treatment'—killing—or whether 'postponement' or 'observation' was appropriate" (Grodin et al., 2018, p. 55). Again, patients, families, and the larger society were not consulted. They too were dehumanized by being judged by the state as unable to grasp its greater needs. Once the panel had agreed that the individual should be killed, this order was accomplished by prescribing strong dosages of sedatives or morphine to the person over time. Falsified death certificates followed.

Sometimes, the individuals to be killed were transferred to one of several killing centers that were located "in isolated areas and had high walls—some had originally been old castles—so that what happened within could not be readily observed from without" (Lifton, 2000, p. 71). In what appears to be intentional misrepresentation of this surreptitious medical activity that was a journey of death, "SS personnel manned the buses, frequently wearing white uniforms or white coats in order to appear to be doctors, nurses, or medical attendants" (Lifton, 2000, p. 70). Some reports indicated that, while those transporting the patients wore white coats, they had SS boots on.

Carbon monoxide gas was used to kill the patients who were led naked to a "fake shower room with benches, the gas being inserted from the outside into water pipes with small holes through which the carbon monoxide could escape" (Lifton, 2000, p. 71). The patients died quickly, and the room was ventilated: "SS men then used special stretchers which mechanically shoved the corpses into crematory ovens without contact" (Lifton, 2000, p. 71). As before, falsification of the cause of death followed.

As part of the process, a series of deceptive letters was sent to the families that notified them initially of the patient's transfer; then that the patent had arrived "safely" at the destination, but that visitation would not be possible because of a shortage of personnel as a result of the war, and that the family would be notified of changes in the patient's condition. A subsequent letter was sent notifying the family of the patient's death (Lifton, 2000). Most corpses were cremated as stated above, but some were dissected. The ashes of the cremated patients were mixed together and sent to the individual families in an urn (Lifton, 2000).

The T4 program was cancelled officially in 1941 after its existence had become more widely known among the general public and more accurate information about the program and its deceptive nature became available. General resistance to the program, articulated by a few Protestant and Catholic religious leaders, was important in its official termination (Lifton, 2000).

Medicalized killing, and the deception associated with it, was not discontinued, however. "Widespread killing continued in a second phase, sometimes referred to ... as 'wild euthanasia' because doctors—encouraged, if not directed, by the regime—could now act on their own initiative concerning who would live or die" (Lifton, 2000, p. 96). Killings of the "unfit" and the undesirable became a matter of personal physician judgment: "Doctors acted on their personal and ideological inclinations, along with their sense of the regime's pulse" (Lifton, 2000, p. 96). Patients were no longer killed by gas but rather through starvation or drugs.

The new incarnation of the killing program was moved to concentration camps and known under the code name 14f13. Lifton (2000) considers the 14f13 program a link between direct medical killing that was previously present in institutions "with the medicalized killing in the concentration camps ... linking the Nazi version of 'euthanasia' with genocide" (p. 134). The term "special treatment" was a euphemism used to describe the fate of those who were considered unworthy of life in the Nazis' programs. It came to be applied beyond the physically or mentally "unfit" to a variety of groups, such as Jews, homosexuals, criminals, and Catholic critics of the state.

The 14f13 program itself underwent a number of changes over time (Lifton (2000). It shifted from an ostensible focus on the mentally ill to others, such as political prisoners, Jews, Poles, and habitual criminals. Lifton (2000) argues that the places where the killings through the 14f13 program occurred became equivalent to, and overlapped with, extermination camps. "Euthanasia" could be applied to almost anyone, but often the victims were Jews and people of non-German nationalities. Selections were made by doctors in the camps. Grodin et al. (2018) cites figures to indicate that under programs such as T4, 14f13 and others, 200,000 to 300,000 people were killed. Hilberg (1992) cites a higher figure: 600,000.

The incorporation of the 14f13 program into concentration camps provided a ready move into a directly genocidal program. Over the course of the years 1941–1945, millions of people (mainly, but not exclusively, Jews) were killed in extermination camps, such as Auschwitz-Birkenau. The methods employed in the extermination camps were similar to those used in earlier killing efforts. Injections (including those with phenol) and beatings occurred, but the most common form of murder was through gassing victims who were led to specially designed chambers under the guise that they would receive showers and delousing sprays. In fact, they were gassed with Zyklon-B, a "technological achievement" that permitted "humane killing" according to its advocates (Lifton, 2000, p. 453). After gassing and certification by doctors or those supervised by doctors that the victims were dead, the bodies were inspected for any valuables that could be used in civilian or war efforts, such as gold teeth. The dead were then burned either in crematoria or in open pits.

All victims transported to killing centers such as Auschwitz were doomed to death. Some, such as prisoner doctors, delayed their deaths if they possessed special skills that could be used by the Nazis in the war effort. Some deaths also were delayed if the prisoner was considered valuable for particular research projects, as in experiments on twins conducted by the infamous Dr. Josef Mengele, who was known in Auschwitz for his extreme cruelty as well as his "larger vision" and "ideology." Dr. Mengele committed himself to "remaking his people and ultimately the people of the world" through his experiments on imprisoned and condemned victims (Lifton, 2000, p. 377). Mengele's approach, consistent with the ideology of the Nazi movement generally, emphasized biology and the importance of biology in revitalizing the Aryan race and in remaking the world. As Lifton (2000) points out, "For a man like Mengele, the ideological mission justified everything" (p. 377). "Everything," in this context, meant that dehumanization, torture, and murder of victims who were often children were entirely acceptable.

The procedures for gassing at Auschwitz were developed by physicians. There was an initial screening by a doctor of those arriving by train. Those individuals who were considered "inappropriate" to continue living because they were too old or too young, women who were pregnant, or those who appeared ill or frail were immediately separated and taken directly to the gas chambers. Those who appeared able to work and contribute to the war effort, usually males who were in late teen years through middle age, were selected for admission to the camp. Individuals who were possible research subjects, such as children who were twins, were admitted to the death camp and sometimes treated relatively better than others who were not of interest for a particular doctor's "research."

There was some tension between the desire to have prisoners work in the war effort to the maximum possible extent and the desire to eliminate these prisoners as quickly and efficiently as possible. Causes of death of prisoners that occurred before their anticipated gassing (or that precipitated gassing) included fatigue, physical injury from beatings or torture, starvation through chronically reduced rations, and diseases, especially typhus, which was frequently present in the camps and difficult to eradicate. Many prisoners also died as a result of the medical experiments to which they were subjected; often this was intentional given the desire to dissect "specimens" to learn the results of the experiments that frequently reflected a callous and sadistic expression of the urge to kill Jews or others who were "not acceptable" for life according to the Nazi regime and its ideology.

The bodies and body parts of victims were plundered before and after death (Strzelecki, 1998). Clothes, money, jewelry, and medicines were taken. Heads were shaved and the hair of the victims was used in industry. Corpses were checked for gold fillings and gold teeth that were recycled for use by the Germans. Human skin was also used for ladies' handbags and other articles (Berger, 1990).

In all cases, physicians were directly involved with the extermination procedures. As noted earlier, the Nazis emphasized that their efforts were intended to effect a "racial cure," using terms that were consistent with a medical model and emphasized the importance of medical personnel involvement. The Nazi leaders felt that, in order to heal a disturbed and sick society, it was necessary to eliminate or kill the cause of the disease, which they argued was the "unfit" individual, very often the Jew. According to this view, the society was the patient; the Jew was the infestation; and the Nazi physicians (who were Aryans) were the true doctors tasked with expunging and killing the infestation.

Other duties of Nazi physicians at extermination camps included providing or supervising medical care for prisoners who sustained minor injuries or medical problems that were considered amenable to brief treatment prior to their return to work and selecting prisoners for removal to the gas chambers if they did not heal quickly enough to merit ongoing care. As noted earlier, some of the doctors had particular "research" interests, and fulfilled these interests using the prisoners, as was true with Doctor Mengele. Several of these experiments reflected the horrific dehumanization and brutality that is linked to the urge to kill and its associated cruelty and sadism, which paid little or no attention to the prisoners' humanity, pain, and suffering.

The Nazis felt that Jews were a subhuman race that deserved the dehumanization and death they received. This did not stop them from considering the "subhuman" Jews suitable experimental subjects whose bodies and biological reactions would provide valuable information for the development of the Aryan race or for the military effort. The experimenters often disregarded the victims' experience of torture, while the experiments, themselves, yielded little or nothing of scientific value given the conditions under which they were conducted and the lack of scientific rigor applied to them. They generally are not considered acceptable for scientific journals (Berger, 1990). The experiments, nonetheless, often were conducted with the cooperation of academicians at recognized medical schools and universities (Perper & Cina, 2010).

Perper and Cina (2010) report that between 1939 and 1945, there were over seventy types of research projects conducted on over 7,000 camp prisoners, Jews and others. Lifton (2000) reports on a variety of experiments that included injection of the cervix in women with a caustic substance to obstruct the fallopian tubes, followed by x-rays to see if sterilization had occurred and the tubes were blocked; brutal and inhumane x-ray and surgical castrations of young men and women followed by laboratory evaluations to determine the effects of the procedures; "anthropological research" to surgically retrieve the skulls of members of the "subhuman" species (the Jews) to determine and differentiate racial classifications; providing heads of victims (and later whole skeletons) to designated institutes to have various anthropological studies performed; using human flesh as a bacteriologic culture medium; using therapeutic agents, such as unproven medications, on various diseases, with the result that some victims died; rubbing toxic substances on prisoners to assess the infected areas and abscesses that developed; performing unneeded surgical procedures; research on dwarfs; experiments with fostering noma (a gangrenous process affecting the mouth and other facial areas) and changing eye color that were performed by Dr. Mengele who injected methylene blue into the eyes in an attempt to change their color.

Perper and Cina (2010) highlight additional "heinous acts committed by Nazi doctors in the name of science" (p. 71). These included: freezing/immersion of prisoners in hypothermia experiments (to simulate conditions of high altitude flight in war); bone, muscle, and joint transplantation experiments (in which body parts from one prisoner were transplanted onto another after the latter's body part had been amputated); artificial insemination experiments (in which women prisoners were told they had been inseminated with animal sperm); and experiments with blood coagulant Polygal that was tested on freshly amputated body stumps.

The extreme cruelty, sadism, and dehumanization of these so-called "experiments" should be apparent to even the most casual observer outside of the Nazi-influenced environment of these secretive camps. The lack of apparent horror felt by the experimenters, the doctors, and some of the other medical personnel is a testament to the strength and widespread nature of long and increasingly severe dehumanization of the Jews and the apparent acceptance of their murder as a culmination of this extreme dehumanization. It speaks also to the cruelty and barbarism that is often more easily perpetrated under conditions of isolation and increased social pressure as occurred in the death camps. Under such conditions, victimizers more easily become blinded to ethical imperatives and the humanity of those victimized. As Shallcross (2020) reported of ghetto environments, concentration camps essentially were necro-topographic zones in which death, its precursors and its aftermath characterized the entire environment.

## Physicians as Collaborators and Perpetrators; Debasement of Ethical Norms; Psychological Issues

Nazi ideology and practice from their early stages were oriented toward the role of the physician, medicine, and "healing." Hitler (1925/1999) had written, for example, "*anyone who wants to cure this era, which is inwardly sick and rotten, must first of all summon up the courage to make clear the causes of this disease*" (p. 435, italics in the original), by which he seems to have meant that the "sickness" existing in German society was caused by "unfit" and dangerous individuals, first of all Jews, and that cure for this sickness required eliminating these noxious agents. Therefore, in Hitler's mind, physicians were crucial to this distorted notion of "healing" that involved the elimination or killing of Jews and other undesirable individuals. Hitler had, in fact, called for physicians to join the party even prior to the 1930s, and, as noted earlier, about forty-five percent of German physicians did join the Nazi party over the course of the Nazi era (Lifton 2000; Perper & Cina, 2000).

The common devotion of most physicians to the health and welfare of individual patients was often replaced, in the Nazi era, by the devotion to the state and its ideology. This shift required that these physicians participate in the active killing of those individuals declared to be enemies of the Nazis and the state. The Nazi perspective was that the various forms in which physicians participated in killing the undesirable individuals and Jews was actually a form of what Lifton (2000) calls "healing by killing." They did not take into account that this practice was also a repudiation of the Hippocratic Oath that speaks of the physician's duty to "abstain from whatever is deleterious or mischievous," that is, to do no harm. The Hippocratic Oath does not speak of the physician's role in attempting to heal the society.

Why did this complete reversal of roles and ethical expectations occur? Why did sizeable numbers of German physicians stray so far from the Hippocratic Oath and the dictate to do no harm to one's patients? Was there something about the nature of medicine practiced in Germany at the time, or the nature of physicians who practiced it, or the activation of the human propensity to kill that produced these aberrations?

Lifton (2000) argues that the attraction of physicians to the Nazi movement was related to the emphasis in Germany and in German institutions on unity and also in part to the strongly "authoritarian and nationalistic tendencies within the medical profession... and to their special attraction as a group to the Nazi stress on biology and on a biomedical vision of national cure" (p. 34). Hitler's dehumanizing emphasis on the comparison of Jews to animals that infested the body and his use of analogies to sickness and curing the society would have kept these images in the forefront and possibly had special significance for some physicians.

Other factors, such as adverse socio-economic conditions that affected the German doctors during the Weimar Republic period, may have contributed to their willingness to join the Nazi cause. Competition from emancipated Jewish doctors might also have contributed to the willingness of German physicians to follow the Nazi rhetoric that would have benefitted them financially.

Another factor not mentioned by Lifton (2000) and Grodin et al. (2018) that may have been influential, at least in some cases of patients with severe mental and physical disabilities, includes the frustrating and emotionally difficult exposure to such patients that is experienced by some doctors who care for such patients in institutions. These are often patients without hope of recovery whose conditions are very stressful emotionally and who place financial burdens on society. These cases may raise ethical questions about caring for such patients when resources for other people in need are deemed to be in short supply.

There are many patients of this type, such as those with severe mental retardation, who are hospitalized for years when their families cannot or will not care for them at home, thus leaving the responsibility to the state. Physicians exposed to this type of patient and the helplessness and frustration they stimulate, may have been more amenable to "euthanasia" than other physicians who treated less severely disturbed patients. Over time, the task of some of these physicians may have come to include the egregious killing of others whom Nazi leaders considered "incurable," such as criminals or Jews. These physicians may have been more vulnerable to the "Nazi image of 'life unworthy of life,' of creatures who, because less than human, can be studied, altered, manipulated, mutilated, or killed—in the service of the Nordic race, and ultimately of remaking humankind" (Lifton, 2000, p. 302). In situations such as these, the actual weakness and vulnerability of patients with severe disabilities may have activated the propensity to kill rather than the dedication to the relief of suffering that is expected of physicians, and considered a manifestation of Eros, or the life force, in psychoanalytic terms.

Through their belief in Nazi ideology and misplaced Darwinian notions of survival of the fittest, physicians (and other killers) in the Nazi era must have had or developed the psychological capacity to actually kill or torture others who had been dehumanized and were considered "subhuman." These physicians must have had the capacity to activate their inclinations toward violence and murder and to turn from healers to killers in order to exterminate prisoners in the camps and to perform experiments on them.

Lifton (2000) and Grodin (2010) address psychological mechanisms involved in these actions at some length. These authors emphasize the ability (or need) of physicians to varying degrees to split off, dissociate, or separate their mental processes or senses of self into different parts. Lifton (2000) calls this phenomenon "doubling," a characteristic familiar to many physicians as a usual part of their healing work that is related to what has been called "compartmentalization."

Doctors are constantly confronted with patients who exhibit and evoke sadness, distress, and pain in the physician. In order to maintain their healing function, and to diagnose and treat their patients' suffering, it is necessary for physicians (and other medical providers) to not become overly identified with the sadness or unhappiness of their patients. Physicians cannot cure all of the pain and suffering they encounter, and they must retain a degree of distance from the emotional pain of their patients in order to objectively assess the patient's situation and formulate a plan to provide the relief that they can provide. They also must be able to endure the pain and suffering that they cause when, for example, they perform physical procedures or discuss terminal or hopeless conditions with their patients and families. These experiences require a degree of detachment and emotional "numbing" that protects the physician, to some degree, from the physical or emotional pain they are producing.

Physicians must consider that the pain and suffering that they are producing is intended to help their patients. The physicians in Nazi Germany who believed that healing the society required elimination of its enemies—who were severely disabled, the Jews, and others thought to be lesser humans—might have brought this same type of understanding to their killing tasks as they had brought to their healing tasks. They might have used various psychological defense mechanisms such as doubling or splitting of the personality, emotional numbness, suppression or isolation of affect (Lifton, 2000), as well as a distorted sense of "ultimate purposes" that would have allowed or, indeed, encouraged the physician to decide another's fate.

Physicians in Nazi Germany may have been particularly prone to activate their own tendencies toward self-destruction and suicide that in some cases may have been stronger than in the usual bystanders. Medical personnel are expected (and socialized) to show concern and empathy for those people who have disabilities and are incapacitated, no matter the degree of their incapacity. The emphasis in Nazi Germany, however, was to do away with those who were helpless, weak, or considered a burden to the Aryan society.

The overwhelming political and social environment in Nazi Germany that emphasized removal of people considered subhuman (those with severe disabilities, Jews, and others) might have activated a tendency toward violence and killing in physicians and challenged their usual values of caring for the weak and the vulnerable. The expression of the propensity to murder or torture those considered subhuman may have "resolved" the ethical dilemma for some physicians, an uncertain number of whom unconsciously would have recognized their own human vulnerability and reacted against this fear by killing or torturing the helpless and disabled among them.

Killing, maiming, and brutalization of "subhumans," regardless of motivation, almost never would have been entirely without emotional consequences for many perpetrators, however. All of these strategies of doubling or splitting usually would not have been entirely effective but would have allowed physicians, if successful, to proceed with their immediate or short-term killing tasks and experimentation. The significant use of alcohol, as Lifton (2000) indicates, also might have been helpful in relieving stress or guilt, at least in the short term. Alcohol use in this sense can be considered an attempt to deny the experience in pepetrators of their inclination to violence and murder that had compelled these individuals to kill their helpless and dehumanized victims, an act that might be associated with guilt and other negative psychological reactions, as described earlier.

The long-term consequences of barbaric medical killing and experimentation for some perpetrator physicians may have been deleterious, although information about this is limited. Lifton (2000) indicates that the suicide rate of Nazi doctors was high, although precise figures are not cited, and it may be that other factors, such as fear of the encroaching Allied armies, might have contributed to increased suicide rates at the end of the war, especially among doctors who were associated with the Nazi party.

Lifton and Hackett (1998) remark, in speaking about the doctors' role in the Nazi era, "There probably has never been an episode in history in which doctors have been as guilty of abrogating their healing function" (p. 315). For many physicians in the Nazi era, as for many other military and civilian persons (Goldhagen, 1997), shifting roles toward the killing enterprise required changes in professional and personal identities that in some sense, as discussed in the next section, resulted in dehumanization, not only for victims but also for perpetrators themselves.

Lifton (2000), for example, reports on an interview he conducted with a military neuropsychiatrist who had treated many members of the Einsatzgruppen, the killing force that had followed the advancing German army through Poland and into the Soviet Union as it was tasked with killing all Jews along the way (as described in chapter four above). These men described problems such as severe anxiety, nightmares, and bodily complaints that seem likely to have been trauma-related. These problems occurred in about twenty percent of those Einsatzgruppen personnel who had actually done the killing. About half of these individuals described what appeared to have been moral questions. Shooting women and killing children especially seemed to have caused the greatest difficulties.

## Other Aspects and Consequences of Dehumanization and Death in the Medical Implementation of Aryan Ideology

In an earlier chapter of this work, I defined dehumanization in part as "the process by which a powerful individual or group (the victimizers) actively deny or withdraw a second group's (the victim's) sense of human worth or personal value. The victimizers' actions are intended to increase their own sense of power and personal worth at the expense of the victimized individual or group. Dehumanization results in the loss of the victims' sense of personal value, self-worth or 'personhood.'"

This definition emphasizes the actions of a victimizer or perpetrator against another person or persons, the victim or victims. Many cases involving perpetrators and victims do not include only these two entities in a direct sense, however. If we make the assumption that parents of individudals with mental or physical disabilities, relatives, and other concerned societal members consider it their right to have information about their loved ones or fellow citizens shared with them, the active failure to do so might be considered an act of devaluation or dehumanization of the patient who has a disability, of the parent or relative, and perhaps of the concerned citizen (or bystander). The parents of a child with a severe disability, for example, are deprived of their own sense of value and agency as parents and as citizens through not being considered or consulted about decisions related to their child.

The various acts of sterilization, "euthanasia," extermination (genocide), and human experimentation discussed in this chapter, therefore, reveal far broader tentacles of dehumanization than those limited to victim and victimizer in a narrow sense. Dehumanization can be understood to occur when parents, relatives, or other members of society are deprived of their abilities (which they consider their rights) to provide input, share concerns, or object to state-mandated decisions about medical procedures or killings that affect their relatives or loved ones directly. The following paragraphs emphasize these considerations in what can be considered a broadened understanding of dehumanization in the Nazi era.

As indicated in earlier sections of this chapter, decisions about sterilization and euthanasia often were made in situations of secrecy or by manipulation. Decisions about who should be selected for these procedures were made by panels (or by physicians alone) without input or consultation from parents, relatives, or others. Depending on the situation, euthanasia patients were transported among facilities, drugged, or starved without the knowledge of family members. Their bodies were cremated without their own or their families' authorizations.

These processes reflect extreme dehumanization leading to death of these individuals. The individual who may or may not have had the mental capacity to consent to procedures such as sterilization or euthanasia seemingly was not considered of sufficient importance, value, or worth to challenge state decisions about them. Relatives also were not allowed a sense of agency or value in decisions about their loved ones. The state decided the fate of its citizens. Individuals with severe disabilities and their families were of less interest and value than the dictates and presumed needs of the state, the ultimate decision maker in what concerned individual lives. Hitler (1925/1999) is clear about these issues, as can be seen from the quotes provided in the first section of this chapter.

The situation was similar, although worse, with later forms of dehumanization that almost always led to death, such as medical experimentation, torture, and extermination in concentration camps where all individual freedoms were taken away and prisoners were essentially slaves whose sadistic mistreatment was not contested. In these conditions, the victims were entirely dehumanized. They were treated as if they had no personal value or worth, which is how their Nazi overseers saw them. These were expectable circumstances for the murder of these unfortunates to become manifest.

Deceptive, manipulative, and cruel procedures were performed consistently from the beginning of the prisoners' time in death camps and up to their deaths. Their ashes were mixed with the ashes of others, thus dehumanizing and disrespecting them even after their deaths and depriving them and their families of their own individualities. In these cases, there was no attempt to notify relatives of the prisoners' fate, which might in fact have been shared by dehumanized relatives in the same extermination camp. Other examples of dehumanization and killing in the Nazi era included starving severely mentally or physically disabled patients in institutions until they died or surreptitiously giving them progressively higher dosages of sedatives that ultimately led to their deaths, and restricting food to concentration camp prisoners while forcing them to perform hard labor under the penalty of death (which would inevitably come).

In the various forms of medical exploitation and experimentation discussed earlier in this chapter, parents, relatives, and concerned citizens were denied accurate information and involvement in decision making. In the context of notions of worth and value that form a part of the definition of dehumanization offered here, the ultimate value was carried by the state. It was in charge of all people's lives, and people were allowed only the freedom and knowledge the state wished them to have or could not keep from them. In this sense, Nazi Germany revealed the extremes of dehumanization that led to the murder of patients, while also requiring that others—parents, relatives, and bystanders—accept their own dehumanization that precluded greater access to information pertinent to their lives and the lives of their loved ones.

Perpetrators also were dehumanized, in at least some cases, by acquiescing against their will to perform what may have seemed like horrific acts (such as assisting in gruesome experiments) or believing they had no alternative to performing acts that violated their own values. As an apparent attempt to ease the emotional burden of killing another human being (although these other humans were said to be "subhuman"), alcohol use/abuse was common in perpetrators in concentration camps, as it was among executioners in mass shootings of Jews in Eastern Europe (Browning, 1992/2017).

The executioners and perpetrators involved in medical experiments and medical-related killings were frequently physicians, although this was not invariably so. If one accepts the psychological understanding of some perpetrator/victimizer behavior described earlier in the discussion of "doubling" or splitting (Lifton, 2000), it becomes clear that perpetrators surrender, often unknowingly, their usual senses of self and drastically restrict the emotional and feeling aspects of themselves in order to take on their killer roles. They develop a personality that includes their usual sense of self, and another—detached, task-oriented, apparently emotionally numb one. It is this latter "person" especially that has become dehumanized and is thereby able to act mercilessly in performing various killing tasks.

Sometimes, as indicated earlier, symptoms such as anxiety, guilt, and sleep difficulties came to the fore as the perpetrators recognized themselves as killers who acted in inhumane ways that they presumably would not have thought possible before being swayed by the Nazi ideology. These perpetrators had been dehumanized in the process of dehumanizing and killing others. They had withdrawn their usual sense of self in favor of a dehumanized, unemotional sense of self. Lifton (2000) provides some evidence that a process of this kind may have been costly, psychologically, both in an immediate sense that involved the regular use of alcohol after selection procedures, and the later experience of what appear to have been posttraumatic symptoms of anxiety, sleep disorders, and guilt. These reactions suggest that perpetrators themselves may experience delayed psychological consequences of the loss of their humanized selves in favor of the dehumanized selves they created in order to fulfill their roles in the death-driven environments of the concentration camps.

# CHAPTER 8

# Summary and Conclusions. Alternative Approaches. Addressing Dehumanization

This book has argued that increasingly severe dehumanization of Jews in Nazi Germany activated in Nazis and their sympathizers an insistent psychological urge toward violence and murder that resulted in the genocide of millions of people, including six million Jews. The dehumanization overlapped with, and served as, a vehicle to activate and maintain this unremitting impulse that was introduced from psychological perspectives as the "death instinct" (later termed the "death drive") by Freud (1920; 1930; 1933) to describe the innate proclivity of human beings to murder and destroy one another. While I have not accepted Freud's original formulation of the death instinct/drive (and have avoided use of the terms "death instinct" or "death drive" as much as possible), I find value in the conceptualization of Freud and other authors from diverse fields, as described in chapter four, of an innate human tendency toward violence and murder that may be activated by particular circumstances, as illustrated in the Nazi Holocaust.

This chapter concludes this book. I will review and provide support for the claim that there is an overlapping relationship between dehumanization, violence, and murder. I will emphasize particular situations or instances that may activate or inhibit the movement of dehumanization to genocide and the murder of others. Finally, I will offer thoughts on approaches to combat largescale social violence and genocide.

# Dehumanization and Death in the Nazi Era: Background and Complexity

Adolf Hitler (1925/1999) hated, despised, and feared the Jews, all Jews. In *Mein Kampf*, written almost a decade before assuming power in Germany, he called for the total elimination from Europe of the Jews, a people he considered an ancient enemy of the Aryan race and its most formidable foe. How to eliminate the Jews from Europe was not clear, however. It could have been accomplished in at least two ways that had been discussed for years in rightwing political circles in Germany: murder or forced emigration (Goldhagen, 1997).

Hitler and the Nazi party were not strangers to violence and destruction. Hitler, and the Nazi party that he led, maintained a paramilitary force in the 1920s and the 1930s that served to create havoc and mayhem for other political parties (as other political parties also did through similar means) (Pulzer, 1964/1988); he was instrumental in the murder of a colleague (Ernst Rohm) who led the famed SA, another paramilitary force of which Hitler grew suspicious; and the Nazi party was suspected in the intentional arson of the Reichstag (German parliament) building shortly after Hitler assumed the chancellorship of Germany in 1933. Hitler and other Nazi members also were involved in a failed rebellion against the government of the Weimar Republic in 1923 (the Beer Hall Putsch in Munich), after which he spent almost a year in jail (during which time he wrote or dictated *Mein Kampf*). The Nazi party was known among the various political parties of the Weimar years for being especially violent (Pulzer, 1964/1988).

All of this might lead one to believe that Hitler would have no compunction about killing Jews, many Jews, if the opportunity was present in 1933 when he assumed the chancellorship after receiving a minority of votes in the previous election. The German public (the bystanders) did have a long history of severe antisemitism but probably would not have tolerated the murder of as many Jews as necessary to eliminate them entirely from Germany that soon into the Nazi rule, however (Landau, 2016).

In any case, the decision about the extermination of the Jews (the "final solution") would have to wait until the Nazi dictatorship was more firmly established, opposition parties and individuals were crushed, a war was being waged, and the German public had become more inured to the dehumanization and social isolation of the Jews that began to happen quickly once Hitler assumed power.

Prior to the decision to exterminate the Jews, the Nazi government tried to force Jewish emigration and to make life unbearable for Jews through terror, violence, harsh propaganda, restrictive legislation, and social ostracism. Many of these policies can be understood to have involved increasingly severe dehumanization, a process of withdrawing or depriving an individual or group in both the victimizer's and victim's eyes of a sense of the victim's humanity (Haslam et al., 2013), worth, or what has been called "personhood."

Dehumanization is intended to demean, belittle, ostracize, and reduce the victim to less-than-human status. A dehumanized individual is considered by the victimizer to act in an unacceptable moral or ethical manner and/or to subsist in behavior or attitudes closer to how a non-human animal (rather than a human being) would act.

Through a legislative onslaught, intense propaganda campaign, violence, social rejection, and isolation, Jews were dehumanized, marginalized, and rejected from German society. The Nazi leadership apparently hoped that this process, which fell short of murder, would be successful and that Jews would be forced to leave from (or flee) Germany "voluntarily" over the course of time.

The program of dehumanization of the Jews that is described more fully in chapters three, four, and five was, in fact, quite successful. At the onset of the Nazi era, there were about 600,000 Jews in Germany; by about 1941, half of the Jewish population had emigrated (Landau, 2016). This dramatic reduction in the number of Jews in Germany does not seem to have been sufficient to have satisfied Hitler's tenacious animosity that required total elimination of all Jews, however. Furthermore, it became clear in the late 1930s, as war to the east was on the horizon, that a whole new group of Jews would soon come under Hitler's dictatorial powers. Germany's war of expansion would bring it into direct contact with a large number of Jews who lived mainly in what had been called the Pale of Settlement in Eastern Europe.

These Jews were poorer, less urban, and less educated than Jews as a group in Germany had been, but they were, nonetheless, still the hated Jews. They would have even fewer opportunities for emigration than German Jews had. How could Hitler eliminate these Eastern European Jews, as he had done to a large extent with the Jews who were German citizens, given the short period of time during his invasion? Would dehumanization work as well as it had in Germany?

The solution to Nazi Germany's dilemma of the relatively small number of Jews remaining there and the much larger number of Jews in occupied lands was largely to abandon dehumanization as it had been used and to institute a policy of extermination. At this point, as described earlier, dehumanization would have prepared many German citizens to consider Jews to be almost non-existent, or to be irretrievably different and lesser than Aryans who were now engaged in a world war. The social isolation of the Jews (see below), the distraction of the war, and the anxiety that would have accompanied the war all would have made the German public less involved with the fate of the Jews.

These factors—increasingly severe dehumanization, social isolation of the Jews, loss of social pressure from part of the German citizenry that would have objected to the wholesale mistreatment of Jews, and the helplessness of the victims—all increased the likelihood that the Nazis' insistent and unremitting pressure to murder Jews (and others thought to be "subhumans") would emerge in full force.

Jews continued to be dehumanized, ostracized, and restricted in their activities and movements as they had been before but, by the late 1930s and into the 1940s, annihilation and extermination became the clear goal. A "final solution" involving the extermination of all Jews was formally agreed upon at the Wannsee Conference in 1942, but the wanton murder of Jews had begun much earlier as the German army stormed across Eastern Europe (Landau, 2016).

By this time, Hitler and the Nazi leadership had reason to be emboldened. German citizens had shown themselves able (or willing) to tolerate dehumanization and social ostracism of the Jews for several years as long as they did not perceive conditions to be too harsh or brutally excessive by their own standards (Bankier, 1992). The German public could practice what Bankier (1992) has defined as "defensive dissociation" (p. 129) or what Lifton (2000), referring to physicians' perpetration of medical atrocities, termed "doubling," or what can also be called "denial" or "avoidance" of troubling emotional reactions in a psychological sense.

Dehumanization during the period from the late 1930s through the end of the Nazi era in 1945 became a horrendous but far shorter interlude for individual Jews as they were herded up and murdered by the Einsatzgruppen (mobile killing units) or Order Police in fields and forests, deported in packed cattle cars to various types of camps, or forced into crowded and disease-infested ghettos prior to their deportation and ultimate deaths in concentration camps. For many Jews living in Eastern Europe, therefore, death arrived swiftly and without pretense toward more gradual dehumanization. Illustrations of these processes are numerous; some are provided in chapters three, four, and five of this book that deal with various aspects of dehumanization and/or murder, especially in concentration camps. A good example is Emmanuel Ringelblum's (Sloan, 1974) description of some incidents in ghetto life.

## Dehumanization, Violence, Murder, and Genocide: What Activates or Inhibits the Process?

The discussion in preceding paragraphs suggests there were at least two approaches to the large-scale murder of Jews employed by the Nazi leadership in the 1930s and the 1940s. One approach was taken in Germany itself over the first several years of the Nazi era, and the other, in Eastern Europe during the World War II years. Both of these approaches involved dehumanization to a degree, but the relationship between dehumanization and murder was different in the two instances, due to factors such as social concerns and social pressures.

There was also a third approach that can be discerned in describing the relationship between dehumanization and murder in the Nazi era. This approach involved the dehumanization and killing of the disabled and those considered "unfit" to live in an Aryan society that has been discussed in chapter six of this book. This third approach did not necessarily involve Jews. It was often applied in secret and involved a disregard for the humanity of the affected individuals as well as governmental attempts to deceive families and the society as a whole (the community bystanders) about what was, in reality, state-sanctioned killing of those whom the state considered "useless" or burdensome.

In the first approach noted above, in which dehumanization had preceded the murder of Jews in Germany through the late 1930s, the apparent purposes of dehumanization from the point of view of Hitler and the Nazi leadership were to restrict, isolate, and punish the Jewish community and to encourage the general population of Germany (the bystanders) to accept and support the mistreatment of Jews that many people witnessed directly or indirectly. The ultimate goal of the Nazi leadership was to coerce the emigration of the Jews out of Europe (Bankier, 1992; Goldhagen, 1997).

During this several-year period from the beginning of the Nazi regime in 1933 until the late 1930s, dehumanization served not only to force Jewish emigration but also as a way to help Nazi leadership gauge the reactions and tolerance of bystanders to the events they were witnessing. In 1938, for example, Kristallnacht made it clear that the German public was appalled by the harshly unfair treatment of the Jews in Germany, and bystander reactions signaled to the regime that the Nazi leadership should cease or at least slow down its violent antisemitic efforts, at least temporarily (Bankier, 1996).

Over time, however, it seems that prolonged dehumanization did shift public opinion away from the mistreatment Jews had received (Bankier, 1996). As Bankier (1996) writes,

> The acceptance of antisemitism as a social norm undermined resistance to the coming persecution in the Third Reich . . . the public gradually grew accustomed to the reality of antisemitism and ceased to notice it . . . acceptance of "mild" persecution paved the way for harsher measures. (p. 129)

The Nazi leadership seems to have understood that bystanders' tolerance for cruelty potentially would have increased over time, and that the "fog of war" would obscure, allow, or "justify" the genocide of the Jews remaining in Germany. Ultimately, as dehumanization continued, and as social support lessened, the murder of Jews no longer appeared as abhorrent as it presumably would have seemed if instituted at the beginning of the Nazi regime.

In the second approach to the relationship between dehumanization and murder, Jews of Eastern Europe were summarily killed in concentration camps, or by forces allied with the German army, or by the Order Police as the German army moved eastward in its attempt to gain territory and subdue the Soviet Union (Browning, 2017). There was no attempt at further dehumanization to coerce flight to other countries before murdering all the Jews who could be found. The conquered peoples (or citizen bystanders) of Eastern Europe were not German citizens and their possible concerns about the murder of helpless people may not have been important to the German leadership in any case. The invading army was under orders to kill all Jews whom they could locate. Forestalling this action, sometimes through removal of Jews to ghettos, was only a delaying tactic. In other cases, as the massacre at Jedwabne, Poland suggests (Gross, 1992), the long history of antisemitism and dehumanization in Eastern European countries made the local populace at times overt or at least passive accomplices to the slaughter that the Germans wanted to occur quickly. Dehumanization of Jews that amounts to torture was extremely severe and malign in concentration camps—but, again, there were no bystanders to object to the processes that were kept secret as much as possible.

These two approaches, which both ended with the genocidal killing of Jews, suggest that a program of dehumanization may be a helpful tactic for victimizers to activate the internal psychological pressure urging toward violence and murder in situations when a stable population of bystanders might disapprove of a regime's actions. An extensive program of dehumanization may be a needless tactic from the victimizers' perspective when circumstances are conducive to murder of the dehumanized, for example, when most potential witnesses are a compliant population of bystanders faced with other concerns such as wartime shortages, casualties, or the desire to settle their own scores.

It is important to recognize in these latter instances that dehumanization is both an external and an internal process. Dehumanization that is reflected in external behaviors is evident to victims as well as victimizers. On the other hand, dehumanization that is the result of an internal process of longstanding subjective calumny and denigration may manifest itself silently and erupt when the conditions are conducive to mass murder, as occurred in Jedwabne, Poland (Gross, 1992).

The third example of a relationship between dehumanization and murder that is described in this book involves individuals with medical and developmental disabilities. In their cases, decisions about life and death were made without the knowledge or consent of these patients (who may or may not have had the intellectual ability to understand these discussions), their families, and the larger society. In these cases, Nazi medical personnel would have realized that patients who had the ability to understand their status, as well as their relatives, might very well have resisted decisions to terminate the life of the individuals with disabilities. These victims and their families were therefore dehumanized as they were denied crucial information and decision-making input about themselves and/or their relatives, thus making the killings easier for Nazi authorities and medical personnel.

Individuals with disabilites, their families, and the larger society in these situations were dealt with as if living or dying for any given individual was a decision the state had ultimate authority to make. Hitler (1925/1999) emphasized that the folkish state *"must set race in the center of all life. It must take care to keep it pure. It must declare unfit for propagation all who are in any way visibly sick or who have inherited a disease and can therefore pass it on, and put this into actual practice"* (pp. 403–404, italics in the original). Dehumanization in these cases of so-called "euthanasia" denied certain individuals the right to live and denied their families the right to participate in choices around the termination of their relatives' lives. For authorities and medical personnel, the strength of the psychological urge toward the murder of severely disabled people in these cases was so great that social involvement and concerns of affected individuals, relatives, and the larger community were minimized.

Considering these three examples involving the relationship between dehumanization and the internal psychological pressures urging toward murdering other human beings suggest that anticipated or actual attitudes and reactions of bystanders (family, society members), or the lack of concern about these reactions, may have affected Nazi leaders' decisions significantly. Social pressures and concerns of bystanders altered (and perhaps lengthened) the course of dehumanization and murder in Germany itself, in prewar years, but made little or no difference in the dehumanization and murder of Jews in Poland and the Pale of Settlement where antisemitism seems to have been widespread even before the German invasion (Gross, 1992). Concerns about bystander reactions forced great secrecy in attempts to hide the killing of individuals with disabilities in Germany itself, and also contributed to the isolation and secrecy surrounding concentration camp environments that employed indescribably harsh and sadistic dehumanizing tactics before their prisoners were murdered.

## Psychological Aspects of the Relationship between Dehumanization, Violence, and Murder

In this book I have described a relationship between dehumanization, violence, murder and genocide, supporting my arguments in part by reviewing the chronology of events from the Nazi era. This section focuses in a more fine-grained way on the psychology of this relationship. At the beginning of the discussion, I would like to move to what may seem a digression but has relevance to the discussion at hand.

One of the many confusing aspects of violence and social interactions in our society involves the cases of homicide and violence against the homeless. The following is taken from a brief account of one such incident in a report published by the *National Coalition for the Homeless* (Leomporra & Hustings, 2018) and its referenced news article ("Boys, 13 and 14, Accused," 2017).

A forty-seven-year-old man was found dead in a park area in Maryland one morning in 2017. He had been stabbed several times. The police investigated and came to learn that he had apparently been stabbed by two adolescent boys, aged thirteen and fourteen. The man may have known one of the boys. The police were told that he was stabbed when he refused to give the boys money. Few other details are provided. He, like many homeless people, is described through a very limited narrative of his life and activities.

This homeless victim apparently was encountered while alone. He may or may not have had any money that is said to have served as an inducement to his murder. Most importantly, he seems to have been a typical homeless person: alone, isolated, without sufficient psychological or physical means or resources to support himself. As a middle-aged man, presumably weakened because of malnutrition, alcohol, or drugs, he may not have been able to fend off two adolescent boys intent on harming or killing him for reasons they themselves would not have fully grasped.

Personal or life circumstances seem to have resulted in this man's severe dehumanization. As a homeless person, he appears likely to have been bereft of usual pillars that describe one's "humanness" in an existential sense. These pillars include various aspects of one's identity, such as social status, human relationships to family and friends, education or occupational position, socio-economic status, religious affiliation, and other "identifiers" (such as place of residence). As described below, the presence of these various identity markers provides context for a person's life; their lack tends to "dehumanize" individuals and may be an inducement to the emergence of the propensity of violence toward them, which, in this case, led to the homeless man's murder.

As described in chapter three, dehumanization, in part, involves the denial or withdrawal of an individual's or group's sense of personal worth and a loss of the victim's sense of personal value or "personhood." As noted above, many of these aspects of dehumanization result from the reduction or loss of the victimized individual's sense of identity, a loose term that is used to reflect various characteristics of individuals or groups that inform, in a psychological sense, who they are and who they believe themselves to be in the family, the society, and the world. These existential assumptions may or may not be correct; they may be articulated or not; and they may or may not be shared by others in the society.

Jews in Germany (and in other parts of Europe) during the Nazi era experienced an increasingly severe diminution of various aspects of their identities as they were personally and collectively humiliated and restricted in their activities. They were, in essence, dehumanized. They lost social and family relationships, occupations, educational standing, socio-economic status, and the ability to practice their religion. They were forced to demarcate themselves from dominant members of the society through behaviors or badges such as Jewish stars. They were isolated, marginalized, and ridiculed. They became what the Nazis called the severely developmentally disabled—"useless" (or worse) to the Nazi regime's goals and aspirations that emphasized a distorted view of race.

As described in the conceptualization of an intrinsic human tendency toward violence and murder offered in chapter four, without social identity, support, or value in the eyes of the Nazi rulers and their sympathizers, the Jews easily became subject to murder, aggression, and destruction that established, both symbolically and in actuality, the dominance, control, and subjugation forced on them by their victimizers. As with the homeless man described above, the loss of pillars of their identities that accompanied their dehumanization ultimately made them helpless both in physical and in psychological sense. This activated an internal pressure towards violence and murder in their victimizers that was unencumbered by usual moderating forces such as taboos against killing fellow humans, or social restrictions on cruel or criminal activities. The Jews in Nazi Germany became socially isolated and powerless, thus creating the conditions for the activation of an intrinsic tendency toward violence and murder in their victimizers and for the expression of this tendency in the murder of the weak and helpless.

While the early years of the Nazi era, with its restrictions and humiliations from the dominant society's perspective, appeared to be focused on the coerced emigration of the Jews, a suspicion that the real goal of the regime was to ultimately dehumanize and isolate the Jewish population so that their genocidal murder would not cause social unrest is appropriate to entertain. In short, it might be argued that increasingly severe dehumanization activated the pressure towards violence and murder that was, consciously or subconsciously, present throughout the Nazi era but could not be activated until the emergence of appropriate conditions—social isolation, helplessness, and wartime confusion—that were conducive to genocide.

The killing of Jews as a reflection of an intrinsic psychological pressure urging toward violence and murder that is activated by external environmental and social forces is more easily understood when it is realized that much of the killing that occurred cannot be satisfactorily explained by examining the necessary or rational goals of the German society or its military. In fact, the killing of the Jews seemed to be counterproductive and detrimental to other social and military goals. Killing Jews in ghettos or fields or transporting them to concentration camps, for examples, appears to have taken precedence over rational planning of resources toward a successful conclusion of the war. It is hard to understand these efforts except for the desire to kill that was camouflaged by wanton and irrational prejudice. This desire to kill may not be verbalized directly by the perpetrators. The zest for killing, the "sport" of killing, the sadistic desire to torture and to experience the suffering of others all suggest the activation of this internal propensity toward violence and murder, however.

## An Alternative Approach to an Understanding of the Relationship between Dehumanization and Murder

Dehumanization and murder are commonly discussed as separate entities (to the degree they are discussed at all). It can be argued that the horrendous act of killing others, in a psychological sense, suggests that murder should be considered a separate process, conceptually distinct from, but susceptible to, activation from increasingly severe dehumanization of victims. Are these two processes truly separate, or might they be considered one entity that is manifested along a continuum? I have argued in this book that there appears to be a continuum involving both processes together. The illustrations in earlier chapters seem to support this contention, although the notion that dehumanization and innate psychological forces resulting in violence and murder form a continuum remains unsettled.

The overlap between the understandings of dehumanization and the human propensity toward violence and murder as offered in this book can be exemplified by returning to the question posed at the beginning of this chapter. How could the elimination of the Jews be accomplished at the beginning of the Nazi era in a society that had deeply antisemitic roots but probably could not, or would not, tolerate the mass murders that occurred (still with some secrecy) a decade later? In this sense, Hitler, other Nazis, and supportive German bystanders harbored a desire to eliminate Jews regardless of the means from the very outset of the Nazi era but genocide, at that time, would have been unacceptable to most Germans.

Dehumanization, which was associated with increasingly harsh restrictions on the Jews, intensely negative propaganda, and social isolation may have been needed to prepare German bystanders for the as yet unplanned (and perhaps unrecognized) extermination and genocide years later. Dehumanizing activities in this sense were an early or less severe expression of the violence and murder that was to come. These "milder" dehumanizing restrictions, prohibitions, and socially isolating activities were "compromises" in a psychological sense. They expressed the balance of considerations available to the Nazi leadership that existed between a desire to totally and quickly eliminate and perhaps exterminate the Jews and the realization that the total annihilation of Jews at the outset of the Nazi era would have resulted in national and international condemnation as discussed earlier.

From this perspective, the desire to exterminate all Jews may or may not have been present from the outset of the Nazi era but could only be expressed in the muted form of dehumanizing actions until the right social conditions came together and the "fog of war" would distract and confuse German bystanders. Approached from this viewpoint, dehumanization in the Nazi era was an early and distinct but muted aspect of an intrinsic pressure toward violence and murder that could not be enacted until dehumanizing actions set the stage for murder.

This understanding of the treatment of the Jews that involves a less severe form of an intrinsic pressure toward violence and murder is consistent with Freud's notion that there are opposing life and death forces that contribute to, and result in, given human actions. The interacting strengths and weaknesses of these two groups of forces then determine the actual behavioral outcome. If we accept this perspective, the genocide of the "final solution" may be understood as the result of a failure in the balance of life and death forces that, in the context of war, resulted in the genocide of the Jews.

The consideration whether dehumanization and the propensity toward violence and murder should be considered separate entities conceptually or whether, as I have argued here, they overlap, with dehumanization representing a less severe form of the propensity toward violence and murder, needs further study. It is clear that they both represent degrees of negative, destructive tendencies human beings exhibit toward one another.

## Prevention of the Progression from Dehumanization to Murder and Genocide

There are many aspects to the question how to prevent or lessen the likelihood of genocide. It is impotant to hold accountable individual purveyors of dehumanization, prejudice, and calumny against the Other as well as groups, political parties, and nations who support or who do not condemn such behaviors. The willingness to take a stand through personal and collective social action against the many forms of dehumanization, prejudice, and social bias against the Other is crucial. All of these statements of intent are, in some sense, obvious, but very difficult to actualize on individual, social, and national levels.

Human beings appear to be endowed with both socially creative and socially destructive forces. Intolerance of the Other and dehumanization of the Other that may lead to violence and murder are all too common in society. As I have indicated repeatedly throughout this book, violence and murder seem readily retrievable from the human repertoire of possible responses when stimulated by personal or social conditions. This is especially true for males, probably at least partly due to evolutionary as well as cultural factors.

Microaggressions have been increasingly cited in the recent past for their potentially harmful effects on the victim. Small slights, such as denigrating athletic abilities in school or variations in dress may be incitements to the types of negative self-appraisal that becomes associated with mental disorders and insecurities. Microaggressions are often dehumanizing, deflating the self-esteem of the victim and temporarily increasing the sense of power and dominance of the perpetrator. The same may be said for bullying, a very prevalent form of dehumanization that has been discussed in chapter six in relation to Jewish children in Nazi Germany. It is for parents, teachers, and other caretakers of children to recognize and react appropriately to dehumanizing statements or deeds of one child against another. Similar recommendations should be made for those involved in the caretaking of older children, adolescents, and even adults.

While longitudinal studies are difficult to perform, case studies of the type reported in this book in which progressively severe dehumanizing actions seemed to lay the groundwork for, or activate a tendency toward, the horrific violence and genocide of the Holocaust suggest that early intervention by outside figures is important in attempts to mitigate the violence and murder that human beings are so capable of committing. As noted above, the outcries of German citizens seemed to forestall, at least for a time, the murderous rampage against the Jews that was known as Kristallnacht. Of course, with the Nazi authorities' ability to divert attention from national social issues to warfare, the unleashing of the most severe forms of Nazi atrocities could not be forestalled for long. Sustained attention to Nazi antisemitism may have helped, although, as demonstrated by the failed Evian conference in 1938, commitment should be maintained and backed up by specific actions if it has a chance to succeed.

In any case, looking the other way in the face of dehumanization and tyranny, in the long term, does not seem to be a viable option if the goal is to preserve human life and forestall violence and genocide. Writing about war, an ultimate form of violence and frequent accompaniment to genocide, Keeley (1996) argues that "the only practical prospect for universal peace must be more civilization not less (p. 179). He cites two factors that have consistently been found to support peace, "employing strong institutions to resolve disputes and punish peace breaking and ensuring that those who keep the peace are rewarded, or at least not punished" (pp. 177–178).

As Samantha Power (2002/2013) has indicated,

> Given the immensity of the harm caused by genocide, its prevention is a burden that must be shared. At the same time, the United States should do certain things in every case. It must respond to genocide with a sense of urgency, publicly identifying and threatening the perpetrators with prosecution, demanding the expulsion of representatives of genocidal regimes from international institutions such as the United Nations, closing the perpetrators' embassies in the United States, and calling upon countries aligned with the perpetrators to ask them to use their influence. (pp. 513–514)

Power (2002/2013, p. 514) is quite specific. She goes on to say that, as dynamics on the ground indicate, the United States should institute economic sanctions, freeze assets of foreign nation perpetrators, and use other resources to combat the perpetrators' aims. Safe areas for refugees should be established and protection for refugees and civilians by peacekeepers should be organized. She writes passionately that, given the assault on American values and interests, "the United States must also be prepared to risk the lives of its soldiers in the service of stopping this monstrous crime."

Early intervention seems to be an agreed upon key to lessen or forestall mass violence, genocide, and war. Actively identifying and addressing dehumanization throughout its lifespan appears to be crucial in this endeavor. We do not know if more active and vigorous efforts of the types mentioned here would have reduced or eliminated the horrific testament to the dangers that humankind poses to itself through genocide, such as occurred in the Holocaust. We do know that, without vigorous sustained intervention, millions died.

## Future Study: Meaning in Life; the Superhuman and the Need for the Subhuman

Another area of study toward which this discussion points involves the question of what Hitler meant by Aryan superiority, how Aryan superiority was (or would be) manifested in the future, and, in a more detailed sense, how it compared with the inferiority he ascribed to Jews who he claimed were the representatives of the subhuman Semitic race. What qualities, in his view, reflected Aryan superiority, or would have more easily reflected it if Aryans were rid of the Semitic Jewish presence?

In a passage in *Mein Kampf* quoted previously in chapter three, Hitler (1925/1999) writes:

> *What we must fight for is to safeguard the existence and reproduction of our race and our people, the sustenance of our children and the purity of our blood, the freedom and independence of the fatherland, so that our people may mature for the fulfillment of the mission allotted it by the creator of the universe.* (p. 214, italics in the original)

What does Hitler believe is the mission allotted to the Aryan people by the creator of the universe?

Elsewhere, Hitler seems to tease at this question without answering it. He says, "*The state is a means to an end. Its end lies in the preservation and advancement of a community of physically and psychically homogeneous creatures... this preservation... permits the free development of all the forces dormant in this race*" (Hitler, 1925/1999, p. 393, italics in the original). A part of this preservation involves "*the promotion of a further spiritual development*" (Hitler, 1925/1999, p. 393, italics in the original). Again, higher spiritual development is a goal, but the meaning of this is unclear; although, for Hitler, the elimination (or extermination) of the Jew was central to achieving it.

Hitler (1925/1999) also wrote, "The mightiest counterpart to the Aryan is represented by the Jew" (p. 300). He argued that it was crucial for the Aryan to eliminate the malign presence of the Jew in order to combat the influence of what he believed to be a Semitic menace. As Vasey (2006) explains Hitler's thinking, "Aryans were, in essence, god-men on earth, but through blood poisoning lost their ruling position" (p. 62). The greater mission of the Aryan race (represented by the German people), from this perspective, was to regain leadership in the world and to produce a higher civilization based on Aryan culture. "If this were done, racially and thus spiritually pure human beings could be produced, ensuring Aryan world domination" (Vasey, 2006, p. 62). Vasey (2006, p. 63) goes on to write: "Once the Jew was purged from Europe, Germany would be able to produce pure Aryans, who would be physically and spiritually perfect human beings... demigod rulers...."

Hitler (1925/1999) seemed to consider his war against Jews to be, in some sense, a religious undertaking. He writes, "I believe that I am acting in accordance with the will of the Almighty Creator: *by defending myself against the Jew, I am fighting for the work of the Lord*" (p. 65, italics in the original). For Hitler, the conflict with the Jews amounted to a holy crusade, a spiritual quest.

This desire or, one might say, "obsession" to raise the Aryans to what Hitler felt was their rightful place as the master race of the world required the dehumanization of the Jew, a lowering or reduction of the Jew's status, and the elimination of Jews from Europe. The Nazi leader believed that, as the Jew was humiliated, broken down, and banished through either emigration or death, the Aryans' superiority over their eternal enemy would be confirmed. This was essentially a cosmic war between good and evil, the spiritual Aryan and the materialistic Jew, that had to be decided once and for all. "Only the total destruction of the Jews could thus save the Germans and enable them to enter the promised land" (Goodrick-Clarke, 1985/2004, p. 203). For Hitler (1925/1999), the increasingly severe dehumanization (and ultimate killing) of the Jews was entirely moral and reflected his attempts to rid society of immoral, impure, and unclean

Jewish elements that resided within it—while also raising the Aryans' worth in order to become the master race he felt they were destined to be.

Many religions, such as medieval Christianity, or the Judaism of the Dead Sea Scrolls, have similar conceptions that involve battles between what are imagined to be the cosmic forces of good and evil or right and wrong. From these perspectives, there are essential or eternal conflicts between light and dark, between the righteous and the unrighteous, or between the holy and the despoiled. In these cases, it is the task of the enlightened, of the righteous, to somehow dehumanize and defeat the evil representatives of another religion, belief, or practice. In so doing, these faiths and their adherents who are willing (or required) to fight for their notions of the divine expect to achieve some type of reward or enlightenment in this or another world.

Hitler had no formal religious beliefs, having rejected his Catholic upbringing at an early age. Yet, following the line of reasoning described here, the strivings of the Nazi party, the ideological belief system that is associated with the greatest genocide in history, had some similarities with religious beliefs that emphasize the spiritual superiority of one group versus another. Religious systems and ideologies throughout history have commonly emphasized the superiority of their belief system over all others, and the importance of violence for many adherents to prove their faith and loyalty to a given dogma in order to gain some higher moral or religious standing. Nazism appears to have had a perverted form of religious or quasi-spiritual belief system that required the subjugation and elimination of non-Aryans in order for the ill-defined Aryan people to achieve fulfillment and reward.

What are the psychological characteristics that require the dehumanization, elimination, or deaths of members of one group in order to prove the superiority of another group and to establish greater meaning for the members of the victimizer group? How does religious or spiritual striving, which Hitler seems to have shown in distorted form, lead to the designation of one's own group as superhuman, and of another group, as subhuman and dangerous?

It is important to learn more about these issues and the psychological imperatives that demand dehumanization, violent, and destructive actions against those who hold different beliefs or who appear different from the victimizer group. Knowledge of this type may help us understand better the aspirational forces that are so important in belief systems, especially when they become distorted and lead to, or require, violence and potential genocide for self-affirmation as happened in the Nazi era.

# References

Antliff, M. (2005). Georges Sorel and the Anti-Enlightenment: Art, ideology, politics. *Studies in the History of Art, 68*, 306–322.

Bankier, D. (1992/1996). *The Germans and the final solution: Public opinion under Nazism*. Blackwell Pub.

Bastian, B., & Haslam, N. (2011). Cognitive and emotional effects of everyday dehumanization. *Basic and Applied Social Psychology, 33*(4), 295–303. https://doi.org//10.1080/01973533.2011.614132

Bauer, Y. (1997). On perpetrators of the Holocaust and the public discourse. *The Jewish Quarterly Review, 87*(3/4), 343–350.

Becker, M., & Bock, D. (2020). Muselmanner and prisoner societies: Toward a sociohistorical understanding. *Journal of Holocaust Research, 34*(3), 158–174. https://doi.org/10.1080/25785648.2020.1794608

Berger, R. L. (1990). Nazi science: The Dachau hypothermia experiment. *New England Journal of Medicine, 322*(20), 1435–1440.

Book burning (n.d.). In *Holocaust encyclopedia*. US Holocaust Memorial Museum. Accessed July 16, 2021. https://encyclopedia.ushmm.org/content/en/article/book-burning

Boys, 13 and 14, accused of killing homeless man in Maryland. (2017, August 11). NBC4 Washington. Accessed February 14, 2023. https://www.nbcwashington.com/news/local/boys-13-and-14-accused-of-killing-homeless-man-in-adelphi/24364/

Browning, C. R. (1992/2017). *Ordinary men. Reserve Police Battalion 101 and the final solution in Poland* (2nd ed.). Harper Collins. (Original work published 1992.)

Burton, E. S. (2015). Sigmund Freud. *Institute of Psychoanalysis*. British Psychoanalytic Society. https://psychoanalysis.org.uk/our-authors-and-theorists/sigmund-freud

Caropreso, F., & Simanke, R. T. (2011). Life and death in Freudian metapsychology: A reappraisal of the second instinctual dualism. In S. Aktar & M. K. O'Neil (Eds.), *On Freud's "Beyond the pleasure principle"* (pp. 128–157). Karnac Books.

Chamberlain, H. S. (1911). *The Foundations of the nineteenth century* (Vol. 1). (J. Lees, Trans.). John Lane Company.

Cohen, N. (1990). Medical experiments. In I. Gutman (Ed.), *Encyclopedia of the Holocaust* (Vol. 3) (pp. 957–964). Macmillan Publishing Company.

Cohen, S. K. (2006). The experience of the Jewish family in the Nazi ghetto: Kovno—A case study. *Journal of Family History, 31*(3), 267–288.

Coolidge, F. L., Davis, F. L., & Segal, D. L. (2007). Understanding madmen: A DSM-IV assessment of Adolph Hitler. *Individual Differences Research, 5*(1), 30–43.

Dawidowicz, L. S. (1989). Thinking about the six million: Facts, figures, perspectives. In M. Berenbaum & J. K. Roth (Eds.), *Holocaust: Religious and philosophical implications* (pp. 51–70). Paragon House.

Dean, M. (2002). The development and implementation of Nazi denaturalization and confiscation policy up to the eleventh decree to the Reich citizenship law. *Holocaust and Genocide Studies, 16*(2), 217–242.

de Gobineau (1853/1854). *The inequality of the human races.* (Adrian Collins, Trans.). Ostara Publications.

DeLara, E. W. (2019). Consequences of childhood bullying on mental health and relationships for young adults. *Journal of Child and Family Studies, 28*, 2379–2389.

De Masi, F. (2015). Is the concept of the death drive still useful in the clinical field? *International Journal of Psychoanalysis, 96*(2), 445–458. https://doi.org/10.1111/1745-8315.12308

Des Pres, T. (1976). *The survivor: An anatomy of life in the death camps.* Oxford University Press.

Ettinger, S. (1988). Jew-hatred in its historical context. In Almog, S. (Ed.), *Antisemitism through the ages* (pp. 1–12). Pergamon Press.

Evans, R. J. (2005). *The Third Reich in power.* Penguin Books.

Fackenheim, E. L. (1982/1994). *To mend the world: Foundations of post-Holocaust Jewish thought.* Indiana University Press.

Felman, S., & Laub, D. (1992). *Testimony: Crises of witnessing in literature, psychoanalysis, and history.* Routledge.

Foster, M. (2019). Johann Gottfried von Herder. In Zulta, E. N. (Ed.), *The Stanford Encyclopedia of Philosophy.* https://plato.stanford.edu/archives/sum2019/entries/herder/

Freud, S. (1920). Beyond the pleasure principle. In S. Freud, *The standard edition of the complete works of Sigmund Freud.* (J. Strachey, Ed.). Hogarth Press.

Freud, S. (1923/1960). *The ego and the id.* (J. Strachey, Ed.). W. W. Norton & Co.

Freud, S. (1930). Civilization and its discontents. In S. Freud, *The standard edition of the complete works of Sigmund Freud.* (J. Strachey, Ed.). Hogarth Press.

Freud, S. (1933). *The Einstein-Freud correspondence, 1931–1932. Why war?* Accessed August 2, 2019, May 7, 2020. https://www.public.asu.edu/~jmlynch/273/documents/FreudEinstein.pdf

Fulbrook, M. (2019). *A concise history of Germany* (3rd ed.). Cambridge University Press.

Gat, A. (2006). *War in human civilization.* Oxford University Press.

Goeschel, C. (2009). *Suicide in Nazi Germany.* Oxford University Press.

Goldenberg, J. L., Courtney, E. P., & Felig, R. N. (2021). Supporting the dehumanization hypothesis, but under what conditions? A commentary on Over (2021). *Perspectives on Psychological Science, 16*(1), 14–21.

Goldhagen, D. J. (1996). A reply to my critics: Motives, causes, and alibis. *New Republic, 215*(26), 1–37. https://www.libraryofsocialscience.com/assets/pdf/Goldhagen-A_Reply.pdf

Goldhagen, D. J. (1997). *Hitler's willing executioners. Ordinary Germans and the Holocaust.* Vintage Books.

Goldstein, P. (2012). *A convenient hatred. The history of antisemitism.* Facing History and Ourselves. National Foundation.

Goodall, J. (1990/2010). *Through a window. My thirty years with the chimpanzees of Gombe.* Mariner Books.

Goodrick-Clarke, N. (1985/2004). *Occult roots of Nazism; Secret Aryan cults and their influence on Nazi ideology.* New York University Press.

Grab, W. (1984). The German way of emancipation. *Australian Journal of Politics and History, 30*(2), 224–235.

Grodin, M. A. (2010). Mad, bad, or evil: How physician healers turn to torture and murder. In S. Rubenfeld (Ed.), *Medicine after the Holocaust: From the master race to the human genome and beyond* (pp. 49–65). Palgrave Macmillan.

Grodin, M. A., Miller, E. L., & Kelly, J. I. (2018). The Nazi physicians as leaders in eugenics and "euthanasia": Lessons for today. *Am. J. Public Health, 108*(1), 53–57.

Gross, J. T. (1992). *Neighbors: The destruction of the Jewish community in Jedwabne, Poland*. Penguin Books.

Grossman, D. (1995). *On killing: The psychological cost of learning to kill in war and society*. Little, Brown and Company.

Grunberger, R. (1971/1995). *The 12-year Reich. A social history of Nazi Germany, 1933–1945*. Da Capo Press.

Gutman, Y. (1988). On the character of Nazi antisemitism. In Shmuel Almog (Ed.), *Antisemitism through the ages* (pp. 349–380). Pergamon Press.

Haslam, N. (2006). Dehumanization: An integrative review. *Personality and Social Psychology Review, 10*(3), 252–264.

Haslam, N., Loughnan, S., & Holland, E. (2013). The psychology of humanness. In S. J. Gervais (Ed.), *Objectification and (de)humanization*. Nebraska Symposium on Motivation 60 (pp. 25–51). Springer.

Haslam, N., & Loughnan, S. (2014). Dehumanization and infrahumanization. *Annual Review of Psychology, 65*, 399–423.

Haslam, N., & Loughnan, S. (2016). How dehumanization promotes harm. In A. G. Miller (Ed.), *The social psychology of good and evil* (2nd ed.) (pp. 140–158). Guilford Press.

Haslam, N., & Stratemeyer, M. (2016). Recent research on dehumanization. *Current Opinion in Psychology, 11*, 25–29.

Herder, J. G. von (1800/2016). *Outlines of a philosophy of the history of man*. (T. Churchill, Trans.). Random Shack. (Orig. publ. Bergman Publ.)

Hilberg, R. (1992). *Perpetrators, victims, bystanders. The Jewish catastrophe 1933–1945*. Harper Collins Publishers.

Hilberg, R. (1997). The Goldhagen phenomenon. *Critical Inquiry, 23*(4), 721–728.

Hitler, A. (1925/1999). *Mein Kampf*. (R. Manheim, Trans.). Mariner Books.

Hitler, A. (1945). *My political testament.* (United States Government Printing Office, Trans.). April 29, 1945. In Office of United States Chief of Counsel for Prosecution of Axis Criminality, *Nazi conspiracy and aggression* (Vol. 6) (259–263). Doc. No. 3569-PS.

Jaffee, M. S. (2006). *Early Judaism. Religious worlds of the first Judaic Millennium* (2nd ed.). University Press of Maryland.

Kaplan, M. (1997). The school lives of Jewish children and youth in the Third Reich. *Jewish History, 11*(2), 41–55.

Kassow, S. D. (2018). *Who will write our history? Emanuel Ringelblum, the Warsaw ghetto and the Oyneg Shabes archive*. Indiana University Press.

Keeley, L. H. (1996). *War before civilization. The myth of the peaceful savage*. Oxford University Press.

Kernberg, O. (2009). The concept of the death drive: A clinical perspective. *International Journal of Psychoanalysis, 90*(5), 1009–1023. https://doi.org/10.1111/j.1745-8315.2009.00187.x

Kershaw, I. (2000). *Hitler 1936–45: Nemesis*. W. W. Norton & Co.

Klein, M. (1946). Notes on some schizoid mechanisms. *International Journal of Psychoanalysis, 27*(3–4), 99–110.

Klein, M. (1955). On identification. In M. Klein, P. Heimann, R. E. Money-Kyrle (Eds.), *New directions in psycho-analysis. The significance of infant conflict in the pattern of adult behavior* (pp. 309–345). Basic Books.

Klein, M. (1965). Love, guilt and reparation. In M. Klein & J. Riviere (Eds.), *Love, hate and reparation* (pp. 57–119). Hogarth Press. (Original work published 1937.)

Kovner, A. (2001). *Scrolls of testimony*. Jewish Publication Society.

Kunzer, E. J. (1939). "Education" under Hitler. *Journal of Educational Sociology*, 13(3), 140–147. https://doi.org/10.2307/2262306

Kuriloff, E. A. (2014). *Contemporary psychoanalysis and the legacy of the Third Reich: History, memory, tradition*. Routledge.

Landau, R. S. (2016). *The Nazi Holocaust: Its history and meaning* (3rd ed.). I. B. Tauris & Co.

Landau, A. W. (2011). *Branded on my arm and in my soul: A Holocaust memoir*. Spinner Publications.

Laub, D. (2005). Traumatic shutdown of narrative and symbolization. A death instinct derivative? *Contemporary Psychoanalysis*, 41(2), 307–326. https://doi.org/10.1080/00107530.2005.10745863

Laub, D., & Lee, S. (2003). Thanatos and massive psychic trauma: The impact of the death instinct on knowing, remembering and forgetting. *Journal of the American Psychoanalytic Association*, 51(2), 433–464. https://doi.org/10.1177/00030651030510021201

Leomporra, A., & Hustings, M. (2018). Vulnerable to hate. A survey of bias-initiated violence against people experiencing homelessness in 2016–2017. *National Coalition for the Homeless*.

Lemkin, R. (1946). Genocide. *American Scholar*, 15(2), 227–230. http:///www.preventgenocide.org/lemkin/americanscholar1946

Levi, P. (1996). *Survival in Auschwitz: The Nazi assault on humanity*. (S. Woolf, Trans.). Touchstone, Simon & Schuster.

Leyens, J-P. (2009). Retrospective and prospective thoughts about infrahumanization. *Group Processes and Intergroup relations*, 12(6), 807–817.

Leyens, J-P., Demoulin, S., Vaes, J., Gaunt, R., & Paladino, M. P. (2007). Infra-humanization: The wall of group differences. *Social Issues and Policy Review*, 1(1), 139–172.

Lifton, R. J., Hackett, A. (1998). Nazi doctors. In Y. Gutman & M. Berenbaum (Eds.), *Anatomy of the Auschwitz death camp* (pp. 301–316). Indiana University Press in association with the US Holocaust Memorial Museum.

Lifton, R. J. (2000). *The Nazi doctors: Medical killing and the psychology of genocide*. Basic Books.

Lind, L. (1991). Thanatos: The drive without a name. The development of the concept of the death drive in Freud's writings. *Scandinavian Psychoanalytic Review*, 14, 60–80.

Lothane, Z. (2012). Freud's *Civilization and its Discontents* and related works: A reappraisal. *Psychoanalytic Inquiry*, 32(6), 524–542. https://doi.org//10.1080/0735169.2012.703601

Lowenstein, S. M. (2005). Jewish intermarriage and conversion in Germany and Austria. *Modern Judaism*, 25(1), 23–61.

Machala, J. (2014). "Unbearable Jewish houses of prayer." The Nazi destruction of synagogues based on examples from central Moravia. *Judaica Bohemiae*, 49(1), 59–87.

MacMaster, N. (2001). *Racism in Europe 1870–2000*. Palgrave.

MacQueen, M. (1998). The context of mass destruction: Agents and prerequisites of the Holocaust in Lithuania. *Holocaust and Genocide Studies*, 12(1), 27–48.

Mastroianni, G. R. (2019). *Of mind and murder: Toward a more comprehensive psychology of the Holocaust*. Oxford University Press.

Mitani, J. C., Watts, D. P., Pepper, J. W., & Merriwether, D. A. (2002). Demographic and social constraints on male chimpanzee behavior. *Animal Behavior, 64*, 727–737.

Money-Kyrle, R. E. (1955). An inconclusive contribution to the theory of the Death Instinct. In M. Klein, P. Heimann, & R. E. Money-Kyrle (Eds.), *New directions in psycho-analysis: The significance of infant conflict in the pattern of adult behavior* (pp. 499–509). Basic Books Inc.

Mosse, G. L. (1978). *Toward the final solution: A history of European racism*. Howard Fertig.

Otterbein, K. F. (2013). Epilogue. In S. Ralph (Ed.), *The archaeology of violence. Interdisciplinary approaches* (pp. 217–279). State University of New York Press.

Over, H. (2021). Seven challenges for the dehumanization hypothesis. *Perspectives on Psychological Science, 16*(1), 3–13.

Parens, H. (2011). Does the death-instinct-based theory of aggression hold up? In S. Akhtar & M. K. O'Neill (Eds.), *On Freud's "Beyond the pleasure principle"* (pp. 154–173). Karnac Books.

Perper, J. A., & Cina, S. J. (2010). The Nazi Murders. In J. A. Perper & S. J. Cina, *When doctors kill: Who, why, and how* (pp. 57–65). Copernicus.

Pine, L. (2010). *Education in Nazi Germany*. Bloomsbury Publishing.

Pingel, F. (1990). Concentration camps. In I. Gutman (Ed.), *Encyclopedia of the Holocaust* (Vol. 1) (pp. 308–317). Macmillan Publishing Company.

Pitch, A. S. (2015). *Our crime was being Jewish: Hundreds of Holocaust survivors tell their stories*. Skyhorse Publishing.

Power, S. (2002/2013). *"A problem from Hell": America and the age of genocide*. Basic Books.

Pross, C. (1991). Breaking through the postwar coverup of Nazi doctors in Germany. *Journal of Medical Ethics, 17*, 13–16.

Pulzer, P. (1964/1988). *The rise of political anti-Semitism in Germany and Austria* (rev. ed). Harvard University Press.

Ralph, S. (2013). Introduction. An interdisciplinary approach to the study of violence. In S. Ralph (Ed.), *The archaeology of violence. Interdisciplinary approaches* (pp. 1–13). State University of New York Press.

Rechardt, E., & Ikonen, P. (1993). How to interpret the death drive? *The Scandinavian Psychoanalytic Review, 16*(2), 84–99. https://doi.org/10.1080/01062301.1993.10592296

Richards, A. K. (2018). The death instinct and its vicissitudes. *Canadian Journal of Psychoanalysis, 26*(1), 121–134.

Rokeah, D. (1988). The Church Fathers and the Jews in writings designed for internal and external use. In S. Almog (Ed.), *Antisemitism through the ages* (pp. 38–69). Pergamon Press.

Ruderman, D. B. (1997). The cultural significance of the ghetto in Jewish history. In D. N. Myers & W. V. Rowe (Eds.), *From ghetto to emancipation: Historical and contemporary reconsiderations of the Jewish community* (pp. 1–15). Scranton University Press.

Sanchez-Pardo, E. (2003). *Cultures of the death drive: Melanie Klein and modernist melancholia*. Duke University Press.

Shallcross, S. (2020). The Muselmann and the necrotopography of a ghetto. *Journal of Holocaust Research, 34*(3), 220–240. https://doi.org/10.1080/25785648.2020.1785089

Shils, E. A. (1950). Introduction to the American edition. In G. Sorel, *Reflections on violence* (T. E. Hulme, Trans.). Free Press.

Sloan, J. (Ed. & Trans.). (1974). *Notes from the Warsaw ghetto: The journal of Emmanuel Ringelblum.* Schocken Books.

Smith, D. L. (2011). *Less than human: Why we demean, enslave, and exterminate others.* St. Martin's Press.

Smith, D. L. (2020). *On inhumanity: Dehumanization and how to resist it.* Oxford University Press.

Sorel, G. (1950). *Reflections on violence.* (T. E. Hulme, Trans.). Free Press.

Sousa, C., & Casanova, C. (2008). Aggression in the great apes: across-species comparison. *Antropologia Portuguesa, 22/23*, 71–118.

Stern, M. (1988). Antisemitism in Rome. In S. Almog (Ed.), *Antisemitism through the ages* (pp. 1–12). Pergamon Press.

Strzelecki, Andrzej. (1998). "The Plunder of Victims and Their Corpses". In Berenbaum, Michael; Gutman, Yisrael (eds.). *Anatomy of the Auschwitz Death Camp.* Bloomington: Indiana University Press.

van Noorden, T. H. J., Haselager, G. J. T., Cilessen, A. H. H., Bukowski, W. M. (2014). Dehumanization in children: The link with moral disengagement in bullying and victimization. *Aggressive Behavior, 40*, 320–328.

Vasey, C. M. (2006). *Nazi ideology.* Hamilton Books.

Vernon, R. (1978). *Commitment and change: Georges Sorel and the idea of revolution.* University of Toronto Press.

Voigtlander, N., & Voth, H.-J. (2015). Nazi indoctrination and anti-Semitic beliefs in Germany. *Proceedings of the National Academy of Sciences, 112*(26), 7931–7936.

Volpato, C., & Andrighetto, L. (2015). Dehumanization. In J. D. Wright (Ed.), *International encyclopedia of the social and behavioral sciences* (2nd ed.) (pp. 31–37). Elsevier.

Wiesel, E. (1958/2006). *Night.* Hill and Wang, Farrar, Strauss and Giroux.

Wrangham, R. (2019). *The goodness paradox. The strange relationship between virtue and violence in human evolution.* Pantheon Books.

# Index

Adam, biblical figure, 34
Africa, 41
Alexander the Great, 20
Alsace-Lorraine, 41
America, 6, 61, 79, 90, 118, 128
ancient Greece, 2, 21
Anti-Christ, 38
antisemitic writings, 18, 35–36
antisemitism, 3, 7–9, 17–19, 21–22, 25, 29–32, 35–36, 39–43, 45, 47, 51, 58, 69, 92, 94, 100–102, 109–10, 115, 123, 131, 139, 167, 171, 173, 178. *See also* political anti-Semitism
Antliff, M., 43
Arabian Peninsula, 23
Aryan race, 1, 14, 36–37, 41, 44, 48–51, 54, 81, 86–88, 115–16, 120, 123–24, 145–48, 155–56, 167, 180
Assyria, 20
Auschwitz, 13, 64, 67, 94, 105, 111, 127, 155
Auschwitz-Birkenau, 119, 127, 154
Austria, 27–28, 41, 79–80, 116, 126

Babylonia, 20, 106
Bankier, D., 169–71
Barbarossa, Frederick, emperor, 26
Bar-Kokhba, Simon, 19
Bastian, B., 4, 142–44
Bauer, Yehuda, 100
Becker, M., 62
Bergen-Belsen, 104
Berger, R. L., 156
Berlin, 114, 131, 138, 152
Bettleheim, Bruno, 61

Birkenau, 119, 127, 154
Bismarck, Otto von, 27
Blavatsky, Helena, 47
Bock, D., 62
Bockel, Otto, 42
Browning, Christopher R., 60, 71, 84, 86, 91–93, 99–101, 106, 164, 171
Buchenwald, 61, 104, 115
Burton, E. S., 126

Chamberlain, Houston Stewart, 43–45
Cina, S. J., 149, 152, 156–58
Cohen, N., 19
Cohen, S. K., 128, 133
concentration camps, 2, 8, 10, 13–15, 59–61, 63–66, 78, 84, 86, 91, 93–94, 101, 103–105, 109–10, 113–17, 119–22, 125–30, 133, 138–40, 144–45, 154, 157, 163–65, 169, 171, 173, 175
Constantine, emperor, 22
Coolidge, F. L., 84, 88
Cyrus, king, 20
Czechoslovakia, 116

Dachau, 61, 94, 114
Danzig, 41
Darwin, Charles, 8, 30, 37, 39, 41, 151, 159
David, king, biblical figure, 20
Dawidowicz, L. S., 122
Dead Sea, 182
Dean, M., 123
death drive/instinct, 3, 5–6, 10, 76–82, 86, 103, 165–66

definition of dehumanization, 9, 57–58, 75, 140, 164
de Gobineau, Arthur, 33–35, 37, 45
DeLara, E. W., 140–42, 144
De Masi, F., 80, 82
Des Pres, Terrence, 63–65, 67, 125, 133
Devil, 22–23
Dreyfus, Alfred, 43

Einstein, Albert, 82
Egypt, 7, 19–20
emancipation of Jews, 8–9, 17–18, 21, 25–26, 28–32, 35, 37–38, 40, 42, 45–46, 68–69, 159
England, 26, 79–80, 126
Enlightenment, 8, 17, 25–26, 28–29, 31–33, 35, 43, 46, 52, 68, 181. See also
Ettinger, S., 18, 22
Europe, 2, 6, 13, 22–24, 26–29, 37–38, 43, 46, 48–49, 51, 58, 88, 94, 96–97, 101, 106, 108–10, 112, 115, 117–18, 120, 122, 129–30, 164, 167–71, 174, 180
euthanasia, 15, 145, 147, 150–52, 154, 159, 162–63, 172
Evans, R. J., 14, 135–36
Evian, 117, 178
evolutionary considerations related to violence, 71–76, 82–83, 177

Fackenheim, Emil L., 66–67
Felman, Shoshana, 102–3
forms of dehumanization, 6–7, 10, 54–57, 71, 111, 117, 123, 130, 134, 139–40, 142–44, 163, 176–77
Foster, M., 32
France, 26, 28, 41, 116–17
Freud, Sigmund, 3, 5, 10, 67, 71, 77–83, 86, 89, 103, 106–7, 126, 166, 176
Fulbrook, M., 26–28, 37–38, 41

Galicia, 94
Galilee, 44
Gat, A., 76
genocide, 1–16, 24, 51–52, 56–57, 64–67, 69, 75, 79, 82–83, 88–89, 93–96, 98, 101–105, 108–109, 112, 121–22, 130, 132, 150, 154, 162, 166, 170–71, 173, 175–79, 181
Germany, 1–3, 6, 8–11, 13–15, 18–19, 21, 26–28, 30–33, 36–41, 43–44, 48, 51–52, 56–57, 76, 78, 87–89, 94, 96–97, 101, 106, 108–18, 120–21, 123, 128–29, 132–33, 135–39, 149–50, 158, 160, 164, 166–68, 170–75, 178, 180
ghettos, 2, 6, 13, 29, 37–38, 47, 59, 62–63, 78, 86, 93–94, 101, 104, 110–11, 113, 116, 118–19, 121, 124–25, 127–30, 133, 139–40, 143, 149, 157, 169, 171, 175
Goebbels, Joseph, 110
Goeschel, C., 102
Goldenberg, J. L., 69
Goldhagen, Daniel Jonah, 11–12, 84, 93–97, 99–102, 106, 109–11, 113–16, 121–23, 130–31, 161, 167, 170
Goldstein, P., 114
Goodall, Jane, 71–75
Goodrick-Clarke, N., 47, 49, 180
Grab, W., 29–31, 38
Grodin, M. A., 149–54, 159–60
Gross, Jan T., 97–99, 104, 171–73
Grossman, Dave, 89–92, 98–99, 106
Grunberger, R., 137
Grynszpan, Herschel, 116
Gutman, Y., 120

Hackett, A., 161
Hamburg, 90
Haslam, Nick, 4, 52–57, 67, 129, 142–44, 168

Heine, Heinrich, 126
Herder, Johann Gottfrid von, 32–33
Hilberg, Raul, 5, 85, 100, 106, 111, 150, 154
Himmler, Heinrich, 66
Hippocrates, 158
Hitler, Adolf, 1, 3–4, 8–9, 11, 14, 28, 31–33, 35–36, 40, 44–51, 53, 56, 66, 74, 81, 84, 86–89, 93, 96, 109, 112–13, 115–18, 120–25, 129, 131, 134–37, 146–52, 158, 163, 167–70, 172, 176, 179–81. *See also Mein Kampf*
human experiments, 15, 54–55, 61, 145–46, 150, 155–57, 159, 161–64
Hustings, M., 173

Ikonen P., 80, 83
Indian continent, 35
Innocent III, Pope, 24
Israel, 19–21, 66, 100

Jaffee, M. S., 21
Jedwabne, 97–99, 171–72
Jerusalem, 21, 137
Jesus Christ, 23–24, 36, 44, 123
Jews
    in antiquity, 7, 17, 19
    in the Middle Ages, 7, 17–19, 21–24, 26, 29, 38, 126. *See also* Enlightenment
    in the modern times, 7–8, 22, 25, 37. *See also* emancipation of Jews
Joseph, biblical figure, 20
Józefów, 91, 93
Judaea, 21

Kaplan, M., 136–37
Kassow, Samuel D., 120, 125
Keeley, L. H., 75, 178
Kernberg, O., 77, 80
Kershaw, Ian, 88, 96, 119

killing of others, 15, 83, 159
Klein, Melanie, 80–81, 83, 86–87, 106
Kovner, Abba, 104, 124–25
Kovno (Kaunas), 12, 95, 97, 128
Kuriloff, Emily A., 79, 82

Landau, A. W., 104–6, 125
Landau, R. S., 2–3, 19, 23–26, 28–29, 31, 39, 110, 112–18, 120, 122, 124–26, 130, 135, 137, 167–69
Lanz von Liebenfels, Jörg (Adolf Joseph), 47
Laub, Dori, 77, 80, 102–4
Lee, S., 77, 80, 102–3
Lemkin, Raphael, 2
Leomporra, A., 173
Levi, Primo, 59–61, 125
Leyens, Jacques-Philippe, 53–54, 57
Lifton, Robert Jay, 15, 145–46, 149–50, 153–56, 158–61, 164, 169
Lind, L., 77, 80
List, Guido von, 47
Lithuania, 12, 94–95, 97, 128
Łódź, 118
Lomazy, 93
Lothane, Z., 79
Loughnan, Steve, 52–54, 57, 129, 142
Lowenstein, S. M., 147
Luther, Martin, 26

Maccabees, the, 21
Machala, J., 112, 124
MacMaster, N., 36, 39, 43
MacQueen, M., 112
Madagascar, 118
Majdanek, 93
manifestations of dehumanization, 68
Marr, Wilhelm, 18, 36
Maryland, 173
Mastroianni, G. R., 79
medical implementation of Nazi ideology, 15, 145, 162

*Mein Kampf,* 9, 31–33, 35–36, 45–46, 49, 51, 84, 87, 110, 115, 131, 134, 137, 146–48, 167, 179. *See also* Hitler, Adolf
Mengele, Josef, 155–57
Metternich, Klemens von, 27
Mitani, J. C., 72
Money-Kyrle, R. E., 77, 82
Molotov, Vyacheslav, 118
Mosse, G. L., 38–39, 44, 46–47
Munich, 167
Muselmann, 61–63, 66, 102

Nazi party (National Socialist German Workers' Party), 1, 9–10, 14–15, 19, 31, 35, 39–40, 45–46, 56, 87, 110, 113, 115, 131, 135–36, 138, 149, 158, 161, 167, 181
Napoleon Bonaparte, emperor, 27
negative eugenics, 15, 150
Northern Kingdom, 20
Nuremberg, 30, 32, 115, 123
Nuremberg laws, 30, 32, 115, 123

Otterbein, K. F., 75
Over, H., 69

Palestine, 118
Parens, H., 77
Perper, J. A., 149, 152, 156–58
persecution, 4, 7, 12–13, 19, 23, 81, 112, 116, 126, 171
Persian Empire, 20–21
Pharaoh, 7
physicians as Nazi collaborators, 15, 124, 145–46, 148–50, 152, 154–56, 158–64, 169
Pine, L., 135
Pingel, F., 64, 119
Pitch, A. S., 133
Poland, 41, 91, 93–94, 97, 111, 115, 118, 161, 171–73

political anti-Semitism, 8, 25, 29, 30–31, 42–43, 69, 92
Poniatowa, 93
Posen, 41
Power, Samantha, 178–79
proclivity toward violence, 3–5, 10, 69, 82, 166
progression from dehumanization to murder and genocide, 12, 15, 69, 101, 106, 108, 129, 177
prohibitions against murder, 5, 10–11, 57, 70, 83, 89, 96, 174–75
propensity toward violence, 10, 70–71, 80, 83, 88, 91, 98–99, 101, 103, 112, 120, 131–32, 142, 158–59, 161, 175–77
Pross, C., 15, 149
Prussia, 27–28, 41
Ptolemies, dynasty, 20
Pulzer, P., 30–31, 39–42, 167

Ralph, S., 75
Rechardt, E., 80, 83
research of dehumanization, 9, 16, 52, 56, 139, 142–43
Ribbentrop, Joachim von, 118
Richards, A. K., 80
Ringelblum, Emmanuel, 118, 169
Rohm, Ernst, 167
Rokeah, D., 22
Roman Empire, 21–22
Roosevelt, Franklin D., president, 117
Ruderman, D. B., 37–38
Russia, 39, 97, 118

Sanchez-Pardo, E., 80
Satan, 24
school aged children, 14, 114, 125, 127, 129, 132–44, 155, 173
Seleucids, dynasty, 21
Shallcross, S., 6, 62–64, 78, 101–2, 118, 157

Shils, E. A., 43
Silesia, 41
Simanke, R. T., 80
Sloan, J., 118, 125, 169
Smith, D. L., 2, 52–53, 56–57, 70, 73–74, 88–89, 129
Sorel, Georges, 43
Sousa, C., 72
Southern Kingdom, 20
Soviet Union, 118, 161, 171
Spain, 23–24
Speyer, 38
stages of dehumanization, 2
sterilization, 15, 145, 147–50, 157, 162–63
Stern, M., 21
Stratemeyer, M., 54
Sudetenland, 116

taboo, 70–71, 89, 99, 174
Tanzania, 71
transition to genocide, 13, 27, 150
Treblinka, 93
Transylvania, 127

United States, 29, 96, 117, 126, 141, 178–79

Van Noordan, T. H. J., 139–40
Vasey, C. M., 2, 47–49, 180
Venice, 37
Vernon, R., 43
Versailles, 41
Vienna, 27
Vietnam, 90
Voigtlander, N., 139
Voth, H.-J., 139
Volpato, C., 53

Wagner, Richard, 43–44
Wannsee, 121, 169
Warsaw, 118
Weimar Republic, 28, 31, 41, 150, 159, 167
Westphalia, 27
Wiesel, Elie, 13, 125, 127–29
witness accounts, 57, 62, 67, 83
Wittenberg, 26
Wrangham, R., 74–75

Dehumanization can be defined in part as a process by which a powerful individual or group (the victimizers) actively denies or withdraws a second individual's or group's (the victim's) sense of human worth or personal value. Dehumanization is an especially harmful form of denigration of the Other and is known to have negative psychological consequences on victims.

Dehumanization of the Jews in the Nazi era was implemented across several domains: social, economic, educational, professional, religious, and personal. As shown in this book, increasingly severe dehumanization may activate a virulent expression of a tendency to kill one's fellow human beings that results in murder and even genocide. Freud described this tendency to kill oneself and others as the death instinct (later called the death drive), a universal tendency in human beings that involves dynamics of aggression and destruction. According to Freud, murder is an expression of the death drive and a means to establish dominance, control, subjugation, or retaliation against the victim.

This book discusses psychological aspects of dehumanization and argues that dehumanization, murder, and genocide potentially form a continuum. It explores how increasingly severe dehumanizing tactics in Nazi Germany activated the perpetrators' insistent pressure toward murder and resulted in the genocide of six million Jews in the Second World War, along with millions of others who were considered racially inferior beings. Increasingly severe dehumanization of the Jewish people in the Nazi era that led to genocide gained "legitimacy" to or acceptance by "ordinary" Germans ("bystanders") through various tactics that included unremitting negative propaganda that blamed Jews for national and worldwide catastrophes, socially isolating the victims (in ghettos and then concentration camps), social pressure on Germans to conform, and distraction of bystanders from horrific events through authoritarian control of information and the social upheaval of war.

A common denominator of these tactics involved the desire and ability of the victimizers to dehumanize Jews (their victims) and establish dominance and control over them by making Jews weak, helpless, unable to defend themselves, and socially isolated from the larger German population. The dehumanization of Jews that preceded their murder in the Nazi era appears to have strong similarities to genocides in other situations. An understanding of the sequence of events from dehumanization to murder and genocide may have implications for the apparent tendency of human beings to harm and potentially kill those who are or appear to be "different" or who are made into the Other under the guise of reprisal or self-justification, as occurred in the Nazi era when Adolf Hitler argued that Jews were the greatest threat to the Aryan race that existed. Efforts to prevent genocide should actively challenge dehumanization of weaker populations whenever possible even when dehumanization appears mild, "insignificant," or "innocuous."

Milton Keynes UK
Ingram Content Group UK Ltd.
UKHW021415201123
432914UK00009B/82